The King of Cash

The King of Cash
The Inside Story of Laurence Tisch

Christopher Winans

John Wiley & Sons, Inc.
New York • Chichester • Brisbane • Toronto • Singapore

Library of Congress Cataloging-in-Publication Data

Winans, Christopher.
    The king of cash : the inside story of Laurence Tisch /
Christopher Winans.
       p.   cm.
    Includes index.
    ISBN 0-471-54923-1 (Cloth)
    1. Tisch, Laurence A., 1923-   . 2. Businessmen—United States-
-Biography.   3. Capitalists and financiers—United States-
-Biography.   4. Millionaires—United States—Biography.   5. CBS Inc.
6. Television broadcasting—United States—Ownership.   I. Title.
HC102.5. T56W56   1995
338.092—dc20
[B]   94-40400

Printed in the United States of America

10 9 8 7 6 5 4 3 2 1

To my mother, Ellen H. Winans
and brother, R. Foster Winans

Acknowledgments

Larry Tisch made it clear in 1991, when first informed this book was in the works, that he and his family saw no need, indeed no market, for such a book. His response to a request for cooperation was that he couldn't imagine more than 12 people being interested in reading such a biography. His explanation was that the story of his life would prove to be remarkable only in its lack of revelations worthy of National Enquirer headlines.

He made it clear, however, that if the book was going to happen, he was willing to help ensure that the final product was as accurate as possible. The research and writing proceeded. Frequently his closest associates rebuffed requests for interviews—on the record or not—because this was an unauthorized biography.

When the book was close to completion, I approached Tisch again. Recognizing that the book was on track to be published, he agreed to review every detail. He identified errors of omission as well as those of commission. He objected to facts and quotes that in his opinion were out of context or given the wrong emphasis and pointed out elements that he believed were irrelevant, yet he never demanded that anything be changed. Neither he nor the rest of his family held back in answering all additional questions put to them.

Tisch's input, along with that of his wife, Billie, and their four sons, was invaluable—especially coming as it did after most of the research had been completed. The family made little effort to control the content of the book or to tone down the more negative anecdotes, reinforcing what I had already concluded: that Larry Tisch possesses the necessary self-confidence not to feel the need to manage the truth.

Many other people assisted in this effort, but two in particular need to be mentioned: Jane Dystel, my agent, helped focus my attention on Larry Tisch as a story worth telling and found a publisher who agreed—and encouraged me to do the best job I am capable of, from conception to completion. Ruth Mills, my editor at John Wiley & Sons, deserves praise for disproving decisively the conventional wisdom that book editing is a lost art.

Contents

PART ONE

THE TISCH TOUCH

1

Larry Tisch: Money Maker

Laurence Alan Tisch came seemingly from nowhere to take control of CBS in the mid-1980s and was still very much in the public eye in 1994 when the CBS turnaround he had engineered seemed poised to crumble. At the end of 1993, CBS lost a bidding contest to keep its lock on professional football broadcast rights, which many viewed as critical to CBS's programming strategy to attract viewers. In May 1994, Rupert Murdoch's Fox network spirited away eight important affiliated stations—a potential blow to ad revenue. A month later, Tisch began serious negotiations to merge with QVC Inc., the leading home-shopping cable channel, and to cede management control to Barry Diller, QVC's chairman. It was a short-lived proposal that nevertheless renewed intense speculation about the next chapter in the eclectic career of Larry Tisch.

Ever since Tisch began to accumulate CBS stock in 1985, the media had sought to make sense of the billionaire's disparate collection of investments. Larry Tisch started his business career by buying up hotels and plowing the profits into a seemingly unrelated collection of businesses: movie theaters (Loew's), insurance (CNA), cigarettes (Kent), watches (Bulova), ships, oil rigs, and finally broadcasting when he became head of CBS. The common thread that Tisch detected was an untapped potential to generate tons of cash. He had no all-encompassing corporate profile in mind as he built his holdings. For Larry Tisch, the game was business and the cash at the end of the day was how you kept score.

Over the years, Tisch sat on the boards of corporate giants such as Getty Oil, Macy's, and others. He counted among his friends billionaire investor Warren Buffett, the influential Federal Reserve chairman Alan Greenspan, and notorious junk-bond king Michael Milken. He influenced a host of world leaders—George Bush, Shimon Peres, Moshe Dayan, Golda Meir—who viewed him as a leading spokesman for the American Jewish community, a role that sprang from his long association with Jewish charities. Presidential hopefuls and numerous other politicians sought his support as a respected member of the business establishment.

Virtually every day of the week, news is reported in the mainstream national media that in some way directly involves Larry Tisch, yet his name is hardly a household word. Throughout his life, he has lived modestly, kept a low profile, and stuck to the fundamental business principle of increasing the value of any investment entrusted to him.

Born in Brooklyn in 1923, the grandson of Russian immigrant Jews, he graduated from high school at the age of 15 and from college shortly before turning 19. He started his business career at 23 by advising his parents—who had started out their marriage literally penniless—to invest $125,000 of their own cash in a New Jersey resort hotel. Within 10 years, Larry was the financial power behind a multimillion-dollar hotel chain, which he quickly transformed into a multibillion-dollar conglomerate ranked among America's largest corporations.

Forbes magazine's 1994 survey of personal wealth put his net worth at $1.14 billion, making him one of the 49 richest Americans. The empire he oversaw encompassed assets of more than $40 billion and generated revenue of nearly $14 billion annually.

What was remarkable was that Larry Tisch accumulated this vast fortune without any apparent ambition to do so. He had no burning desire to be rich. At no point did he visualize his future success and devise a plan to get there.

"I never thought in those terms," Tisch said. "I just enjoyed business and we were doing business. I never thought of it as money-making. You're involved. You're doing business. You try to build it up. You do the best you can everyday. And whatever happened, who cared? It was never a question of accumulating money as such. Fortunately, right from the beginning, money was never a problem. It was the game."

His life-style reflected a singular lack of attachment to the accoutrements of practically limitless wealth. He drove Pontiacs purchased at his brother-in-law's dealership. The decor in his homes and offices, tastefully understated, would scarcely strain the budget of a midlevel executive with one one-thousandth of Tisch's net worth. He was the antithesis of conspicuous consumption, as sensitive to an overpriced hotel meal as he was to an overvalued Fortune 500 company.

He was a genius not of planning and design but of swift decisiveness driven by instinctively good common sense. Asked whether he ever had anything like a five-year plan for achieving certain goals, he replied, "I don't have a one-day plan."

What worked for Tisch wasn't having a plan but having a clear set of principles for determining when to buy an asset and when to sell, whether it was a business, a commodity, or a security. He looked for bargain-priced assets whose values were depressed only temporarily— typically, because of mismanagement. His overriding requirement was that he would put no more into an investment than he could reasonably expect to get out of it under a worst-case scenario. Once he owned an underperforming asset, he aggressively rooted out the cause of its stagnation and made the changes necessary to turn the tide, often by gaining ownership control and taking over management himself. A key element was Tisch's ability to quickly determine whether an investment met all his requirements and to act fast.

Tisch's boardroom coup at CBS had less to do with having a strategy to take over the company than it did with moment-to-moment, circumstantial decisions. He was a brilliant opportunist, quick to adapt to changing conditions though never one to take inordinate risks. He always made sure that, based on all available information, the odds for success were stacked heavily in his favor. That was the case when he became a CBS stockholder. From day 1, his CBS stake represented a high-potential, low-risk investment that grew stronger and safer as time passed, even though the company itself was experiencing some of its darkest days. His rapid progression from investor to director to chief executive had more to do with a leadership vacuum at CBS than with Tisch's desire to run the company. His main motivation for wanting to take the helm initially was to protect his investment until a permanent, effective leader could be found.

It wasn't the first time he had more than made up for the lack of a plan by having acute radar for a rare investment opportunity, a ready load of cash, and the unshakable self-confidence to move swiftly. Those were the qualities that, in the span of 20 years, transformed Tisch the hotelier into Tisch the conglomerateur—all the while proving himself one of Wall Street's smartest smart-money investors and one of corporate America's most sought-after board members.

His prominence in matters of business and finance often drew Tisch into the center of some of the most highly charged moments in the recent history of capitalism. He found himself at the center of the Equity Funding insurance scandal as one of its biggest investor-victims in the early 1970s. When he sold his stake in the Franklin National Bank, also in the 1970s, to a shady European financier—Michele Sindona—who then brought the bank to the brink of insolvency, the sequence of events nearly sparked a national banking crisis. He was often consulted for his levelheaded clarity in complex business controversies. Gordon Getty turned to Tisch for advice in the bitter feud between Texaco and Pennzoil for ownership of Getty Oil in the early 1980s—a feud that ultimately put Texaco on the losing end of a record $10 billion lawsuit, forcing it temporarily into bankruptcy. And Tisch came to the rescue of CBS amid the leveraged-buyout craze of the 1980s.

Taking Over as CBS Chairman

The opportunity for Tisch to assume a white-knight role unfolded in 1985 when Senator Jesse Helms, the archconservative Republican, took a shot at spearheading a shareholder revolt against CBS News's supposed liberal slant. Any vague nervousness company officials may have felt about Helms's quixotic effort quickly blossomed into outright fear when cable-TV cowboy Ted Turner emerged soon after with a precarious but potentially serious takeover bid.

In the tradition of the riskiest of the 1980s leveraged buyouts, Turner's offer was heavily dependent on junk-bond financing—lowgrade, high-risk debt—and the sale of numerous CBS assets to service that debt. Still, the offer posed a real enough threat that CBS had to mount a costly defense. That's when Tisch began to build a stake—with the quiet encouragement of then CBS chairman Thomas H. Wyman. CBS employees and the general public began to ask, "Who is Larry Tisch?" Even CBS founder William S. Paley, still the company's largest single shareholder, wasn't sure, assuming at first it was Robert Tishman, the real estate developer.

The confusion was understandable: the Tisches were also heavily involved in real estate. Tisch and his brother, Preston Robert ("Bob") Tisch, along with their parents, built the foundation of their family fortune on a chain of luxury hotels and related real estate deals. By 1985, however, the hotel business was a small part of the family's rich empire. The Tisch holdings by that time encompassed Bulova, Lorillard, and more than 80 percent of CNA, as well as a large block of CBS—all under the umbrella of parent company Loews Corp. Loews was the last vestige of the movie theater chain the Tisches had bought into during the late 1950s in their first stock-market play—a purchase that would establish the Tisches' reputation as savvy corporate bottom-fishers.

The Tisch investment strategy was to acquire bargain-priced stock of publicly traded companies that held assets far more valuable than the average investor perceived. Some companies' stock was cheap despite potentially valuable assets, because management hadn't figured out how to transform those assets into ever-rising profits. In those situations, the Tisches weren't shy. They became activists. CBS was no exception, but when Wyman welcomed Tisch's investment, the CBS chairman and chief executive was betting that this time would be different. By March 1987, Wyman had lost that bet—and his job—to Larry Tisch.

PUTTING THE SHAREHOLDERS FIRST

To Tisch, the purpose of every business was to generate decent profits for its owners. That article of faith went without saying, and it applied to the mom-and-pop candy store on the corner as well as to his own sprawling conglomerate. This nugget of common sense had served him well in all his business ventures. But from the time Tisch first emerged as a major CBS stockholder in the summer of 1985, it gradually became clear that almost no one in the company seemed to think common sense applied to a company like CBS.

"There's nobody in this business at ABC, NBC, or CBS who doesn't know one thing," Tisch said. "The show is the thing. But by the same token, if you carry that to extremes, it's like the guy who drowned in an average of 12 inches of water. Sure the show is the thing. Everybody knows that; but do you sit around having the money pour out in waste while you go around saying the show is the thing?"

Along with the other two top broadcast networks, CBS was perceived as a public trust. With the government's blessing and oversight, the three major networks used the airwaves to provide a public service—the transmission of useful information. In return, they earned the right to air whatever else they believed would interest people enough to sit through all the commercials that paid the rent. The people who worked for the news operation—the core of the public service function—developed a hybrid personality: part public servant, part celebrity. Of almost no interest to many of these people was whether their work enriched the shareholders of the companies that ran the networks. Small wonder. For years, it was a tradition at the networks to keep the news divisions from showing profits for fear of eroding their aura of public service.

Profitability, however, of the news unit and every other network function was of growing interest to a new breed of investors—businesspeople who generally failed to see the payback in stroking on-air egos, especially in an environment of upstart networks and 50-odd cable alternatives.

By the time Tisch had displaced Wyman in September 1986, the Tisch family had acquired a 25 percent stake in CBS, and it was clear to Larry that the network's executives had been mismanaging the shareholders' money. CBS's board wasn't used to Tisch's no-nonsense, bottom-line-oriented management style. When Tisch walked through the front door at CBS's 36-story, Canadian black granite headquarters in midtown Manhattan on the morning of September 11, 1986—the day after being named chief executive officer—he already was tuned into what he saw as evidence of appalling waste: too many rent-a-cops in the lobby. As he made his way through the building, he accumulated proof that CBS executives had forgotten whose money they were spending. He saw too many dining rooms, and too many layers of top executives camped out in too many richly decorated suites of offices. To Tisch, it hinted of a spendthrift culture in an atmosphere of arrogant indifference toward shareholders.

He intended to change that culture fast—as had Wyman—but much of what Tisch viewed as waste former President Frank R. Stanton had purposefully built into the CBS mindset. As William Paley's prime corporate image maker at CBS, Stanton had crafted the network's so-called Tiffany image partly by sparing no expense to create an ambiance of pricey but tasteful elegance and by encouraging a cradle-to-grave generosity toward employees. The ambiance was an extension of CBS's aim to be known as the network of quality programming.

In Tisch's view, however, CBS no longer could afford a spare-no-expense approach to the network's quality. "Survival was the issue," Tisch said, "not the comfort of management." CBS was throwing money into a pit where it had no chance to grow and return a reward to the all-important owners. There was no greater corporate sin.

Worrying about maintaining a well-heeled public image, with money no object, was no longer appropriate.

"Sure we had public obligations which we fulfill," Tisch said, "but if we don't run it as a business we're not going to be here tomorrow. It's a funny kind of a business that nobody understands. Our network, ABC network, NBC network—each grosses about $3 billion a year and, among the three of us, I don't think we make $300 million in the network business. So that's $9 billion of gross with $300 million total profit for the three networks," for a measly combined return of less than 4 percent.

In a good year, CBS might earn $150 million. "It's nothing," Tisch said. "If you don't run it as a business, our fixed costs in a down year could destroy us, because when we start the season, say September 10, if our programs don't work, there's no cost to cut. I can lay off six people or eight people, but it's not like a manufacturing plant where you have a cost of goods. Our costs are all preordained. It's fascinating. It's a very interesting business for that reason. There's no leeway once you make the mistake."

Did Tisch understand these dynamics when he bought into CBS? "Not all of them" he admitted, but he wasn't completely green. His initial CBS stock purchase in 1985 was little more than a trading opportunity, but he had been exposed to the business through his friends Leonard Goldenson, CEO of ABC, and Warren Buffett, CEO of Berkshire Hathaway and the second-wealthiest man in America in 1994, with a net worth estimated at $9.35 billion.

THE TISCH-BASHING BEGINS

One of the dynamics of the network business Tisch hadn't fully appreciated was the public's appetite for gossip about it—and CBS's own fear of bad press. Wyman, for example, before Tisch arrived, had told the board of his plan to reduce the broadcasting division's staff by 500 people to help cope with the phenomenon of disappearing earnings.

"The board was very pleased with the announcement," Tisch noted. "It was the right thing to do. So six months later I got here and I spoke to the head of personnel, who told me that of the 500 announced layoffs only 25 or 30 had been laid off. I said, 'What happened?' Well, everyone was afraid of an article in the *New York Times.*"

Such publicity might make managers uncomfortable, but managers who dared to put their own comfort ahead of that of the shareholders were, to Tisch, as low as the lowest of corrupt ward-heeler politicians. In his first 40 years in business in a variety of enterprises, that belief seldom failed him. On the infrequent occasions when the media noticed him prior to the CBS years, he usually was praised for such convictions.

In 1960, for example, *Fortune* magazine ran an admiring feature on how he and his brother had built a chain of highly profitable luxury hotels by taking over mainly troubled properties, sprucing them up, subjecting them to strict cost-accounting management controls, and aggressively promoting them. The *New York Times* in 1968 used the occasion of the Loew's acquisition of Lorillard to identify Tisch as one of the nation's most successful corporate empire builders. In 1971, *Fortune* revisited Tisch, focusing on his role as the champion of shareholders' right to hold management accountable for corporate performance. And in 1976, a *Business Week* headline was: "How Loews' Lean Management Fattened the Profits at CNA."

When Howard Stringer made the layoff announcement at CBS, there was no praise for such tough-minded, cost-accounting discipline. Tisch was about to be lambasted for having had the nerve to suggest that CBS should be forced to measure up to the same performance standards the Tisch family had applied to all its other investments. The most fundamental of those standards was that every dollar spent in the course of doing business was viewed as an investment expected to yield at least as good a return as that of no-risk government bonds.

In the first sixth months of Tisch's tenure as chief executive, the journalists at CBS came to view him as a hero. His first day on the job, he fired news president Van Gordon Sauter, widely viewed as having displaced news values with an overemphasis on entertainment values. Richard Cohen, the "CBS Evening News" senior producer in charge of foreign coverage, danced through the newsroom singing "Ding dong, the witch is dead." Tisch encouraged staffers to view him as someone whose chief mission was to restore the network's news integrity, protecting it from ideologues and spending cuts that might hurt its quality. Staffers already had undergone a demoralizing water torture of incremental—and frequently only threatened—cut-backs ordered by Wyman late in 1985. In conjunction with other cost-cutting moves, Wyman had jettisoned a number of stumbling nonbroadcast operations such as toys and musical instruments. With Tisch at the helm, many employees assumed a full-scale bloodletting would be averted. What they didn't understand was that the board felt betrayed by Wyman: he hadn't delivered the deep cuts he had promised.

From the beginning, Tisch called for managers to finally implement those cuts and to find ways to slash even more costs at every level. Never one to write memos, he made his wishes known face-to-face, leaving it to individual managers to figure out how to carry out the directive.

Stringer, whom Tisch named to succeed Sauter, was among those managers ordered to cut the annual budget. From the news division, Tisch wanted a $50 million cut, to $250 million. "I saw waste and inefficiency and redundancy," Tisch said. "CBS News had an operating budget of $89 million in 1978. And it skyrocketed to $300 million in 1986! If you took the normal inflation increase, it would have been just $145 million in 1986."

Stringer agreed with Tisch that the news budget was bloated. He agreed that hyperinflation in the salaries of celebrity newscasters—especially Dan Rather, who was about halfway through a 10-year, $22 million contract that quickly turned out to be the minimum wage for network anchors—was a major cause. Stringer knew the division had to become profitable. And he knew his career depended largely on being able to meet what in any other business would be considered a reasonable business goal: to make money. But when Stringer disclosed the layoffs as his first step toward achieving that goal, the troops, via the media, attacked Tisch and began to sound mutinous.

In a flash, Tisch was to be stripped of his hero's mantle. He would be depicted as a short, bald miser who drove his late-model Pontiac station wagon to the front door of Paley's classy "Black Rock" skyscraper to rummage through a prestigious institution in search of anything that could quickly be converted into cash and reinvested in bonds or anything else that might yield a safe, respectable return.

"Tisch has gone to great lengths to present himself as a conciliatory fellow almost overwhelmed with reverence for the proud traditions of CBS," *Fortune* magazine reported in October 1986. "Don't be fooled. This short, bald dumpling of a man, who looks so profoundly out of place in the extravagant confines of Wyman's old five-room office suite, is without question going to stand CBS on its ear."

And, that's exactly what Tisch did. He forced CBS to abandon its reputation as a cradle-to-grave civil-service employer. No longer would tenure have any meaning. The company's payroll was cut by thousands as Tisch jettisoned everything that wasn't broadcasting— including CBS Records, a music publishing division, and its magazines. He forced the remaining operations to slash even more costs—more than 200 news division staffers were let go. He promoted a culture of such frugality that, at times, the cost cutting seemed to reach ludicrous proportions.

At the nadir of his popularity after buying into CBS, the ultimate example of what Tisch supposedly was all about involved cutting corporate waste not just in the board room, but in the rest rooms. One of Tisch's minions, Edward Grebow, hired in 1988 as senior vice president in charge of personnel, facilities, and data processing, discovered an underpriced sanitary napkin dispenser, boosted the price, and turned it into a profit center. It was true that Tisch and a handful of trusted managers were rooting out waste at every level, but this anecdote he vehemently denied. "This sanitary napkin thing just didn't happen," he said, meaning he personally didn't make such a decision. But it did happen.

Stringer clarified that Tisch was not directly involved with the decision. Grebow was merely an enthusiastic lieutenant. In dollars and cents, it probably wasn't worth it. Grebow's reasoning was that the underpriced dispensers were being tapped for home supplies. Nevertheless, the media seized on such tales of penny-pinching taken to extremes.

For a long time, the media would lose interest in the substance of Larry Tisch. They were interested in his style—in more stories like the one about sanitary napkin profit centers. Tisch was beginning to feel picked on. In fact, as his managers hacked and slashed their way through the fat at CBS, selling whole divisions and eliminating layers of executives, staffers started referring to being "Tisched" as a synonym for "fired." A May 1988 *New York Magazine* article was even headlined "The Tisching of CBS." This surely wasn't how Tisch, then 65 years old, had hoped to be remembered. Nearly two years later, when the pieces seemed to be in place for Tisch's CBS to turn around—it had shed noncore lines, was cash-rich, had started to build a strong schedule of programs like "Murphy Brown" and had a "special events" strategy to showcase them—the media still remained skeptical.

In February 1990, Kenneth Labich's piece in *Fortune* carried the headline: "Has Tisch Lost His Touch?" The article, which angered Tisch, carried this comment: "He seems to relish the spotlight, as if unaware of how unkind it has been to him."

What Labich was missing—indeed, what nearly all the writers on the Tisch beat seemed to miss—was the source of Larry Tisch's motivation. It wasn't being in the spotlight, or having good press, or having more money than anyone else. "Your standard of living," he said, "doesn't change after the first million." What drove him was being in the game. He lacked the kind of ego that craves public adulation; the love and acceptance of his own family was all the approval he needed. Anything beyond that was secondary. Tisch wasn't unaware of how hard the media were hitting him, but, in the long run, their blows didn't matter a whole lot to him.

In the context of his stewardship of CBS, Tisch faced a public perception challenge that, for the first time in his career, posed a threat to his ability to lead. The media clamored that he was about to meet his Waterloo—the type of prediction that tends to be self-fulfilling in its effect on an already fragile employee morale.

Whatever the negative coverage might do to undermine his authority at CBS, Tisch wasn't about to cave in. Unlike some leaders who are driven by internal voices of self-doubt, Larry Tisch held his ground. His irritation at the media didn't translate into a weakened resolve. None of the criticism convinced him that he was on the wrong track—only that he was in a new kind of business that was driven by creativity and stars and huge audiences, and was covered incessantly by the media.

Nearly four years passed before the press and its insider sources grudgingly stopped second-guessing Larry Tisch's every move at CBS—and then, only after success seemed certain. Costs got in line, the cash mounted, and ratings were poised to rebound. Tisch would achieve all this not by altering his strategy for CBS, but by adapting his personal management style to the unique culture of television, the stock market of commercial creativity and talent.

By 1994, when Tisch at the age of 71 was casting about for a way to leave the helm at CBS, the company's constituents—employees, shareholders, and the all-important advertisers—would experience as much anxiety about the prospect of his departure as they did at his arrival. Even before the Diller proposal surfaced, insiders fretted over the reality that Tisch wouldn't be there forever yet had no obvious successor. In the corporate landscape, few leaders could match Tisch's record of amassing cash and bringing rock-solid financial stability to so many companies.

2

The Hotel Years: Learning the Acquisitions Game

"I was always thankful to him for coming to America."

—Larry Tisch, referring to his grandfather.

Like many American Jews, Laurence Al Tisch traces his U.S. beginnings to the massive migration of East Europeans around the time of the assassination of Alexander II, a tolerant czar, in 1881. The czar's death unleashed a torrent of renewed anti-Semitism. The Jews, who lived between the Baltic and Black Seas, in an area known as the Pale, began to prepare for an exodus inspired not just by persecution but by hope. The revival of attacks on Jews coincided with a time of explosive intellectual and spiritual growth within the Jewish community. At the same time, America, the new promised land, beckoned them from their slumlike shtetls.

Between 1881 and the start of World War I in 1914, one-third of Eastern Europe's Jews emigrated. Among them was the family into which Larry's father, Abraham Solomon Tischinsky, was born in 1897 in Dnepropetrovsk, about 200 miles north of the Black Sea and 500 miles south of Moscow, on the Dnepr River in what is now Ukraine. Abraham, who had two sisters, was about three years old when he arrived in New York. Like tens of thousands of Russian Jewish immigrants, he was destined to work in Manhattan's flourishing garment industry.

The details of how Abraham's parents, Solomon and Dina, decided to emigrate were lost when they died—Dina in the 1930s, Solomon in the 1940s.

"The reason people left was they were at the bottom of the heap," Tisch said. "The rich Mexicans don't come across the border." In Russia, to be poor and Jewish was a deadly combination.

What experiences pushed individuals to leave for America? "People didn't talk about it a lot," said Billie Tisch, Larry's wife. "I think it was painful when they came here, and people weren't really interested in that until it was too late."

The family's oral history begins with the arrival in America. Larry's grandfather, Solomon Tischinsky, was a furrier, a trade he pursued successfully in New York. He lived around the corner from a synagogue in the Bensonhurst section of Brooklyn and was active in its affairs. When Larry himself became a grandfather for the 11th time, he would still be wearing his grandfather's gold ring, handed down to Larry by his own father.

"He was a wonderful man—a decent, intelligent, hard-working, good citizen," Tisch said of his grandfather. "I was always thankful to him for coming to America."

The ring, its inscribed initials all but worn away, symbolized the tradition of working hard and enjoying it in the service of family and community. It was a reminder of one particularly spiritual family leader who placed a high value on integrity.

Abraham attended public schools in New York, which is where his prowess on the basketball court first emerged. In high school—the same school Larry would graduate from—Abraham's friends simplified his name to Al Tisch.

By the time he had graduated from City College of New York (CCNY), Al had been captain of the basketball team and a college All-American around 1917. At that time, 5' 10" was a normal height for a basketball player. Abraham was 5' 10½", or about two inches taller than Larry became in adulthood. At CCNY, Al formally adopted Tisch as his last name.

In 1920, Al Tisch married Sayde Brenner, whose parents had immigrated from Lithuania earlier in the exodus, before Sayde's birth in New York in 1899. The day Sayde married Al Tisch, he had 30 cents in his pocket—the change left after purchasing their marriage license at City Hall in Manhattan. On their way out of the building, Al gave a third of his money to a panhandler and then used what was left for their subway fare home. That impulse to share—which would be passed along to their two sons—gave Sayde and Al Tisch the right to claim they had started out, literally, with nothing.

In the early years of their marriage, Al Tisch worked for a children's clothing manufacturer on Fifth Avenue. He came to the job through a family reference, but had no burning desire to be in that business. Still, he worked hard at it and soon left with one of the company's top salesmen, Hymie Handelsman, to produce their own line of low-priced clothing for boys under the company name of Tisch-Handelsman. Tisch managed the manufacturing, and Handelsman managed sales. Their operations centered along lower Fifth Avenue, between 14th and 23rd Streets—at that time, home to numerous makers of boys' and men's clothing.

Sayde, meanwhile, pursued her own career as an assistant to movie mogul Harold Lubin, who, in 1921, paid her the then-astronomical salary of $200 a week. Lubin built the famed Roxy Theater in New York. When Sayde worked with him, his office was at 1540 Broadway, which later became the home of Loew's Theatres Inc. when her sons made it their base of operations and built the foundation of a multibillion-dollar family fortune.

"Sayde was an extraordinary woman," recalled journalist Elizabeth Drew, daughter of Sayde's brother Bill. "She was unusually bright and I think in another era and culture might well have been a CEO in her own right. She had a tremendous amount of energy." Al Tisch she remembered also as "no slouch. He was very strong, very smart."

Said Larry Tisch: "My mother was a remarkable woman. She always had a good figure—thin, well dressed, well groomed. She was also very bright." In no sense did she fit the mold of the traditional Jewish mother, putting her career on hold when her children were young.

Responding to one observer's characterization of Sayde as "a nice old Jewish woman," Tisch protested. "My mother was never a nice old Jewish lady," he said. "Never. If you met my mother, no one ever thought she was Jewish. She looked Irish. She was never an old lady; even when she was old she was never an old lady." She was at least as entrepreneurial as her husband and surely modeled for her sons a spirit characterized by an exuberant willingness to work hard and to work smart.

Larry, born March 5, 1923, was the Tisches' first son. At the time, they lived on the ground floor of the two-family house Al's father owned in Bensonhurst. Solomon and Dina Tischinsky occupied the second floor. Larry's only other sibling, Preston Robert, was born three years later, on April 29, 1926. Bob recalled an early indication of Larry's unusual intelligence. They would sit on the front steps of their Bensonhurst home, and Larry, no more than eight years old, would call out the make of each car as it sped past.

With their two young sons, the Tisches moved to the Flatbush section of Brooklyn, where Larry attended P.S. 99 for about two years. From there, in about 1931, they moved into a new, six-story apartment building in Brighton Beach—like Bensonhurst, a community of Jewish families, many of East European origin. They would live there about six years.

Judith Pere Goldman lived next door to the Tisches, on the third floor at 125 Brighton 11th Street. These were one-bedroom apartments that rented for $65 a month. The Tisches' two children shared the one bedroom and their parents slept on a pullout bed in the foyer. "That's the way everybody lived," said Dr. Goldman, who was a few years behind Tisch at P.S. 225. "We thought we were rich."

Brighton Beach in the 1930s was a secluded, almost provincial neighborhood. The children went to the Brighton Baths in the summer, or to Manhattan Beach and Oriental Beach on the ocean. Although they were Jewish, they seldom went to temple, except on high holy days. "When we were growing up," Dr. Goldman said, "the emphasis was very much on assimilation. I don't even understand Yiddish."

The Tisches were different. "My family was never interested in assimilation," Tisch said. "We were always Jewish. We never had any interest in being anything else other than Jewish." Indeed, the family's earliest business ventures were related to serving the Jewish community: summer camps for Jewish children, and hotels that catered primarily to Jews. "We were always identified with the Jewish community."

At P.S. 225, Tisch started to skip grades, pushed along by teachers because of the obvious speed with which he mastered every subject he encountered. He paid a price for this rapid advancement. "I was always the youngest one in the class," he said. The age difference made it harder to make friends. He briefly attended Abraham Lincoln High School before the family moved to West End Avenue and 78th Street in Manhattan. Larry graduated from Dewitt Clinton High School in the Bronx in 1939 at age 15.

Throughout these Great Depression years, Al Tisch built his business, though not without problems and not without wondering whether it was the right business for him. He managed it successfully in spite of the Depression. Because its focus was on low-priced clothing, A. S. Tisch Co. (Handelsman, much older than Al Tisch, had retired) remained profitable, but a chain of clothing stores he owned in New England—Newton Clothes—began to hemorrhage.

"It was a very successful chain," Larry Tisch recalled, "but when the Depression hit in 1930–31, affecting New England towns like Lowell and Lawrence and Fall River and New Bedford, his stores went bad, but he never went into bankruptcy. He paid everybody 100 cents on the dollar."

Any losses Al Tisch incurred in business weren't detected at home. "There was never a period that I remember a hardship in the family," Larry said.

Even if hardship had been a part of their growing up, Larry and Bob are not likely to have turned out much different. "They had a very firm but loving upbringing by their parents," said Elizabeth Drew, their cousin, and the brothers were raised to be close and would always remain close.

FIRST JOB

Larry and Bob, as teenagers, worked in their father's business, starting out as shipping clerks. "We did everything," he said. "We enjoyed work. My father was a very easy man to work for. Very kind. Never tough on us." While still in his teens, Larry established his own accounts, making sales to jobbers on Orchard Street on the Lower East Side on Sundays. "It was interesting," he said. "These people were always interested in price. They were intelligent. They all were in business for themselves. My job was to make sure I didn't give away the store."

Larry's next job was in the summer camp his parents bought in 1935, when Larry was about 13 years old. They bought the camp as a shared business venture. Sayde, who had taken some courses in Freudian child psychology, decided she wanted to go back to work. Al told her: "People will think I can't support you. If you want to work, we'll do something together."

"My mother wanted to be in a business," Bob Tisch recalled, and perhaps her interest in child psychology played a part in the decision to look for a summer camp to operate. Besides, Bob suggested, "The lure of a children's camp was that it was a clean business for a young husband and wife." The main motivation for Al was that he had had enough of the clothing business. It was time for a change.

The Tisches bought the Lincoln and Laurel summer camp, in the rolling hills of Blairstown, in northwestern New Jersey, from Frank Dees of Jersey City. The camp was divided in half—one half for boys, the other for girls—and had a shared dining hall. For Al Tisch, this venture was an opportunity to share some of the pleasure he took in being an avid athlete and team leader. He continued to run A. S. Tisch Co., but increasingly left the clothing business's affairs in the hands of one of Al's brothers-in-law. For Sayde, the summer camp was a way to stretch her entrepreneurial wings. She directed camp operations while Al managed the finances.

The camp accommodated roughly 125 Jewish children, ages 6 to 15, with tuition set at $125 a season. To drum up business, Sayde would call on parents in their homes and show them film footage of the camp's activities. She worked hard to sign up these word-of-mouth referrals.

"That was a very good experience for my brother and myself, because in the off-season we would go up there every weekend and work," Larry Tisch said, "and we were there during the summers."

The way Sayde and Al worked together and gave their sons useful roles in their enterprises left little doubt in Larry's mind that he would be a businessman when he grew up. It mattered little what business it was: the appeal was in running an enterprise that generated cash.

Sayde once said in an interview: "My husband and I never shielded our children from business talk. We've always been a close-knit family and my husband's business philosophy was founded on integrity. On occasion, someone would propose a business partnership in some venture and my husband would always bow out with the same saying: 'I have three partners already, my wife and two sons, and that's enough.'"

The summer camp led the family in the direction of the resort business. The Tisches had built a few cabins for vacationing adults at the camp, and that led them to think about pursuing that kind of business in a bigger way.

Besides, after 11 years in the camp business, Al and Sayde Tisch were ready to move on. Al's interest in the clothing business had all but evaporated.

COLLEGE ON THE FAST TRACK

Bob progressed through school at a normal pace; Larry continued on a fast track. In 1941, just three years after graduating from high school, he graduated cum laude from New York University's School of Commerce. He had picked NYU because he was too young to go away to school, and, within the city, NYU had one of the best business schools. At that point, Larry knew only that he wanted to be a businessman; he had no idea what kind of business he would aim for.

At NYU's School of Commerce, Larry Tisch met and studied under the legendary Marcus Nadler, whose ideas about the international money markets and the role of central banks would later influence Tisch and a group of devoted followers. Perhaps the most famous member of the group was investor Henry Kaufman, who spent 26 years at Salomon Brothers.

"Nadler had an extraordinary ability to simplify complex financial practices," said Kaufman, who studied under Nadler several years after Tisch. "He did not have a pet theory, but he was an anti-inflationist." Perhaps Nadler's greatest quality was his step-by-step approach to problem solving, a hallmark of Tisch's future business strategy.

Nadler developed an enormous following of former students. His classes on current economic and financial problems frequently were attended by former students, many of whom joined the Money Marketeers, a group that met several times a year for dinner and to hear Nadler speak. Nadler was a major influence in formulating Tisch's views on money supply fluctuations and the implications for inflation, interest rates, and the economy.

When Tisch graduated from NYU in February 1942, just before his 19th birthday, Nadler offered him a job as an assistant. Tisch wasn't as inclined as Kaufman to take up the anti-inflation crusade, but Nadler must have viewed him as a potential protégé. With World War II raging, Tisch had another offer that fit in better with his plans to fulfill his military obligation: a chance to get a master's degree in two semesters from the Wharton School of Finance and Commerce at the University of Pennsylvania in Philadelphia. He asked Nadler what he would do if it were his choice. Get the master's, Nadler said. Tisch took his advice and graduated from Wharton in January 1943 with a master's in industrial engineering, a misleading name for what essentially was a master's of business administration.

Shortly before graduation, Tisch tried to enlist in one of the Navy's officer training programs, "the only time in my life that I ever felt anti-Semitism." He failed the physical for high blood pressure, something no doctor ever detected before or since. "It was a form of 'We don't want any more Jews for Naval officers,'" Tisch said, "so I enlisted in the Army."

During basic training at Fort Dix in New Jersey, Tisch was picked up by the Office of Strategic Services, predecessor to the Central Intelligence Agency, and transferred to Washington. Although still attached to the Army, he worked in cryptanalysis—code breaking, enciphering, and deciphering. "Everything that came in from every agent around the world came through our office," he said, except dispatches from Gen. Douglas MacArthur's theater of operations. Tisch found this work very interesting; often, what was most interesting was the extent to which incoming reports would prove to be exaggerations. Following a bombing run, the dispatches would give an impression that the city of Stuttgart, for example, was gone. Reality would turn out quite different. Within hours, rail lines would be back up and running.

When Larry Tisch was discharged from the Army in 1945, he was unsure where he was headed. A friend was planning to attend Harvard Law School, and Tisch's father urged, "Why don't you go to law school? It's a good education." Larry said he didn't want to be a lawyer.

"You don't have to *be* a lawyer," his father told him. Said Larry: "My father was a very intelligent man. I was 23 at the time. So I said, 'All right, I'll put in an application. They'll never take me.'" Harvard accepted him for classes beginning that summer. Meanwhile, Larry knew his parents were looking for their next opportunity. In a family as close and hard-working as the Tisches, it seemed logical that the family somehow would move forward as a team.

As Larry prepared for his studies at Harvard, Al and Sayde began in earnest to pursue their next business goal: to get into the resort hotel business in Florida. They figured correctly that Florida was on its way to becoming a major mecca of tourism. The only problem was, the speculation was overheated. "It was like trading sardines," Larry Tisch said. A deal agreed to in the morning might be scuttled by the end of the day because of a higher bid.

"We got fed up with that kind of business ethic," he said. "We were interested in Florida, but we wanted to go first-class in Florida. We didn't want to end up with second-rate hotels."

As part of the process of raising money to bankroll such a venture, the Tisches sold the Lincoln and Laurel summer camp. Proceeds from the sale, combined with the family's savings, amounted to about $125,000.

With Al's brother-in-law gradually winding down A. S. Tisch Co., Al and Sayde headed for Florida.

Tisch's First Acquisition

In February 1946, Tisch, who had just gotten out of the Army and was preparing for his first semester at Harvard that summer, spotted an ad in the *New York Times:* Laurel-in-the-Pines, a Kosher 300-room resort hotel in Lakewood, New Jersey, about 60 miles south of New York City, was on sale for $375,000. In a town with 100 hotels, Laurel-in-the-Pines was considered far and away the best, although it badly needed a face lift. Larry and his father drove down to Lakewood to evaluate the aging luxury resort hotel and decided to go forward. "After Florida, Laurel-in-the-Pines seemed like a terrific buy," Tisch said. "In Florida, for 50 rooms you were paying $500,000, $600,000."

Larry was just 23 years old. That anyone so young could play a key advisory role in his parents' decision to make the $175,000 investment necessary to take over the hotel was remarkable. The amount of the investment would be equivalent to more than $1 million in 1994 dollars. Al and Sayde Tisch recognized that their son's intelligence far exceeded that of an average 23-year-old. They respected it and deferred to it. Even as a youngster helping out in the family clothing business, "My father treated me as an adult," Tisch said. "Anything I wanted to do was my decision."

As Larry's oldest son, Andrew, put it, Al Tisch "really lived his life for the boys. He bet everything he had on Larry and Bob with Laurel-in-the-Pines and on their ability to do the right thing."

Larry was the Tisches' child prodigy. He was ready to enter the business world without ever having worked for anyone except his parents and the U.S. Army. His parents treated him as an equal partner. His age and experience were insignificant compared to his native powers of reasoning—abilities Larry and his parents were eager to capitalize on in the pursuit of their next opportunity.

Frank Seiden, the owner of Laurel-in-the-Pines, and Larry Tisch looked at the hotel and saw sharply different pictures. Seiden believed he had some good reasons for being willing to sell his New Jersey hotel at one-eighth the per-room price Florida hotels were fetching. Like a lot of people at the end of World War II, Seiden was convinced the Depression had never ended—that the effort to produce arms for the war had only put it on hold. The hotel had prospered during the war, catering to the need for the war-weary to get away from it all when they had little time to get far away and meager gasoline rations. Seiden, figuring property values would stagnate and the economy would swoon, was eager to get out while the getting was good. Indeed, at the time of the sale, the hotel's postwar return was waning.

Larry Tisch saw a different future for postwar America, a different vision perhaps influenced by Professor Marcus Nadler's view of the world's economy. The key element was that, compared with the United States, competing economies in the rest of the world were in a shambles. With Germany and Japan in ruins, along with many of the countries where the two nations had won and lost their battles, the United States was one of the few industrialized nations that had been spared physical destruction. Tisch sensed that the demand for U.S. goods and services was about to explode, fueling a continuation of the industrial output that previously had been powered by the war effort.

Besides, for the first time, the government was subsidizing home mortgages—at low interest rates. Under the GI Bill, it also was paying all expenses for war veterans who wanted to attend college. Tisch foresaw that cheap and easy loans for housing would produce a building boom, which, in turn, would fuel strong economic growth. At the same time, the work force was about to undergo a rapid upgrading just as the foundation was being built for strong overseas demand for American output. Where Seiden saw gloom and doom, Tisch saw a can't-miss boom.

The Tisches believed a well-run, renovated Laurel-in-the-Pines could easily generate $100,000 a year in profit. It was a strong, reputable business. At a purchase price of $375,000, the downside risk appeared minimal. Even if they had to settle for just $100,000 a year, the hotel would pay for itself quickly and remain the resort's most salable property. With a little effort, the profit potential was even greater.

In August 1946, the Tisches, hedging their bet, signed a lease for the hotel, a Thanksgiving-to-Easter/Passover operation. Part of the initial investment for leasing and renovating Laurel-in-the-Pines came from Sol Henkind, a New York real estate investor and a friend of Sayde. For $50,000, Henkind got a 25 percent stake, which he would sell back to the Tisches after one year of operation. With Larry having started at Harvard Law in June, Sayde and Al Tisch geared up for their first season as resort hoteliers.

The Laurel-in-the-Pines deal, Larry Tisch's first big deal, encompassed two themes that would characterize practically all of his investment decisions. First, he showed an unshakable confidence in his own instincts and a willingness to defy conventional wisdom that didn't make sense. Second, he showed his inclination to avoid overpriced investments—such as Florida hotels—and their accompanying higher downside risk. The family resisted the temptation to be swept up in the speculative fever in Florida. Instead, they went into a far more conservative deal—one that left plenty of room for error—on terms that gave them a few years to make a go of it before committing to an outright purchase.

"I LIKE THIS BUSINESS"

At the Christmas break at Harvard in 1946, Larry Tisch gathered up his law books and headed home to Lakewood. "My family had just opened the hotel in November," he said. "We'd just taken it over, and when I got there I realized, Jeez, I like this business. And I said 'What am I doing in law school?' So I left law school."

Lakewood, as a resort town, didn't always welcome Jews. Before World War I, it had been a popular winter vacation spot for the wealthy blue bloods of New York City. The season opened around Thanksgiving and closed after Easter/Passover. To the fine hotels in Lakewood they came by train for good food, card games, entertainment, and perhaps a little gambling and romance. Around 1915, Jewish industrialists who were being refused service in Lakewood responded by building their own hotel, the Lakewood. Rival hotels soon dropped their barriers and began to actively court the same Jewish vacationers who flocked to New York's Catskill Mountains in the summer. By the 1940s, many of the biggest hotel operators in Lakewood also ran hotels in the Catskills, a pattern the Tisches would briefly follow.

Built in 1898, Laurel-in-the-Pines was big and lavish, with a fireplace in every room. "Laurel-in-the-Pines was the Grand Hotel of New Jersey," said George H. Buckwald, mayor of Lakewood in the late 1940s. It was perched on the north shore of man-made Lake Carosaljo, a mashing-together of the names of the developer's three daughters. Lakewood's year-round population was about 8,000; at Passover, it would reach 40,000.

For the first two years, the Tisches leased Laurel-in-the-Pines, and in that time installed an indoor pool and an outdoor skating rink— unusual features in those days even for a resort hotel. No stunt was too offbeat to promote this new and improved operation, including having reindeer brought in from Finland to pull a sleigh across the skating rink, and staging basketball games on ice.

In 1948, the Tisches bought the hotel from Seiden, essentially with the hotel's profits plus a small mortgage. The cash from the sale of the summer camps provided only a small portion of the financing, and A. S. Tisch Co., winding down to a standstill with nothing left to sell, provided even less. Seiden's nephew, Charles stayed on to help the Tisches manage the hotel.

The Tisches added to the hotel's appeal by bringing in the day's top entertainers, among them Red Buttons and Alan King. In the process of booking such acts, Larry Tisch got his first taste of the entertainment business and the tender egos that drive it. "You realize after a while they're very fragile," he said. "If somebody doesn't applaud enough you ruin their week. It was interesting." Years later, the same phenomenon reappeared with perhaps even more intensity in the television business; at CBS News, it would become more than "interesting"—it developed into a major headache that could affect the profitability if mishandled.

Managing talent at the resort hotel level, however, was a relatively small challenge for the Tisch family, which was proving to be a top-notch management team in all aspects of a new line of business that required expert management skills.

Alan King remembered Sayde Tisch as "a tough bird. If she saw me tummeling around, she'd say to me, 'Behave yourself, young man! You're not in the Catskills now. You're in Laurel-in-the-Pines.'" Said Red Buttons, "She was the boss, she was the queen."

Al Tisch, on the other hand, was mild-mannered. "He was not a tough businessman," said Larry Tisch, whose own reputation for toughness would become almost legendary.

Sam Christopher, a young local newspaper reporter at the time the Tisches arrived in Lakewood, remembered Larry clearly as "the numbers man. He tended more to the business side. Bob was the man in the lobby, the official greeter."

The family clearly worked well together. Al was the boss as well as an ambassador of good will to the community. He served as president of the Lakewood Hotel Association. Sayde was in charge of buying food and furniture. Bob, while still studying at the University of Michigan, worked on holidays. Larry worked on the front desk, booked talent, and oversaw all financial matters.

Sidney Zweben, whose family owned and operated the rival White House Hotel in Lakewood, was a magistrate in Lakewood at the time—"the best judge money could buy," he said of himself. He remembered Larry as the brains in the family, the strategist who got things done. On one occasion, Al and Larry asked Zweben what local politicians could help the Tisches get a license to buy a small loan company in Lakewood. Zweben introduced the two to the county's Republican leader and to a state senator. "I don't know what they did, but they got the license," Zweben said. "From then on, Larry was promoting, wheeling and dealing."

Bob Tisch graduated with a B.A. in economics from the University of Michigan in January 1948. Two months later, he married classmate Joan Hyman. They moved into a cottage near the high school in Lakewood, and jumped into the family business full-time. Bob excelled as supervisor of dining room operations. Managing people was Bob's strong suit, and his people skills left a strong impression in Lakewood. Nearly 50 years later, Bob, more so than Larry, would be remembered for his warmth.

In 1948, the Tisches' 7-day weeks, working 18 hours daily, were still confined to Lakewood's winter resort season. During that summer, Larry had time to fall in love.

Soon after Bob's marriage, mutual acquaintances set up a blind date in June so that Larry could meet Wilma "Billie" Stein, daughter of a successful car dealer who owned Pontiac and Cadillac agencies in Asbury Park, about 15 miles northeast of Lakewood. Billie had graduated from Skidmore college four days earlier and had taken a position as a trainee at prestigious *Time* magazine in Manhattan.

That summer, Larry was overseeing construction of the indoor pool at Laurel-in-the-Pines. "Larry was kind of his own boss," Billie Tisch recalled. "It was essentially a free summer for him and that was fine." He was living with his parents in Deal, near Asbury Park.

On their first date, Larry spent most of the time visiting with Billie's father.

"My mother was having a gall bladder attack," Billie recalled, "so mostly we stayed home. I was tending to my mom and Larry had a lot of conversation with my father. He was a pretty good talker and I guess we went out for a soda or something afterward."

As dates go, it wasn't the stuff of romance novels, but it was enough to give Billie a clear sense of what was special about Larry Tisch.

"Larry was a grown-up person," she said. "He was not a boy. I liked his values. I liked his intelligence. I liked his sense of direction. I can't recall that we discussed life in general. He was a real person. He'd been through the Army, he'd been through school. He had a sense of direction."

Not that he had a grand design for the future. "He won't read a fortune cookie," Billie said. "He has this flexibility. He is, more than anybody else I know, a work in progress. Everything is a possibility."

Tisch enjoyed visiting with Billie's father, Joseph F. Stein, almost as much as his time with her on their first date. "He was a brilliant man," Tisch said, and coincidentally had been a classmate of Al Tisch's at Dewitt Clinton High School. While Al went to CCNY, Stein was at Columbia University earning a degree in journalism.

After college, Stein went to work for United Press. One day his boss invited him for dinner and told Stein what a great job he was doing, but "when Joe realized how little money his boss was making, he said, 'What am I doing in journalism?'" Tisch said. In 1920, Stein and his brother-in-law bought the Pierce Arrow automobile agency in Asbury Park, then a prosperous city. At the time, Pierce Arrow was one of the highest-priced cars in America. When Stein closed the deal to buy the agency, the man who sold it to him said, "Boy, I admire you young fellows, because as far as I can see, everybody who wants a car has a car." Stein went on to do a whole lot better financially as a businessman than he probably would have done as a journalist.

Tisch was impressed with Billie's intelligence and the fact that she had been picked from among an army of fresh graduates who applied for one of the most sought-after entry-level jobs in New York. Unlike her father, Billie's focus was more on publishing than on writing. "Billie was very smart, very nice," Tisch said.

When they met that June, Billie was commuting to New York and planning to look for an apartment in the city. She never did find one. Their summer romance culminated in their engagement in September. A month later—just four months after their first blind date—they were married at the Berkeley Carteret Hotel in Asbury Park before 120 friends and relatives. Their first home was a six-month house-sitting arrangement in Lakewood, right behind the Tisches' hotel. Housing at that time was in short supply. Soon after, they bought a newly built little house in Lakewood.

Billie didn't stay long at *Time* after they were married. "In those days, you didn't have two-career families," Tisch said, although his own parents, a generation earlier, were clearly an exception. His mother's career had been put on hold by her pregnancies, but they did not end her worklife.

Nine and a half months after their wedding Billie gave birth to Andrew, the first of four sons, in nearby Long Branch. Five months earlier, Bob and Joan Tisch had had their first child, Steven, the first of their two sons and a daughter.

For Billie and Larry, the children came in rapid succession. All four were born within the space of five years and two months. "It was very noisy," Billie said, but not unplanned. "We always felt that one child took all of our time and we might as well have as many as we wanted and as quickly as we wanted."

At one point in these early years, Larry and Billie and Bob and Joan rented a house together in Atlantic City. In this house, Billie and Joan grew to be best friends, and Larry and Bob developed the business chemistry that eventually would make this family one of America's richest. It was an idyllic time.

Early in their marriages to his sons, Al Tisch made it clear to his daughters-in-law that only they had the power to undo his sons' intense closeness and loyalty. "He talked to them both separately," Larry said. "He meant it in a very positive and friendly way."

Jack Lamping, then Ocean County's PR director, remembered the Tisch brothers as high-energy managers. "They overwhelmed you with their graciousness," he said. "You had only to see one coming or going to see things getting done. They were all over the place."

Of the parents, Lamping said: "They were really gung ho. Al himself was a real bull in a china shop. He was anxious to put the boys forward to see what they could do. He was always in the background. He gave them their independence, contributing to their training but not

second-guessing them. If they made a mistake, it was their mistake."
Said Larry: "He was easy, very nonjudgmental. We had a very good
relationship."

THE FOUNDING OF TISCH HOTELS INC.

By 1950, Larry and Bob, still only in their 20s, had established what in
retrospect would be the first glimmer of the Tisch touch. In 1949, the
Tisches used profits from Laurel-in-the-Pines to buy the Grand Hotel
summer resort in Highmount, New York, in the Catskill Mountains,
for $300,000. The two seasonal properties produced a year-round op-
eration. The Tisches turned both the Laurel and the Grand hotels
into money machines and established their corporate identity as Tisch
Hotels Inc. They did it with minimal debt, relying instead on cash
generated by the enterprises themselves and on the Tisches' considerable hard work.

The cash was piling up fast, and the pile—now measurable in millions—was outgrowing their immediate personal and business needs,
an entrepreneur's dream come true. Al Tisch, however, wanted to
teach his sons that with success comes the responsibility to give something back to the community. One summer, he turned part of their
Lakewood hotel property into a camp for needy minority children
from the city. They were fed, clothed, and cared for. His sons would
adopt Al's values in the pursuit of ever-multiplying wealth. With all
that capital available, the Tisches were in the hunt for a new and bigger home. They were prospering on Lakewood's borrowed time as a
winter resort for the rich.

A few years later, the resort suffered an accelerated decline,
brought on by two developments. The first, around 1950, was an effective crackdown by the state on illegal gambling in the Lakewood
area. The second was the death blow: the advent, in the late 1950s, of
three-hour, affordable flights to Florida and Puerto Rico. Lakewood
was robbed of even its most loyal winter vacationers. They found it

nearly as cheap to fly to Florida as it was to go to Lakewood. The town was stripped of its status as a winter resort. All but one of its 100 hotels and boarding houses eventually shut down.

The Tisches, however, exhibited perfect timing; they moved quickly enough to avoid getting caught in the decline. While Bob concentrated on running the hotels they had, Larry prepared a war chest and went looking for new worlds to conquer. The Tisches stepped back from Laurel-in-the-Pines and the Grand Hotel simultaneously, leasing them to Charles Seiden, whose uncle had sold the New Jersey property to the Tisches. The hotels were destroyed by fire within two years of each other in the mid-1960s.

The Grand, an all-wood building, was damaged beyond repair and torn down in 1965. As Lakewood entered its twilight years, Laurel-in-the-Pines became the scene of a series of suspicious fires, the last of which occurred in 1967 and, as one local resident put it, was "successful." The Tisches were never questioned about the cause. The remains of the once luxurious hotel were bulldozed and replaced with run-of-the-mill townhouse condos. Of the luster that once graced the north shore of Lake Carosaljo, not even a glimmer would remain. The Tisches recovered both losses through insurance.

For Larry, the destruction of Laurel-in-the-Pines was no cause for tears. Indeed, one of his strengths as a businessman was emotional detachment from investments. "You just don't fall in love with your assets," son Andrew said. That detachment allowed the Tisches to build equity fast. They traded hotel properties much the way a Wall Street money manager works the stock market. They bought or leased or built. They added value. They sold them. Sometimes they leased them back.

"By the late 1960s, we had 13 hotels," Andrew noted. In 1994, "we still have 13 hotels, though not all the same hotels. We leased them, sold back leases, managed them. Each deal has been a profitable deal unto itself. We never had to be somewhere. Even in the hotel business, we've just been trading assets."

For the Tisches, the brief Lakewood–Catskills adventure had been long enough to showcase all the elements of the family's low-risk investment strategy. They bought low, ignoring the majority view that values would sink even further in a postwar resumption of economic decay. They managed costs carefully, but spent wisely on amenities that attracted business. They lived modestly. They didn't get emotionally attached to their businesses, and they shifted out quickly when they saw a more compelling investment opportunity— or, in this case, an opportunity to get out of waning resorts.

What distracted the Tisches from Lakewood and the Catskills was a new and bigger project that surfaced in 1950 and was to challenge Larry and Bob's expanding financial and management abilities. Both Laurel-in-the-Pines and the Grand Hotel, in terms of the number of rooms each had, had reached the limits of their growth potential. What followed was a rapid-fire series of deals that quickly made those first two hotels look puny.

THE MAKING OF A HOTEL TURNAROUND ARTIST

Frank Gravatt, then in his 60s, had more real estate than he wanted, and he decided to raise some cash. His Traymore Hotel, a 575-room Atlantic City landmark built in 1915, was an ideal candidate. It was taking in $3 million a year but losing money on high operating costs. He printed up a handful of brochures touting the property, one of which ended up in Larry Tisch's hands—a reflection of his family's growing reputation as hotel turnaround specialists. With that level of revenue and some disciplined cost-accounting management, Tisch was confident that he could coax profit of about $750,000 out of the hotel in one year.

Gravatt wanted about $4.5 million for the property, more than Tisch was willing to pay. They couldn't find a middle ground, so they settled on a $520,000 annual lease, with a $500,000 deposit. Tisch figured he could clear $230,000 in the first year. The Tisches used $100,000 of their own money, borrowed another $100,000 from an Asbury Park bank, and signed a note for the rest. Completion of the deal on May 1, 1950, made the Tisches the first Jews to manage a big

Atlantic City hotel, and it got off to an inauspicious start. The hotel's top manager quit the day they signed the deal.

"We felt pretty lonely standing there in that huge lobby," Larry said. But they didn't waste time sulking. They went on the attack—shedding employees, cutting entertainment costs, upgrading the menu, and hiring Herbert A. Hofmann, a Harris Kerr Forster hotel-management consultant Gravatt had contracted for advice on the dining room. Hofmann, then about 34, was hired to enhance Tisch's own skills at finding ways to increase revenue while cutting costs. Hofmann, a Native New Yorker, was a 1937 business administration graduate of St. John's University. He would prove to be one of the Tisches' best hires, quickly establishing a reputation as a brilliant hotel operations strategist.

After the Tisches' first year in the Traymore, Gravatt agreed to sell them the hotel for $4,350,000. The deal called for a total down payment of $700,000, including the $500,000 he'd already received. The $200,000 balance was a fraction of the first year's expected profit. Adding to the transaction's appeal was the tax benefit of a $420,000 annual depreciation allowance the buyers could take over 12 years. Identifying potential tax benefits in such deals would become a hallmark of Tisch's approach to minimizing investment risk. Such benefits would become even more useful in later years as he diversified his holdings (the most stunning example of this was CBS, where Tisch essentially recouped his entire initial investment and still held more than 18 percent of the company). A favorable tax treatment often could convert what might seem a gamble—buying a distressed business—into an investment in which the worst-case scenario was breaking even.

Gravatt apparently sensed that Tisch knew more than Gravatt did about the Traymore's potential. Perhaps the deal he was about to accept was too good to the buyers. At the last minute, he became so indecisive, he decided to flip a coin to settle the issue. Tisch wouldn't allow it. He grabbed Gravatt's arm. "I just couldn't let him toss that coin," he said. "Once he did, we had only a 50–50 chance." Perhaps Gravatt was right to pause, but Tisch correctly calculated that his own reassuring delivery and powers of persuasion gave him better odds than heads-or-tails. Gravatt finally signed.

As in the case of Laurel-in-the-Pines, the Tisches weren't acquiring a mature property operating at the peak of its potential. They were buying the Traymore's unrealized potential, confident now of their ability to greatly enhance the asset's value by investing their own time and money for a far better profit margin. Again, they quickly turned the hotel around, installing an ice rink, indoor and outdoor pools, modernizing the marquee, foyer, lobby, and most of the rooms, and, finally, raising prices 25 percent while at the same time boosting occupancies. Result: annual net profit averaged about $1 million for the next five years, more than the hotel's purchase price.

As the cash rolled in, it was never allowed to rest. The Tisches seemed unlimited in their capacity for what they felt they could manage. They bought the Sand & Surf Hotel and two cabana colonies in West End, New Jersey, in 1951, the year Larry and Billie's second son, Daniel, was born, and Laurie was born to Bob and Joan.

Around this time, the Tisch brothers and their families shared a house and a bank account in Atlantic City for about a year. "It was wonderful," Billie said of that time, a kind of Utopian existence free of want and characterized by automatic sharing. The environment was a direct reflection of Al and Sayde Tisch's influence through the sons. "Larry's parents both really believed in family and that what was in the family belonged to everybody and that people wouldn't take advantage," Billie explained. "I think that is the basis for the great trust that Larry and Bob have for each other and that Joan and I learned and have tried to transmit to our kids."

A Success Formula Emerges

The Tisch investment formula was coming into sharp focus: Avoid risk, which included avoiding debt. Exploit hidden tax benefits. Buy low, or don't buy at all. If the price is too high, rent it; owning the cash flow is good enough. Hire top-quality professional managers, and keep the chain of command short for speed of notification when things go wrong.

Word of repeated successes travels fast within any industry. The hotel business is no exception. The Tisches already were building a reputation as highly effective managers with deep pockets. It made them automatic targets for pitches by owners of poorly performing hotels who wanted to either sell or lease them to someone who could do a better job operating them and would improve their resale value. The Tisches were becoming adept at making money on both sides of the equation: owning and operating and then leasing, or leasing and operating and then buying. In a given time and place, they went for whatever arrangement seemed to promise the highest investment yield.

In October 1951, they leased the Ambassador Hotel in Atlantic City. Tisch Hotels Inc. was well on its way to qualifying as a major chain of luxury hotels. The Ambassador posed a low-risk opportunity because of the tax write-off potential, which was even higher than the Traymore's because the deal didn't call for any lease payments for 18 months. With the combined genius of Herbert Hofmann and Larry Tisch and Bob's superb management skills, the Ambassador in just two years was returning $750,000 a year.

Between the Ambassador and the Traymore, the Tisches' total tax shelter for 1951 was a staggering $620,000. Tisch's penchant for erecting such fortifications against downside risk made him no less aggressive in building the scope of their operations.

In 1952, after meeting the Tisch brothers at a cocktail party, Joe Levy, owner of the Crawford Clothes chain, gave the Tisches their first hotel opportunity in Manhattan. Levy owned the 1,500-room McAlpin Hotel at Broadway and 34th Street. He wasn't pleased with the $4 million a year it was pulling in. Levy figured that leasing it to the Tisches for 30 months, with their sterling management record, could greatly improve the operation and enhance its value.

By the time Levy sold it to Sheraton Hotel Corp. for $9 million in 1954, the Tisches had cleared $1.5 million on the deal after investing $1 million on renovations, raising room rates 30 percent, and increasing occupancy 20 percent. The Tisches purchased the two adjacent office buildings from Levy for $500,000 at a time when values were appreciating at nearly 20 percent a year.

In addition to running the Traymore, the Ambassador, and the McAlpin, the Tisches bought the run-down Brighton Hotel in Atlantic City and leased the 800-room Belmont Plaza on Lexington Avenue in Manhattan, across the street from the Waldorf-Astoria.

They decided not to upgrade the 75-year-old Brighton yet—they waited four years before spending $4 million to transform it into the 275-room Colony Hotel, offering an ice rink, a pool, double-sized rooms, two restaurants, and a lounge. The Belmont deal, however, was similar to the McAlpin. Coral Management Corp., principally owned by Alfred Kaskel, owned the Belmont Plaza, and Kaskel wanted to upgrade the hotel but didn't have the necessary cash. He gave the Tisches a 21-year lease at $450,000 a year and simultaneously borrowed $1.4 million from the Tisches at 5 percent. The Tisches liked the Belmont's proximity to the Waldorf. They also foresaw that, with the dismantling of the Third Avenue elevated subway a block away, the neighborhood was about to undergo a renaissance.

The Tisches spent $1 million on the Belmont's improvements. They put in a new bar and dining room, stripped the green paint off the oak-paneled lobby, refurnished the rooms, and installed televisions. The top two floors were turned into rented office space. Room rates were raised 20 percent. In two years, they had recovered their investment.

With three hotels in Atlantic City, two in New York, and other smaller properties, Tisch Hotels Inc. was one of the nation's first two luxury chains. The Hiltons had the other. The formula was to create year-round income by attracting convention business and by adding indoor and outdoor amenities. The formula worked: the hotels were generating annual profit of $3 million to $5 million.

By 1955, just nine years after the family moved its relatively modest assets into the hotel business, the Tisch brothers, still in their 30s, were awash in cash. Keeping it invested without taking inordinate risks was a challenge.

Their desire to own a hotel in Florida, but only on their own terms, hadn't gone away. Indeed, Florida was turning into more of a winter vacation mecca than had been originally envisioned. The Tisches followed the growing migration south, but, remembering their pre-Laurel-in-the-Pines foray, they still believed that, to do it right, they would have to build their own hotel—one that would set new standards for luxury. Larry found 10 acres of beachfront property in Bal Harbour and bought it for $1,350,000. The site was less than five miles north of the finest hotels in Miami Beach.

The Traymore was sold for $15 million. Tisch Hotels stayed on to manage it and retained some property, valued at $250,000, leasing it out for $25,000 a year. That same land, years later, would be cashed in for a huge profit when casino gambling was legalized in Atlantic City.

Also in 1955, the Tisches sold their lease on the Ambassador for $5 million, but retained management control. Meanwhile, the company started building the 780-room Americana Hotel on the beach in Bal Harbour. The project ultimately would cost $21.5 million. A major part of the strategy to bring business to this hotel was to actively promote it as a convention destination.

Even while it was being built, Bob traveled the country drumming up convention bookings. "Behind it all was Larry's mind," a builder on the project said. "When they were doing an area over, he could compute how many tables and how many people could fit into the room. He was like a computer before there were computers."

In addition to booking conventions, Bob supervised operations in the North. Larry moved his family to nearby Bay Harbor to oversee construction, commuting to the site by bicycle. Around the time the Americana opened for business in December 1956, Alfred Kaskel, of the Belmont, paid his $1.4 million debt to the Tisches, and they sold their lease on the Belmont Plaza for $1.7 million, all of it profit.

The Tisch family now was worth about $30 million, more money than the entire family would ever need. No longer did Bob and Larry feel compelled to check out every proposal that met their requirement for a 12 percent pretax return on their investment. Larry Tisch was carving out a reputation as a persuasive negotiator—the kind who frequently gets what he wants by virtue of holding so many of the marbles. Fortified by the self-confidence that comes from sitting atop a mountain of cash, Tisch was an overwhelming adversary not just because of his financial strength, but because of his ability to rapidly grasp the complex details of any transaction and identify the weaknesses in a seller's pitch about value.

On December 1, 1956, the Americana opened on time, without overtime and without a mortgage. Bob Tisch made a series of personal connections that started with a broadcast industry publicist whose mother was a longtime guest of the Traymore and ended with his spiriting away the National Broadcasting Co. (NBC) from a smaller Florida hotel and booking NBC's 30th anniversary festivities into the Americana. Just two weeks after the hotel opened, the Americana became the backdrop for three national broadcasts in three days, rife with plugs for both the network and the hotel amid a parade of stars, including Gina Lollobrigida and Groucho Marx. The opening garnered coverage on all four TV networks.

"They believed in us," Bob Tisch said of NBC. "It was a big plus in making it known and successful." The convention business at the Americana was off to a fast start.

Once again, the Tisches reached for the unusual to set the Americana apart from its rivals. With rooms going for as much as $175 a day, the hotel featured a ground-floor rock pool occupied by live alligators. The reptiles' greatest health hazard proved to be the guests, who had a habit of flicking plastic toothpicks into the pool along with more than $100 a week of coins—items the alligators swallowed, sometimes with fatal results. A glassed-in garden of orchids and other tropical flowers had an open roof to capture rain. The lobby featured Italian travertine marble, the balconies were set with Panamanian tile, and the fixtures combined brass and Venetian blown glass. On the Americana's 600-foot beach, "lanai suites"—cottages with bedroom, living room, and two baths—rented for $68 a day (versus $32 for a hotel room).

Said Americana architect Morris Lapidus on opening day, the hotel was "more dedicated to the spirit of play than any hotel I have ever created." Comedian Jackie Miles joked, "Another $17 would have spoiled it." It was the most luxurious and expensive hotel in Miami Beach. The *Times* called it a "bizarre design."

Bizarre or not, the Americana put the Tisch brothers on the map. They were an unstoppable, cash-rich team, with a loaded convention calendar that turned their Florida venture into an instant success. In the first year it was open, the Americana took in $12 million. Suddenly, the Tisches had their pick of the deals. For Larry Tisch, the pickings would become almost too easy.

3

On to Wall Street and New Investment Horizons

"I think of stocks as businesses."
—Larry Tisch[1]

With the opening of the Americana and the resulting torrent of cash, Larry Tisch was primed for new investment horizons. The Tisches expanded their hotel activities in ways that eventually led to Tisch's first foray into the stock market.

While they were upgrading the Brighton in Atlantic City, converting it into the luxurious Colony Hotel, they built an economy motel—the 55-room Aristocrat Motel—for just $600,000. Before it was finished, they decided they shouldn't be distracted from the luxury hotel business and leased out the Aristocrat.

But the idea of developing affordable city hotels still intrigued them. With that in mind, they had started negotiating with Rockefeller Center to purchase the Roxy Theater—built, coincidentally, by Harold Lubin, whom Tisch's mother worked for in the 1920s. Their idea was to build a 40-story midtown motel with reasonable rates and cutting-edge enhancements like closed-circuit TV check-in, elevators to bring guests to their rooms in their cars, orange juice and coffee on tap in the rooms, and self-service food.

The Roxy deal collapsed because of a problem over air rights, but the Tisches still liked the concept of downtown motels. Against this background, Nathan Cummings, chairman of Consolidated Foods Corp. in Chicago (later known as Sara Lee), brought the Loew's opportunity to Tisch's attention. At the time, Cummings was widely admired in the Jewish business community for his success in a business not traditionally dominated by Jews.

"I bumped into Nate Cummings early one morning in the lobby of the Americana Hotel in Miami when I was running the hotel," Tisch recalled. "We went down and had a cup of coffee together in the coffee shop and he mentioned to me that he was buying stock in Loew's Inc. and why didn't I take a look at it. I had never been involved in the stock market. Never at that point. So I looked at it and I started buying some stock and I'd speak to Nate from time to time."

What Tisch saw in Loew's stock was something hoteliers lust for: a gold mine of high-traffic downtown real estate. Buying stock in Loew's Inc. would be a proxy for buying that real estate cheap. It didn't matter that many of the Loew's theaters were slightly rundown at the time.

What led to the Loew's opportunity was a government antitrust drive to break up the big theater/studio conglomerates. Loew's was founded in 1919 by Marcus Loew, the nickelodeon-era pioneer. It began life as a film exhibitor, branching quickly into the film-production business by acquiring Metro Pictures Corp. a year later. In 1924, Loew's bought Goldwyn Co. and Louis B. Mayer Pictures to create the Metro-Goldwyn-Mayer movie production division. This vertical integration of film producers and exhibitors was what had incurred the government's antitrust wrath and led to the breakup of Loew's. Throughout 1957 and 1958, Loew's Inc.'s fate worked its way through federal courts.

In October 1958, the company agreed to spin off Loew's Theatres Inc., then in possession of 102 theaters. Metro-Goldwyn-Mayer would be the surviving company. In November, a federal district court approved the spinoff; the next day, the Supreme Court upheld the ruling that forced Loew's, RKO, and others to end their film production-theater ownership ties. The company's misfortune would provide the Tisches with a base from which to build the quintessential, modern-day conglomerate.

It also would give Larry Tisch his first intoxicating taste of the stock market.

A MARKET STRATEGY EMERGES

As an investor, Tisch wasn't interested in handing his family's cash to a money manager and then sitting back to wait for quarterly reports on how he was doing. For Tisch, buying stock wasn't a passive act. It was buying *ownership*, and with ownership came *responsibility*. For Tisch, that meant understanding a company's business fundamentals, its financial strengths and weaknesses, and its management. After just 10 years of active business management experience, Larry Tisch wasn't thinking retirement. He was aiming for a bigger arena. His motivation?

"The game," said longtime friend Leonard Stern, chairman of Hartz Group Inc., the pet supply company. "That's what motivates him. He lives modestly, he has no use for money himself. He neither shows off nor exercises power. He's just fascinated with trying to solve the problem at hand."

Tisch's youngest son Tommy went deeper perhaps than his father might in analyzing the underlying appeal of problem solving in the context of the financial markets, what he called "a world made only for complete psychological misfits." In Tommy's view, "It's very alluring in terms of the broad quest for truth in the world. Every buyer and seller has very rational reasons for doing what they're doing. You have to look at the rationale on the other side of the trade."

Tisch's fascination with market psychology and finding hidden value led him to discover Michael Milken long before even the most prestigious Wall Street houses had heard of him.

Tisch was always open to discovering tomorrow's financial genius. Milken captured Tisch's attention in the late 1970s because the young bond trader had a new way of looking at the world of corporate debt. Tisch was always an active player in the bond market, and here was someone actively making a market not just in the traditional, narrow confines of highly rated investment-grade debt but in the below-investment-grade universe typically shunned by cautious investors.

Michael Milken, the so-called junk-bond king, practically invented the financing philosophy that made the 1980s-style leveraged buyouts possible. Milken ultimately went to prison in connection with the insider trading scandals of that era, but as early as 1978, Tisch saw him as a visionary. Milken recognized that the risk of default in the universe of unrated debt was much lower than was suggested by the high interest rates these bonds paid. It wasn't a new idea. What *was* new was Milken's resolve to apply his considerable salesmanship at the firm eventually known as Drexel Burnham Lambert—later dragged under amid Milken's legal morass—to give junk bonds the one feature that kept them out of the investment mainstream: liquidity.

By 1978, Mike Milken was a household name in the Tisch household, yet when Tommy Tisch went to work at Goldman, Sachs & Co. in 1979, Geoffrey Boisi, a pivotal figure in the Getty Oil takeover battle (among others), responded to the mention of his name, "Who's Mike Milken?"

Said Larry Tisch of Milken: "He was the only one around who took the time to read every debenture and to understand each company and bond. He was brilliant."

When Milken was about to be sentenced in late 1990, Tisch was among those who wrote letters on his behalf, even though Tisch had long since decided Milken's operation was too closely connected to the predatory practice, rampant in the 1980s, of putting companies in play to force highly lucrative stock buybacks from takeover players who never intended to take over anything.

Not that Tisch didn't dabble in the junk-bond market—and ultimately incur a whopping loss, for example, in Macy's debt.

Larry Tisch's attraction to the stock market, in 1958, didn't mean his appetite for risk had grown. In fact, central to Tisch's game was discovering, in a deal or a company, hidden value that no one else appreciated—and gaining the upper hand early in the game. Such an opportunity had been evolving since 1952, when the federal government laid the groundwork for breaking up the movie giants that owned both studios and theaters.

Investing in the stock market in general appealed to Tisch. It was liquid; it could be converted to cash practically overnight. It provided an opportunity to learn how other businesses were run. It also appealed to Tisch's love of gamesmanship. With the right strategy and market discipline, an investor could reap high rewards with a minimum of risk. The underpinning of that strategy was value investing. "I'm a businessman," Tisch said. "I think of stocks as businesses."

The comment closely tracks the basic theme of the "bible" for this kind of investment thinking, *Security Analysis,* by Benjamin Graham and David Dodd, first published in 1934 (McGraw-Hill). It argued that an investor should use the same approach in purchasing a stock as in buying the whole company. It was and remains the guiding principle for a high proportion of successful investors, including Larry Tisch and the legendary Warren Buffett, chairman of Berkshire Hathaway Inc., a wildly successful investment vehicle that would one day require an investor to pay more than $120,000 for the privilege of owning just one share. Indeed, Graham became Buffett's mentor at Columbia University.

"Graham and Dodd" today is synonymous with value investing, which stresses the importance of strong asset value and cash flow. The value investor buys a company's shares when they are underpriced relative to the broad market on the belief that the investing public is temporarily underestimating the company's true value.

For the average investor, the stock market is a giant casino. For people like Larry Tisch, it is a bazaar where the educated shopper finds high-quality, bargain-priced goods.

How do investors know a stock is underpriced? Divide the current stock market price per share by the company's earnings per share for the most recent year. If the resulting price/earnings multiple—or P/E ratio—is less than the average for the entire stock market, that means the stock is relatively cheap. But is it cheap for a good reason? That's where Graham and Dodd come in. Looking at bottom-line earnings numbers on a balance sheet isn't enough. Tisch was one of those investors who was sharp enough to look beneath the surface of a company's annual report and find fundamental sources of strength and weakness. Often, that meant talking to management.

Tisch took the candy store approach. How much money was left over that didn't have to be reinvested in the store to keep the customers coming and the money rolling in? He called it free cash flow. "Profits that have to be reinvested in more capital outlays may not really be profits at all," he said. Companies routinely list as an asset money spent on upgrading factories and equipment—so-called capital spending. They call it reinvesting profit. The rationale is that if the owner decides to sell the candy store, the expanded shop will fetch that much more because it's bigger and better. But Tisch believed such expenses were part of the cost of generating sales.

"More and more, a big company has to go on spending money just to maintain its existing earnings stream. Isn't that really an expense, rather than something that should be considered as a true increase in value?" Tisch said. "In what we call 'smokestack America' there often isn't any accumulated free cash after capital outlays. The companies in many cases aren't really making money."

It was right out of Graham and Dodd, as was the notion of evaluating a company's underlying assets. Tisch liked insurance companies and banks, for example, because their asset values—in the form of cash, stocks, bonds, mortgages, and real estate—were simple to assess and fairly easy to access. A steel company is different; its value depends more heavily on the state of the economy and a slew of hard-to-measure variables: Is demand strong for cars, heavy appliances, and other things made of steel? Is inflation high? Is labor expensive? Are foreign rivals selling low, forcing the domestic producer to charge less and earn less? Is there pressure to invest heavily in more efficient machinery?

In the case of Loew's, the underlying asset was real estate, a relatively simple commodity to value and trade.

A FOOTHOLD AT LOEW'S

By the end of 1958, Nathan Cummings's group had acquired 235,000 shares from dissident Loew's Inc. directors at $22 each. Buying with him were his brother Maxwell Cummings, a real-estate operator and developer in Montreal, and Paul Nathanson, a Canadian film distributor. The move ended the threat of a proxy fight by a director, Louis A. Green, who had clashed with management over what he viewed as mismanagement of the Metro-Goldwyn-Mayer movie-producing unit.

Other sellers included two other dissident directors—Joseph Tomlinson and Jerome A. Newman. Tomlinson, a year earlier, had threatened a proxy fight over management's plan to spin off Loew's Inc.'s Canadian and U.S. movie theaters and its WMGM radio station, leaving MGM as an independent studio—a plan the courts had approved. Cummings's aim was to ensure that the plan could be completed. He wanted to end up with MGM after the spinoff.

By 1959, the Tisches had accumulated $69 million in hotel profit. Buying Loew's shares ultimately would require tapping about 15 percent of that cash. That March, Loew's Theatres was formally separated from Loew's Inc.—soon to be renamed Metro-Goldwyn-Mayer. Existing shareholders got a half share in each of the two new companies for each pre-breakup share held.

Tisch called Cummings and said, "What do I do now?"

Cummings offered to buy Tisch's MGM shares. "So I sold him my MGM stock and I still owned the Loew's Theatre stock, and at that time the price of the stock was $14. I knew enough to know that $14 for a company without debt and $10 or $12 [per share] in cash plus 100 theaters and a radio station was awfully reasonable—plus the office building in New York and other office buildings. So I just kept buying the stock at $14. The stock was always $14."

Tisch wasn't playing the market. Loew's was an asset play made attractive by a persistently low, stable stock price.

Soon Tisch had close to a 20 percent stake. It was time to meet the company's executives. "They told me to get lost, in effect. I just kept buying the stock." Always at $14. With plenty of cash and an unshakable conviction about Loew's untapped value, Tisch was giving the business community its first glimpse of his disarmingly direct style, an irresistible force impervious to intimidation.

"Everybody wanted MGM," Tisch recalled. "Nobody wanted Loew's Theatres. MGM was the glamorous company—studios and everything else."

Tisch would say he wasn't interested in the "glamour end of the business" that became MGM, but he gradually was cultivating a keen interest in the business end of glamour—the Hollywood-driven business of television.

Throughout the summer of 1959, however, Tisch was content to quietly but steadily accumulate more and more Loew's Theatre shares. He would use the same strategy in later conquests, most notably that of CBS. Rather than storming into the market to gobble up huge blocks of shares, or launching a takeover bid, Tisch employed a tactic that would come to be known derisively as the "creeping tender offer." Just keep buying shares in the market without making any announcements, except those that the Securities and Exchange Commission requires. The tactic prevents the stock price from running up too quickly and allows the buyer to acquire shares in the early stages at better prices than at the end. Once the buyer reaches the desired ownership goal, the average cost per share is less than the market price. The goal is modest. It isn't necessarily to own 100 percent of a company, but to own just enough shares to control its management, perhaps with the support of other large shareholders.

That's what Larry Tisch meant when he said he thinks of stocks as businesses. For Tisch, buying a stock *is* buying a business. It becomes *his* business. To make sure that the business is sufficiently profitable, Tisch was an owner who liked having some say in who ran the company and in setting policy, goals, and strategy.

At the time of the Tisch purchases, Loew's Theatres had a book value—assets minus liabilities—of $60 million, but that valuation was based on grossly outdated real estate values. Tisch figured the real property value was easily closer to $80 million, yet in the fiscal year ended in August 1959, the theaters produced just $2 million in profit. That worked out to a paltry 2.5 percent return on assets, about what the money would earn in a passbook savings account, and 10 percentage points below what Tisch viewed as a minimum acceptable level. Loew's had the perfect investment profile: lots of hidden value hampered by poor management. But a stock isn't a lottery ticket; it's a business. Once an investor like Tisch gets his foot in the door, he aims to see it run like a business and will happily do it himself, if necessary.

By September 1959, the Tisches owned enough of Loew's that the board was obliged to make them members. When the stake reached 25 percent, Tisch's lawyer, Simon Rifkind, then of the New York firm Paul Weiss and later a federal judge, negotiated active roles in the company for both Larry and Bob. "That was the start of our involvement in Loew's," Tisch said. Larry grudgingly was named chairman of the finance committee and Bob head of the executive committee, two of the most important board positions for influencing a company's management.

Loew's posed a major challenge for the Tisches' management skills. It was a neglected business that needed major surgery. Each of the more than 100 theaters had to be evaluated: Was it profitable? If not, why not? Should it be renovated, sold, or converted to some other use, such as a hotel or motel? Larry moved his young family from Florida to Scarsdale, New York, to supervise the winnowing process. Bob's family made their home in Bay Harbor to stay on top of the Americana. Sayde and Al were winding down their involvement, spending summers in Deal, New Jersey, and winters in Bal Harbour.

DIVERSIFICATION BECAME THE GOAL

Rejuvenating Loew's wasn't the only reason Tisch wanted it. He viewed it as a launching pad for diversification, the soon-to-be buzzword of the decade that was about to begin. To gain a freer hand in Loew's, Tisch said, "I wouldn't mind having more stock." As would be the case with

CBS years later, his aim wasn't to take the company private, but simply to own enough of it to control it. Already his strategy was being put in place, with Loew's selling unprofitable theaters and renovating the more promising ones.

With the Loew's campaign, the media began to take greater notice of the young Tisch brothers. They had gotten a smattering of mentions in the daily business press, but in October 1959, *Time* magazine acknowledged their success in building the largest U.S. chain of resort hotels—seven, with a total of 2,800 rooms. Larry was perceived as the Tisch team's main strategist. *Time* chose to run Larry's photo with its brief Tisch profile. Even then, the bald 36-year-old bore a striking resemblance to the actor Telly Savalas.

Those who thought, in the mid-1980s, that Tisch's interest in CBS came out of nowhere had missed a detail in this *Time* article: Tisch— along with real estate and industrial companies—had included radio and television on a short list of businesses that appealed to him in pursuing a diversification strategy for Loew's. The appeal of broadcasting was twofold: It was oligopolistic and inflation-proof.[2]

By the end of 1959, Tisch Hotels controlled 28 percent of Loew's, having paid an average of $14 a share, or about $10.5 million. At the time, Loew's total stock market value was $37.2 million, a tiny fraction of the $6.14 billion it would be worth by mid-1993. The family never sought to buy even a majority of the stock. After all, it was a New York Stock Exchange traded issue. As such, it gave them the flexibility to sell shares as needed to raise money for other opportunities, and to buy them back when the price was low. Besides, the goal was to manage the investment for a high return, not to own everything. The Tisches weren't megalomaniacs.

In Larry Tisch's view, ego was the number-one stumbling block for effective management. "The manager wants the company to grow and grow even if it isn't making any more money as a result," he said. "He wants a bigger plane and a bigger office. That may not be at all the same thing that's best for his shareholders." The number-two menace for managers? Surrounding oneself with yes men.

MANAGING A BURGEONING PORTFOLIO

Beginning in 1960, Bob joined Larry at Loew's to focus on managing day-to-day operations while Larry concentrated more on managing the assets. That meant rapidly working through the theater chain's real estate portfolio: bulldozing old, out-of-date theaters, leasing out the ones they didn't want to keep running themselves, and building new theaters and hotels on the sites of old theaters. For example, the Summit Hotel in New York would be built on top of a former theater, in what architect Morris Lapidus called "tongue-in-cheek Aztec style."

The Tisches were on their way to being involved with eight New York hotels in a variety of deals, including construction of the 1,850-room, 50-floor Americana begun that summer—the tallest hotel in the world at the time—and the Regency, the family's pride and joy. The Americana, which opened in 1962, embodied many of the innovations the Tisches viewed as essential to beat the competition. Built to attract convention business, it offered parking for 350 cars, ballrooms, exhibition space, and a shopping promenade.

The Americana in Florida was already generating gross annual profit of $3 million, or 25 percent of revenue. And that profit wasn't reached by cutting corners. Tisch knew the hotel's return could be made even higher, but not without cutting costs and ultimately reducing the hotel's appeal. Three employees, for example, did nothing but polish copper fixtures in one of the dining rooms. The polishing could have been done by just two men and "we wouldn't serve any fewer meals," he said, "but I'd rather have the compliment."

By the end of the 1950s, the Tisches were bragging that they had turned down a $28 million offer for the hotel. Some analysts at the time thought the Tisches would be in no rush to sell the Americana, not so much because it was the crown jewel of their burgeoning empire, but because it had 19 years of tax-reducing depreciation left in it.[3] Two months later, however, they did sell it.

Al Tisch died February 1, 1960, at the age of 63, in a Houston hospital where he'd gone 15 days earlier for treatment of a heart ailment.

Shortly after his death, the Americana was sold to New York real-estate developer Kratter Corp. The hotel was booked through 1966 with $50 million of convention business. The deal, for more than $16 million, included a 35-year leaseback to the Tisches. Effectively, the Tisches were perfecting the art of having their cake and eating it too: they retrieved much of the cash invested to build the Americana and rented the resort back, along with its annual revenue of $12 million.

IN THE DRIVER'S SEAT

The Tisch family now had an estimated net worth of $65 million; its enterprises generated annual profit of more than $6 million. By May 1960, the Tisches had gained management control of Loew's, named five new directors, and let it be known the company had $50 million available for acquisitions. It made sense. Through their stock holdings, they had become intimately familiar with how other businesses operated. In fact, their interest—both financial and intellectual—in other enterprises was beginning to win them invitations to serve as outside directors at other companies. Within a year of gaining control of Loew's, for example, Larry would join the boards of Sun Chemical Co., Sterling Bank & Trust Co. of New York, and Fulton Industries, a collection of industrial concerns.

The trend only accelerated the growth of Larry Tisch's capacity for understanding a broad range of businesses and their unique financial needs. His reputation within the business community as a financial strategist grew as well.

In September 1960, Loew's Theatres could no longer deny Tisch what he already had essentially paid for: the right, by virtue of being the largest shareholder, to the company's top titles. Tisch was elected chairman, succeeding Leopold Friedman, and added the title of chief executive officer, which was ceded to him by Eugene Picker, who remained president and took on the title of chief operating officer.

By the time he chaired his first Loew's annual meeting, in December, Tisch faced a mostly friendly crowd. He announced plans to sell radio station WMGM in New York for $11 million, then fielded comments from shareholders, including Martha Brand, who asserted that shareholders were "being raped" by the company. Whatever she meant, it surely wasn't reflected in the stock price. The growth in the value of her $14 shares, if she kept them, would multiply in value by the hundreds, far outperforming the rest of the stock market.

After the breakup of Loew's and MGM, Eugene Picker was named president and Leopold Friedman chairman of Loew's Theatres. They may not have known it at the time, but their positions were temporary. A similar pattern recurred later at CNA, Bulova, and CBS, where the management of underperforming companies attracted Tisch with potentially fertile assets. Picker clung to the titles of president and operating chief less than two months. He clashed with Tisch over the diversification strategy and was ousted. Tisch viewed him as an obstacle in the process of unloading money-losing theaters and converting a theater at 51st Street and Lexington Avenue into the Summit, one of the first new hotels to be built in Manhattan in 30 years. The $25 million hotel opened in the summer of 1961.

By June of that year, the Tisches had put in place a plan to build two motor hotels, an apartment hotel, and a movie house, all in Manhattan, and a 450-room Americana resort hotel on five acres of waterfront in San Juan, Puerto Rico. To effect the massive plan and in the wake of the Picker experience, the Tisches started to bring their own people into Loew's. They brought in their favorite hotel-management pro, Herbert Hofmann, to be a senior vice president. They had recruited Hofmann 10 years earlier from Harris Kerr Foster, the hotel management consultants, and they knew that Hofmann's value went beyond hotel-management expertise. He was able to facilitate the contributions of Larry and Bob, two very different personalities, to the venture. Larry, the prodigy whose parents exhibited unquestioning confidence in his intelligence and judgment, seemed to have never been plagued by self-doubt—nor did he need to seek his brother's advice. Bob was above average, his talents only a half step behind the family's leader. Larry depended on the personnel and cost-control skills Bob brought to their operations, but he confided less in his younger brother than he might have if he had been less sure of himself or had needed consultation for his decisions.

Bob was not inclined to second-guess Larry's investment moves. The rationale behind the Loew's purchase, for example, was undeniably brilliant. Over the years, Bob had seen no downside in letting Larry develop such opportunities. As the brothers laid the groundwork for merging their destiny with that of Loew's—establishing a hotel division within it and nursing the theater chain into greater profitability—they positioned themselves in roles they would hold for more than two decades: Larry became chairman and CEO, and Bob assumed the presidency of Loew's Hotels Inc. and remained chairman of the parent company's executive committee.

To speed the process of repositioning the theater chain, the Tisches raided the competition, bringing in Bernard Myerson as executive vice president of Loew's Theatres. Myerson had 25 years of experience at movie-house operator Fabian Theatres. His mission was to cut away the dead wood. He became one of a small core of managers the Tisches would depend on over the years to implement their strategy for growth and high returns.

The following year, the Tisches once again went to a competitor for a key player, hiring as general counsel Lester Pollack, a 32-year-old lawyer who, on behalf of National General, had outbid Loew's for two hotly sought-after theater leases. Pollack would one day go on to make his own headlines in the mergers-and-acquisitions game of the 1980s with Odyssey Partners.

THE VIEW FROM THE TOP

In June 1964—the first year of the New York World's Fair—Loew's bought the Drake Hotel, at Park Avenue and 56th Street in Manhattan, from William Zeckendorf's troubled Webb & Knapp Inc., once again taking advantage of his own strong cash position and an anxious seller as in the case years earlier of Frank Gravatt and the Traymore.

With the Drake, the Tisch organization became the city's largest hotel operator, with a staggering 5,350 rooms in six hotels.

Larry Tisch knew that once the World's Fair shut down, New York's hotels would experience a slump, but said, "We expect to do a better job than the next fellow." It wasn't just a boast. The concept of thriving (being the best in a tough market) was a hallmark of Tisch's conservative approach to business. The same principle would be applied in later ventures: Become number one if the field is so competitive that only the top player can make decent money.

Even before the World's Fair opened, the Tisches enjoyed a 15 percent higher occupancy rate than their rivals in the city's hotel business. Why? Bob Tisch attributed it to having newer properties and bigger rooms. Also, unlike their competitors, the Tisches were promoting their hotels at their 74 movie theaters and were even taking hotel reservations at the theaters. One former executive pegged their success in large part to having assembled the finest hotel sales force in the world. More important, Bob suggested, was having management housed just a few blocks away. "We are sitting on top of our operations and are not absentee owners," he said.

Their emerging formula for success, regardless of the business, had a strong factor of hands-on management without a lot of intermediary layers. Their response time to operating problems was practically instantaneous—a Tisch trait that came through, sometimes annoyingly, even for top executives of companies whose shares the Tisches were only just beginning to accumulate. Years later, for example, for one full day in the late 1980s, the Tisches occupied the investor relations office of a New England bank whose shares they had been buying, and demanded answers to tough financial questions.

Whatever misgivings the Tisches may have had in the mid-1960s about the hotel market in general, they didn't reduce their appetite for deals. In fact, their interest may have even increased. A slump in any market can be a buying opportunity. Within a year's time, Loew's would buy the brothers' leasehold on the Americana in Florida, acquire the Warwick Hotel in Manhattan and the two Ambassador

Hotels in Chicago, and gain a 99-year lease on the Mark Hopkins Hotel in San Francisco. To the Tisches, it made little difference whether they leased or owned, as long as the cash flow was powerful enough to deliver a competitive investment return.

INVESTING WITH WARREN BUFFETT

By 1965, the Tisch strategy was firmly in place in Loew's. The stage was set for a transformation into something more than a hotel-and-theater operation. Increasingly, Tisch was looking at the universe of publicly traded companies for new opportunities. He also was looking at investors who were already successful in that environment. It was then that Larry Tisch sent an unsolicited check for $300,000 to a then relatively unknown investor named Warren Buffett.

"I got an envelope addressed to Buffett Partners," Buffett recalled. "It actually came in a couple of days late. For some reason it had been misrouted through Honolulu. Inside was a check and Larry's card and a note that said, 'Count me and my brother in.' When I finally did get a chance to talk to him I said, 'I haven't met you, but I like you already.' He's a very decisive guy. I liked him. We could talk the same language and he's fun to be with."

In Buffett's view, Tisch's acumen in the ways of Wall Street and business had less to do with who his mentor was or whose investment theory he subscribed to. It had to do with character. "If Larry hadn't got past kindergarten, he'd still be terrific," Buffett said. "He's very down to earth. No pretentions."

The investment in Buffett Partners—disbanded in 1969 at a stock-market top, after growing thirtyfold—was an example of that decisiveness. Indirectly, Buffett's own mentor from Columbia University—Ben Graham, the famed value investor—played a role in bringing Buffett to Tisch's attention. Howard Newman, son of Jerry Newman, Graham's partner in their own investment firm, had told Tisch of Buffett's successes. At that time, Buffett Partners was running assets of between $15 million and $20 million, not a lot of money, considering Buffett's rise in 1993, if only briefly, to the top of the Forbes 400 rich list, with an estimated net worth of well over $8 billion, but, as Tisch said, "Everybody knew Warren was up and coming."

So was Tisch.

The envelope was the beginning of a close friendship between the two soon-to-be giants of Wall Street who independently adopted strikingly similar investment principles around the same time: buy the shares of undervalued stocks with great long-term potential, contribute to strong management, and hold the stock indefinitely. They weren't speculators—those supposedly savvy day traders who jump in and out of stocks at the expense of the market's compulsive gamblers. Buffett and Tisch bought companies, not stocks. Culturally, they were vastly different. Buffett was an Omaha, Nebraska, Midwesterner; Tisch, the Brooklyn-born son of a Russian immigrant. But as investors they were nearly indistinguishable, moving down parallel paths toward major investments in the network television business.

Tisch eventually became one of a group that joined Buffett every two years on a one-week trip for business leaders and investors. Others included the likes of Tom Murphy of newspaper publisher Capital Cities, Katharine Graham of *The Washington Post,* and William Ruane, whose investment fund focused on media stocks; they met in places such as Aspen, Colorado, or en route to Britain via the *Queen Elizabeth II.* "Half the time we discuss the media and media stocks and investments," Tisch said of these trips. "Certain things in the investor world when you don't have a working knowledge, you sort of shy away. When you get a familiarity with the subject, it makes it easier to take a position."

As much as Tisch and Buffett had in common as investors, they rarely worked together. The one notable exception, Buffett said, occurred in the summer of 1985, when he, Tisch, and Richard Ravitch, former chairman of the Metropolitan Transportation Authority in New York, formed a group to take over Bowery Savings Bank for $100 million in a bailout backed by the Federal Deposit Insurance Corporation.

"This came up after a lunch with Larry and the four [Tisch] boys," Buffett recalled. "He mentioned it as we walked back to the Loew's office, then at 666 Fifth Avenue. It worked perfectly. The return was decent. We held it two years. After tax we made 60 percent," a profit taken in a sale to a Los Angeles-based savings and loan holding concern, H. F. Ahmanson & Co., just two weeks before the stock market crashed in October 1987.

The investment, however, was the exception to the rule. "The Bowery deal was very unusual for me," Buffett said. "It may be the only one I've done like that as a private deal."

Tisch's approach to business even spilled over into his leisure activities: Buffett noted similarities in Tisch's bridge game. Said Buffett: "He's enormous fun to play bridge with. He's very decisive and smart. He plays it like he does business. If he makes a wrong play, he forgets about it and goes on to the next round. He's very good at seeing the essence of a thing. I've never seen him lose his temper."

Indicative of the extent to which Larry Tisch had risen in stature in the business and investment community was the company he was keeping. In addition to Buffett, his friendships now included Alan Greenspan, the future Federal Reserve Board chairman. He also became close friends with Felix Rohatyn, the Lazard Frères investment banker whose name would surface in connection with numerous high-profile financial deals, including the plan that would bring New York City back from the brink of insolvency in the mid-1970s.

ABC: THE FIRST FORAY INTO TV

Ironically, Tisch first became involved in the television industry by acting as a go-between for the legendary conglomerateur Harold Geneen, chairman of the sprawling ITT Corporation, and Leonard Goldenson, founder of the American Broadcasting Company, the upstart television network.

In December 1965, Tisch was playing tennis with Goldenson and told him Geneen was interested in adding ABC to ITT's growing collection of companies—which included the Sheraton hotel chain. Tisch arranged for Geneen and Goldenson to meet. ABC was struggling. It was the only one of the three networks that still hadn't converted to color, and it was losing ad dollars to CBS and NBC. Even so, it had only two competitors. In those days, before cable, it was hard to lose money on a network.

This wasn't Goldenson's first news of ITT's interest in ABC. A year earlier, money manager Gerald Tsai, Jr., of the Fidelity Fund, had brought to Goldenson a feeler from ITT, but the price was low and the timing wrong. Now, coming off a year of battling unwanted advances from Norton Simon, a Geneen wannabe who had built his own mini-conglomerate with Hunt Foods & Industries, Goldenson was ready to take ITT's interest seriously.

Personalities were a factor. Goldenson viewed Simon as a takeover nuisance who hadn't much of a reputation for running companies. Geneen, who would eventually acquire over 350 companies at ITT, was known for his ability to make successes of his acquisitions. His biggest flaw may have been that he built a company so sprawling that only Geneen could grasp its totality enough to manage it.

Or did Goldenson decide to listen to Geneen because Larry Tisch urged him on? Goldenson respected Tisch's judgment. In fact, a deal was hammered out and ABC's board approved it in December 1965. But legal hurdles loomed. After efforts to derail the acquisition failed at the Federal Communications Commission (FCC), the Justice Department sued to block it on antitrust grounds. One of the government's concerns: ITT had an interest in the then-nascent cable-television business.

On New Year's Day, 1968—two years after ABC had accepted the offer, and before the court had ruled on the lawsuit—Goldenson once again was playing tennis with Tisch. They were in Nassau, where Loew's had just opened the Paradise Island resort hotel. In the middle of the game, Goldenson was called to a telephone. ITT's board had voted to back out of the offer, invoking an escape clause that gave both sides the right to do so if they hadn't merged by that date.

On the way back to the tennis court, Goldenson passed Gerry Tsai, who had transmitted the first ITT feeler to him. Tsai's Primerica Corp. would one day merge with Commercial Credit Group Inc., a consumer-loan company that Larry Tisch already was considering taking over. Clearly, Tisch already was close to the center of corporate finance in America.

As later chapters will show, the ITT–ABC situation wouldn't be the last time Tisch would surface at the vortex of a major takeover deal. Yet, it was the nature of Larry Tisch to happily avoid becoming a household name even as he freely mingled with and counseled some of the day's most powerful business leaders. He wasn't interested in fame. What he had was far more valuable: respect—both on Wall Street and on Mahogany Row. To him, his relative anonymity was icing on a cake. The attention he attracted was the only kind he wanted: smart people came to him with interesting investment ideas. He was playing the biggest game in town, and Tisch was enjoying the luxury of being able, by virtue of controlling so much cash, to be choosy about his investments, to set the terms, and to act fast—and win.

After getting to know Buffett, who reinforced his interest in media stocks, and seeing all the acquisition interest surrounding the networks, Tisch was cultivating a similar appetite. All he needed was a buying opportunity.

In the meantime, the money was rolling in to Loew's. As of August 31, 1967, the end of Loew's Theatres' fiscal year, the company had racked up $15.8 million of profit—eight times what it had earned in 1959, the year of the spinoff. Revenue was $136.8 million. It owned 108 movie theaters and 12 hotels and motels.

As Tisch had promised when he moved into Loew's, diversification was coming. In October 1967, soon after posting the annual numbers, Tisch made it clear that he wanted to acquire another service company. The series of deals that followed would run the gamut in degrees of difficulty and would bring Tisch stunning success and total failure.

4

A Conglomerate Is Born

When the business press gets lazy, it describes companies like ITT, General Electric, and Gulf & Western as "diversified conglomerates." Their numerous and varied holdings defy any effort to describe in a few words what they do for a living. Sometimes it's hard to discern, let alone explain, the core business of some of these companies.

In a sense, that's the point. Investing in a broad array of businesses is meant to prevent a company from being too heavily dependent on any one of them. Diversification can be the ultimate low-risk business strategy. The best built conglomerates include subsidiaries that, at any point in the economic boom–bust cycle, flourish when its siblings don't.

Larry Tisch's close friend, Warren Buffett, started in 1969 to build such a company. He used a struggling textile maker, Berkshire Hathaway, to gobble up other companies, eventually including businesses that sold candy, furniture, newspapers, jewelry, uniforms, encyclopedias, vacuum cleaners, and insurance. Try describing that kind of company in three words or less. To make matters even murkier, the cash flow from this potpourri was then plowed into large chunks of underpriced stock in companies with strong, steady earnings—companies like Geico (insurance), Coca-Cola, Capital Cities/ABC, and Washington Post Co.

Tisch was moving down a similar path when the 1970s began. It would lead to investments in insurance, tobacco, oil rigs, and wrist watches as well as hotels. The exact businesses or products of his diversified purchases were not part of a conscious plan, Tisch said, "though it looked that way."

Intentional or not, diversification had another benefit for a publicly traded company: it could help reduce stock-price volatility. Wall Street firms maintain stables full of industry analysts who make informed investment recommendations to their clients. If an influential tobacco analyst says sell tobacco stocks, the prices of such stocks tumble almost on cue, even before investors have had a chance to figure out whether the analyst was right. Frequently, the price of such stocks bounces back, once the market recovers its composure. The benefit of a Loews-type operation, in which tobacco is one of several diverse businesses, is that it doesn't get caught up in a tobacco stock price downdraft to the extent that a single-product cigarette company does.

Stock-price volatility is no benefit to a company's management. It scares away buy-and-hold investors, the people corporate executives most want as owners because they add to a company's stability. Speculators, on the other hand, love volatility. A stock on a roller-coaster ride can generate big gains—or losses—in the course of a few days. The ownership becomes transient. The managers start to focus more on how to prop up the day-to-day stock price than on how to build a healthy long-term business.

When a stock moves slowly but steadily higher and pays decent, regular dividends, the owners tend to be in it for the long haul, and management can concentrate on keeping the business strong enough to support the stock's steady appreciation.

FIRST FAILURE: COMMERCIAL CREDIT CO.

As Tisch was building Loew's, he did not succeed in acquiring all his targeted companies, although many of his unsuccessful attempts would prove to be profitable investments. There was one notable exception. In 1968, Tisch's on-the-job training as an empire builder covered the extremes of victory and defeat.

In April 1968, Loew's Theatres bid to acquire Commercial Credit Co., a commercial and consumer-loan business with assets of $3 billion. At the time, Loew's assets totaled just $273 million.

As was typical in his approach to acquisitions, Tisch wasn't pursuing a grand plan. Of Commercial Credit, Tisch said, "It was just an undervalued financial situation. It was a good company with some potential in a business we thought we could understand."

The Baltimore-based company took less than a week to vote down the offer and hire the Wall Street firm of Kidder Peabody to seek a friendly suitor—someone who would outbid Tisch and leave management alone, which Tisch probably would not have done.

To succeed, Tisch would have to launch a hostile tender offer, a move that stood a good chance of pushing the stock price to an overvalued level and eliminating the company's principal appeal to Tisch. Being a disciplined value investor, Tisch did not buy overvalued stock. No matter how badly he wanted something, he would not be pushed to overpay for it.

Tisch's bid had an added problem: it was perhaps a little too clever. He had invented a way to reduce takeover cost by building in a substantial tax benefit, thereby turning the tax laws to shareholders' benefit. He weighed a broad range of financial factors when he assessed risks, and he structured a deal with the worst-case scenario in mind.

His Commercial Credit offer was set up so that the dividend on the shares he bought, combined with the tax benefits, would give Loew's a profit, no matter what the outcome. Here's how it worked.

If his tender offer succeeded, he would be buying the shares of a company that paid a large dividend—$1.80 a share. He would use the dividends to cover the interest payments on the money he had borrowed to buy the shares. The effective tax rate on the dividends, since they would be paid to another corporation, Loew's, would be just 7.5 percent. That meant the after-tax value of the dividend payments to Loew's would be $1.66 a share. Meanwhile, the interest on the money to be borrowed for the acquisition would work out to $2.47 a share, all of which would be tax-deductible against Loew's income, resulting in a tax saving of $1.235, assuming a 50 percent tax rate. That would make the after-tax interest cost $1.235 a share. Subtract that cost from the $1.66 after-tax income from the dividend, and Loews would end up with an after-tax profit from the Commercial Credit dividend of 42.5 cents a share. The effect would be a takeover completed with interest-free debt and a built-in price discount on the share purchase.

Not much risk was involved in that deal—except that it outraged Capitol Hill. After all, wasn't the U.S. Treasury the ultimate source of that discount and interest-free loan? What outraged Capitol Hill was a source of utter delight on Wall Street, where the sheer brilliance of the formula was irresistible. It would be copied in at least two other deals: (1) when DWG, a cigar company turned holding company, acquired Southeastern Public Service, and (2) when Charles Bluhdorn of Gulf & Western Industries used it in a bid for Associates Investment Co.

Despite a U.S. senator's attempt to prevent the offer from going forward, Loew's won clearance from the Securities and Exchange Commission (SEC) to launch its bid in June 1968. That day, however, Commercial Credit announced it had agreed to be acquired by Control Data Corp., Minneapolis, in a friendly takeover for $579 million.

Tisch went to war for two weeks, trying every conceivable ploy to defeat Control Data, short of sweetening his bid. Declaring his offer "far superior" to Control Data's, Loew's tried to lure shareholders to tender to its bid by promising to return all their shares if the offer failed. Finally, Loew's tried a lawsuit to block the white-knight bid, seeking $25 million in damages, even as the Control Data and Commercial Credit boards approved the merger. A week later, Tisch conceded defeat, booked a $28 million profit on the Commercial Credit shares owned by Loew's, and dropped the lawsuit.

Tisch's interest in Commercial Credit was serious, but it didn't go unnoticed that his failure was hugely profitable. He drove his quarry into a takeover deal that ran up the value of the shares Loew's accumulated in its pursuit. The marriage of Commercial Credit and Control Data made more obvious sense than a Loew's deal. Control Data was a computer and financial services concern; Commercial

Credit was a finance company. But Tisch's appetite for expansion remained. With his war chest that much fatter, he was primed for the next opportunity.

ACQUIRING LORILLARD

Hard on the heels of the failed Commercial Credit bid, Felix Rohatyn informed Tisch later that summer that Larry's longtime friend and fellow Scarsdale (New York) resident Manuel Yellen, chairman of cigarette maker Lorillard Corp., was looking for a merger partner.

Lorillard's products included Kent, True, Newport and Old Gold cigarettes, Tabby and Three Little Kittens cat food, and Reed's, Sir, Look, and Big Hunk candies. Tisch had a more-than-passing awareness of Lorillard. Lewis Gruber, whom Yellen succeeded as chairman in 1964, had been a Loew's board member since 1960 and was considered a stronger leader than Yellen. Gruber's retirement had hurt Lorillard.

Tisch felt that Lorillard's cigarette market share could be boosted to 15 percent; Yellen seemed to be trying half-heartedly for diversification, with limited success. In 1967, one year after acquiring Reed Candy Co., Yellen tried to acquire Schenley Industries Inc., the liquor company, and failed. When Tisch entered the picture, Lorillard was, of all the tobacco companies, the most heavily dependent on cigarettes. Its stock was a market underperformer, an absolute requirement for Tisch to begin to get interested.

The cigarette business in general was appealing. It was the ideal consumer business, something Tisch had been on the lookout for. The manufacture of cigarettes was uncomplicated, compared with that of other consumer products. Tobacco growers enjoyed federal agricultural subsidies. Unlike many other consumer products, tobacco products weren't subject to federal regulations governing the sale of food and drugs. Yet cigarettes had the same business appeal as food and drugs: people tended to buy cigarettes no matter what the economy was doing. They might put off buying a house or a new sofa or new car, but they would always eat, drink, smoke, and take medicine.

One element that didn't figure prominently in Tisch's decision on Lorillard was the health hazard associated with cigarettes, despite the fact that just a few years earlier, the U.S. surgeon general had issued a warning linking cigarettes to cancer. Generally, the harmfulness of smoking was still being dismissed as unproven.

Years later, Tisch would suggest that he might not have bought the company had he known at the time what he knew in 1994 of tobacco's impact on health and health-care costs. "Am I happy with what I did? I don't know. I'll never know. What am I going to do, go flog myself every day?" Even as he said this, his son Andrew was preparing to face Congress, along with the rest of America's top tobacco company executives, and explain why cigarettes shouldn't be regulated by the Food and Drug Administration (FDA) as an addictive substance.

"Would we buy such a company today?" Billie Tisch said. "Absolutely not. But having it, there is a responsibility to the industry."

In 1968, however, the public health issue was not prominent in Tisch's mind. Lorillard appealed to Tisch because the stock was a "growth stock"—that is, it could be depended on to generate 15 percent annual growth in profits in good economic times and bad. Investors who buy such stocks usually don't expect to pay bargain prices, but the stocks are still considered good buys because these companies can dependably pay strong dividends. Lorillard had the potential of a growth stock, and Tisch, the value investor, was about to get it for a bargain.

It took just one week for the details of a noncash merger pact worth more than $400 million to be worked out in a series of secret meetings in Scarsdale. The negotiations were kept so quiet—to prevent an artificial runup in the stock price—that Loew's shares actually fell in the first two trading days of the week, and inched up only 62.5 cents before the announcement, after which it shot up $15.50 to close at $110.50 a share. Lorillard gained $2.625 a share to close at $60.75. With 6.5 million shares outstanding, that put Lorillard's market value at $394.9 million.

Even two of Loew's public relations officials were taken by surprise. They had to abandon a meeting in Atlantic City and rush back to

New York to deal with the breaking news that even they hadn't been prepared for.

The beauty of the deal was that it required not one penny of Loew's cash to acquire a company three times its size. For each share of Lorillard, shareholders got a Loew's $62 principal amount, 25-year subordinated debenture paying 6⅞ percent, plus one-quarter of a warrant to buy a Loews' common share for $110. Analysts' estimates of the value to Lorillard shareholders ranged between $66 and $75 a share, or a total of $429 million to $487.5 million. Wall Street analysts estimated that Loews' profit for the fiscal year ended August 31, 1968, rose about 27 percent to $20 million on a 32 percent sales gain to $180 million. Lorillard's calendar 1967 results showed a relatively slim $31 million of profit on sales of $565 million.

Among Yellen's woes, Tisch said, was the fact that at least two-thirds of the board consisted of company executives. "Every vice president, practically, was a director. Everything was a compromise; you couldn't interfere with the next guy because you could get voted off the board." Nevertheless, Yellen managed to sell the board members on the deal, partly by persuading them to view the deal as a merger and not a takeover. Indeed, Lorillard was the bigger of the two companies, but it surely was being taken over, with negative implications for Lorillard's entrenched management. The deal was settled within 30 days—less time than it takes to close even the most basic real estate transaction.

"This company [soon to be renamed Loews Corp., dropping the apostrophe] is going forward as a consumer-products company," Tisch said.

A *New York Times* profile of Tisch a few days after the Lorillard deal carried the headline, "Hotel Man With a Bankroll." Calling him "perhaps the most prominent hotelier in the world next to Conrad Hilton," the story went on to say: "Tisch is one of a handful of executives who have achieved prominence in recent years through just such imaginative financial management. They are the creators of the conglomerate concept—the multi-industry corporation—and shares of their companies have become the darlings of Wall Street."

By then, Loew's Theatres owned 108 movie houses in New York, Los Angeles, and Phoenix (Arizona), and Tisch sat on the boards of Sun Chemical Corp., Grand Union Co., Madison Square Garden,

Northwest Industries Inc., and the Manhattan Fund, an organization founded by Gerald Tsai, who, like Tisch, had had a role in the near-acquisition of ABC by ITT.

The fact that Tisch was on Tsai's Manhattan Fund board is an indication that Wall Street respected Tisch for his stock-picking acumen as well as for his liquidity. Tisch's popularity as a corporate board candidate reflected growing respect for his skills as a business strategist.

By the end of November 1968, the boards of both Loews and Lorillard had approved the merger. Soon after, Bob Tisch was named president and chief operation officer of Loews Corp.; Larry remained chairman and chief executive. In the wake of the brief, competitive fight for Commercial Credit, Lorillard was a cake walk.

"It wasn't necessarily a bargain," Tisch said, "but it was a sensible transaction at the time, an opportunity to do a deal on very favorable terms—and a friendly deal."

Bob Tisch immediately launched a high-speed, hands-on analysis of Lorillard's inner workings. He toured cigarette factories and warehouses throughout the South, and combed through the corporate headquarters in New York. Things were worse than the Tisch brothers had expected. Lorillard's strongest cigarette brand, Kent, which had been a winner in the 1950s, was losing market share to Marlboro and Winston. The company had no framework for developing new products, and it nearly destroyed its mainstay menthol brand, Newport, by changing the blend, a move that cost it 20 percent of its volume. The candy company, Reed, which was earning $1 million a year when Lorillard acquired it, was now losing $1 million. Lorillard wasn't a bad business; it was a badly run business. Larry was certain it had the potential for 10 percent annual profit growth.

It took Tisch a little over four months to ease out J. Edgar Bennett as president and replace him with someone who would join the short list of professional managers at the core of Loew's suddenly diversified and expanded empire. Bennett's successor, Curtis H. Judge, then 46, was named president of the new unit. Formerly vice president, marketing, and head of domestic sales and advertising at R. J. Reynolds, he had quit over a policy dispute. Before Reynolds, he was with Colgate-

Palmolive. Yellen would stay on as chairman of Lorillard for just another year.

The move to hire Judge, clearly an operating manager, silenced the critics who had predicted that Tisch aimed only to suck cash out of this latest target's assets. The criticism was understandable. Tisch frequently sought to convert assets into cash, but his purpose wasn't simply to raise cash. The assets earmarked for sale were always those that didn't yield a decent return and held little potential for doing so in the near future without a costly overhaul. Lorillard was no different. The candy and pet-food lines didn't meet Tisch's requirements for cash flow. Ultimately, they would go. In time, Loews would come to depend heavily on the cigarette business for much of its earnings.

In Tisch's view, if a business had no prospect for yielding the magnitude of returns he could get in the highly liquid stock and bond markets, then that business should be sold and the cash added to the investment portfolio until something better came along. The Tisches put Lorillard on a crash diet. Besides Bennett, six more top executives left. Their jobs "simply vaporized," according to one executive, leaving behind "a residue of bitterness" that Tisch acknowledged.[1]

"Whether it could have been done in a more politic way, there's plenty of room for doubt," Tisch said. "We just took out a layer of management." It wouldn't be the last time Tisch would respond to charges of insensitivity in personnel matters. As in those later cases—most notably at CBS—his concessions had to do with how the firings were handled—not whether they should have happened. In Tisch's view, sparing people's feelings by prolonging their tenure generates no savings and amounts to an injustice to shareholders.

LOOKING AHEAD TO THE NEXT ACQUISITION

As the Tisches began the process of digesting Lorillard, they also nibbled at the edges of other potential deals. By January 1969, Loews had become B. F. Goodrich's largest shareholder, although Tisch insisted he never contemplated making a run for the company.

Within a month, Northwest Industries—another conglomerate-minded operation, with interests in industrial, consumer, and chemical products—launched a takeover bid for the tire maker. Goodrich immediately sued everyone in sight, including Loews and Larry Tisch. Larry was a director and member of the executive committee of Northwest by virtue of his having been a director of Philadelphia & Reading when Northwest took over that conglomerate in 1968.

Goodrich's suit was rejected, but the company ultimately escaped the clutches of Northwest and its chairman, Ben Heineman, who had little appetite for waging a battle for control. A few months later, the federal government, in the third such attack by the Nixon Administration against conglomerates, sued Northwest on antitrust grounds. Soon after, Northwest ended its six-month pursuit, blaming the declining stock market.

At about the same time the Tisches were shaking up Lorillard and tilting toward Goodrich, Loews also formed a $200 million joint venture with a California residential builder, J. H. Snyder Co., to build homes outside San Diego. At the time, Jerry Snyder described the Tisches as "true entrepreneurs, and they run the company just like a little store." Tisch may have been a true entrepreneur, but he didn't make the common mistake of growing so emotionally attached to his creations that he didn't know when to move on. The Snyder partnership would last roughly 10 years, when Loews shut it down, following two years of losses totaling $19 million. As Tisch explained it, the building projects it undertook—including one in Coronado—were plagued with legal problems. "It was so difficult building in California," he said. "They'd sue you every time you'd try to sell it. If a nail was missing from a 2-by-4, it wasn't earthquake-proof. It just wasn't worth it."

A search for a theme in Tisch's business ventures throughout this period could be frustrating. A trial-and-error approach seemed to be at work. On the surface, it appeared he was pursuing a carefully orchestrated diversification. In fact, Tisch judged each opportunity on its own merits, one at a time. He wasn't executing some grand scheme to achieve synergy or recession insurance. He approached business acquisitions in the same way he had handled hotel deals. He pursued a deal only if it made sense internally and was a business he could understand.

The hotel operations of Loews Corp. continued to operate in that fashion. Near the end of 1969, the company's Loew's Hotels unit launched plans to build a $60 million hotel in London as part of a larger strategy to expand in Europe. Other ventures in France, Monte Carlo, and Hamburg (West Germany) were planned. The ultimate driver in all these deals was a combination of elements, but timing was perhaps most critical.

Individually, none of these deals necessarily reflected macroeconomic considerations. Decisions were based more on whether Tisch perceived the successful convergence of local factors: good location, good market, good real estate prices, and good financing arrangements. As always, the idea was to keep risk at a minimum by using cheap money to buy low-priced, high-quality assets. Tisch applied his investment rules as stringently and dispassionately to hotels as he did to stocks and entire conglomerates.

In the wake of the lightning-fast Lorillard deal, investment banker Felix Rohatyn had another prospect for Larry Tisch: Radio Corporation of America (RCA).

RCA was a $3.5 billion behemoth comprising broadcasting, electronics, publishing, car rental, frozen foods, and carpeting. In sharp contrast, Loews was a mere $800 million-a-year company. Yet, in some ways, Loews was the stronger of the two. RCA's profit—and its stock price—was under pressure. In 1970, RCA earned only $91 million, down 43 percent from $160 million in 1969, because of an ill-fated computer venture. Two large shareholders on the board were pressuring RCA chairman Robert W. Sarnoff, son of founder Gen. David S. Sarnoff, to act remedially.

Early in 1970, Robert Sarnoff quietly began to put out feelers for a friendly merger partner. Lehman Brothers and Lazard Frères were RCA's investment bankers on the board. Andre Meyer and Rohatyn approached Larry Tisch, who had met Sarnoff at the Century Country Club in Purchase, New York.

The idea that Tisch, through Loews, might be able to gain an active role in the much larger RCA, one of America's household names and a conglomerate in its own right, was naturally enticing. Tisch, however, wasn't impressed with the company's long-term plan. "One of the problems was they wanted to use our financial resources to further their role in the computer business," he said. "We didn't want that. I didn't think RCA was going to make it in the computer business, because IBM was just too strong." Ultimately, he wasn't interested in becoming a shareholder in the company if "from the first day I would be opposed to management."

Without citing the computer business commitment as the reason, Tisch said, "We called that deal off. . . . There was no confrontation."

RCA, however, told a lightly different story. After Sarnoff and Tisch met, Tisch made a written stock-swap proposal to Sarnoff under which Loews shareholders would receive preferred shares and Tisch would be named chairman of the executive committee. That role for Tisch was cited by Robert L. Werner, RCA executive vice president and chief legal officer, as a major reason *not* to pursue the deal. Tisch's positioning of himself for maximum influence was a familiar feature of his buying into companies. It had worked at Loews, where he gained a foothold early on via the executive committee. Werner told Sarnoff, "If you sign this agreement, you will be reporting to Mr. Tisch."[2] Sarnoff, apparently not interested in trading job security for a partnership with the well-capitalized Loews, didn't push the deal any further. A few years later, RCA gave up on its computer industry hopes and sold that division.

Tisch attributed the failure of the RCA deal to "a basic philosophic difference," perhaps a veiled reference to top management whose desires for executive-suite longevity tended to cloud their concerns for shareholders' interests.

By now, Tisch's crusade was well known. Larry Tisch was "a dangerous subversive" in the eyes of many businesspeople.[3] In an era when America was racked by civil unrest over the Vietnam War and the nation's youth widely viewed big business as the scourge of the planet, these words carried greater impact than they do today.

"We've lost the concept that the stockholders own the company," Tisch said. He was the corporate equivalent of the student radical chanting, "Power to the people!" And he knew it. "If you want to change management," he continued, "you're labeled a raider, and the next thing to a criminal is a raider. We leave rebellion to the youth; maybe that's our problem."

What gave Tisch the right to lecture on the topic? His own record. He was rapidly growing Loews toward the $1 billion mark, and he was doing it with a minimum of risk. Not that Loews carried no debt. As a percentage of equity, debt would reach a relatively high 68 percent in mid-1971, but the company was managing a huge stock portfolio— $300 million—which generated half the company's profit.

"Larry Tisch is hard-nosed, a good thinker, and asset-oriented, which at this phase is a lot more than these guys who are interested only in earnings per share."[4] This description, by Smith Barney President Bill Grant in 1971, summarized approvingly Tisch's value-oriented investment style. In contrast, investors dedicated to the growth approach, in which an investor targets stocks of companies whose profits grow 15 percent or more a year, were driving up the stocks of companies known as the Nifty Fifty (Polaroid, Sony, Digital Equipment, and McDonald's, for example), with total unconcern that the prices were reaching the stratosphere relative to the rest of the market. What Grant envied at least as much about Tisch was liquidity: "He's got one of the greatest reserves of cash in American business today."

5

The Sindona Affair: A Brush with Scandal

"It was one of those situations where with hindsight everybody became a genius."

—Larry Tisch

If there was a vulnerability in Larry Tisch's approach to business and investing, it was his belief in integrity. Tisch operated under the assumption that the person on the other side of the bargaining table was rational and played essentially by the same rules. Agendas might conflict, strategies might include elements of hype and borderline deception, but an environment of flat-out dishonesty and cheating was dangerously chaotic and unpredictable.

Tisch, for whom success depended on being able to accurately assess the risks in a given deal, had to be able to trust that people—even highly ambitious, competitive people—were predisposed to playing fair, at least trying to do the right thing.

In the early 1970s, Tisch found himself at the center of two highly controversial business situations that punished him in varying degrees for his faith in human nature. Both involved stock purchases that seemed to fit Tisch's profile for the ideal investment: (1) they were undervalued companies that he understood and (2) he could get a big enough stake to get a seat on the board and influence their management.

76

THE FRANKLIN BANK DEBACLE

He made the first of his two ill-fated purchases in 1970. Tisch liked Franklin New York Corp., parent of Franklin National Bank on Long Island, the nation's 18th-largest commercial bank, with assets of $3.4 billion. "I thought the bank had some potential and tried to straighten it out when it started to have some problems," Tisch said.

By May 1970, Loews had accumulated a 15 percent stake in this stock-market underperformer. The bank's president, Harold W. Gleason, welcomed Tisch as a potential director, noting that Loews had no intention of acquiring more than 25 percent of Franklin. To do so would have forced Tisch to decide between the banking business and Loews because of restrictive Federal Reserve Board ("Fed") rules on controlling both a bank and a commercial enterprise. Tisch formally joined the board in October of that year.

This seemingly innocuous investment, however, would prove to be a major headache, albeit an immensely profitable one for Loews. It put Larry Tisch at the vortex of what was arguably the most bizarre tale of international corporate corruption the business world had ever seen.

In 1971, the Loews' stake in Franklin neared 25 percent, setting the stage for a potential determination by the Fed that Tisch now effectively controlled the bank. The prospect of such a finding forced Tisch to decide which he wanted to control more, a conglomerate or a bank. "We never intended to go past 25 percent," Tisch said. "We figured there was not much more that we could do. We couldn't go any further, and we never wanted to be active managers." But being a passive investor in a troubled business wasn't a role Tisch relished, and Franklin had a high-risk profile.

The bank was losing money because the interest it had to pay its depositors was higher than the rate it was collecting on its investments. Franklin had gotten into this fix by putting its money into long-term fixed-interest municipal bonds while short-term interest rates were climbing. The interest the bank was paying on certificates of deposit was soaring.

For Tisch, the situation was intolerable, but there appeared to be no immediate solution. The more he managed Franklin's affairs, the more likely the Fed would demand he relinquish control of Loews, something he was unwilling to do. It was easy to see why. Since 1960, Loews' profit had grown in every quarter. Its five-year profit growth rate had outperformed many of the biggest conglomerates. Tisch's value investing approach had turned Loews into a stellar growth stock. The Tisches owned a hefty 32 percent of Loews, a major reason for their personal net worth being valued at about $400 million.

Tisch wasn't about to dismember Loews for the sake of a badly wounded bank. It was time to dump the Franklin shares. Any attempt to do so, however, would surely devastate the stock price before Tisch could have a chance to get out completely—unless a single buyer could be found for the entire stake, in a private transaction.

The economic landscape at the time provided Tisch with another compelling reason to seek such a buyer. Tisch believed the economic cycle and an overpriced stock market were headed for big falls. If he was right, it was time to raise cash—not just to avoid incurring losses in the downturn, but to be ready to snap up bargains amid the wreckage.

The Franklin shares weren't the only assets Loews wanted to liquidate. Throughout most of 1972, Loews would sell a number of assets: Lorillard's Reed candy business, 48 movie theaters, and several hotel leases, including a $200 million, 25-year lease on four hotels to American Airlines. American would later try unsuccessfully to get out of the agreement, admitting that the deal's timing, on the eve of a severe recession, couldn't have been worse.

"THE POPE'S BANKER"

Amid this evolving scenario, Michele Sindona entered the picture—an Italian described as "Italy's Howard Hughes . . . one of Italy's richest and most respected financiers."[1] Sindona was also the banker for the Vatican. Sindona wrote to Tisch in November 1971: "You must be seeing what is happening at Franklin National Bank. The earnings of the bank are declining. You are a substantial stockholder and I am looking to you to take the necessary corrective action."

Tisch had another idea. Sindona had made it known he wanted to make a major investment in the United States. Two months after Sindona's letter to Tisch, Kuhn, Loeb & Co., the investment banking firm, informed Sindona that Tisch might like to sell Loews' 1.1 million Franklin shares, a 21.6 percent stake. Kuhn told Sindona the incentive for Tisch to sell was to avoid having the Fed classify Loews as a bank holding company, which would then force Loews to shed its nonbanking businesses—everything but Franklin.

Meantime, Franklin's woes were deepening. By March 1972, bank examiners identified $211.1 million of classified and criticized loans—those that stood a good chance of being defaulted on—or an extraordinarily high 11.6 percent of total loans and 91.2% of capital. Based on these numbers, the bank should have been declared insolvent or forced to merge with another, but regulators decided to wait. Maybe management would make good on its assertion that it could nurse the bank back to health.

Tisch, however, was getting nervous. The pressure was on to do something to save himself and other shareholders from incompetent management. Under Harold Gleason, from 1968 through 1970, as Franklin's problems were being created, the bank's salary expense soared 50 percent. Shareholders didn't rank high among management's priorities. The more Tisch tried to influence decisions at Franklin, the more intensely the Fed pursued the question of whether Tisch, even though he controlled less than 25 percent of the bank's stock, effectively was exercising control as a director.

Among Tisch's last acts to turn Franklin around was his luring of Paul Luftig from Bankers Trust to Franklin as president and chief operating officer, supposedly, said the media, with the idea that he would replace Gleason as chairman in a few months. Luftig, however, said he wasn't aware of any plan to oust Gleason. Tisch wasn't about to wait around long enough to implement a turnaround.

Tisch was torn between negotiating a deal to get out of Franklin and executing a plan to fix it. While laying the groundwork for beefing up

Franklin's management, Tisch sought Gleason's support in dealing with Sindona. In May 1972, Tisch, on the way into a meeting with Sindona in New York, assured Gleason his job would be secure under Sindona—a hint that a sale might be imminent. What Tisch didn't know was that Gleason, as well as Luftig, would ultimately land in jail.

In the 15-minute meeting that followed, Sindona said little as he folded a piece of paper into the conical shape of a papal hat. Finally, he asked Gleason what his daughter-in-law's maiden name was, obviously already knowing the answer. Gleason told him the name was Bracco, adding that she didn't speak Italian. Sindona smiled approvingly. The next morning, Gleason asked Sol Kittay, a Franklin shareholder and director, for his opinion of this eccentric Italian. Kittay had nothing but praise.

Later that month, Sindona told a luncheon of bankers and money managers at the Recess Club, in Manhattan's financial district, that he intended to make a large investment in the New York banking business. He did not name a specific bank.

A little over a month later, on July 5, Tisch told Gleason: "I've sold my stock to Sindona. Sorry you weren't kept informed, but I tried to reach you earlier."

ACQUISITION THROUGH DEBT FINANCING

Sindona then set in motion a complex series of bank transfers designed, he claimed, to let him buy the shares while drawing minimal attention to the process, so as not to affect Franklin's stock price. This maneuvering made little sense: Sindona's purchase price was set with Tisch and not subject to open-market influences. Price fluctuation was a nonissue.

Sindona was actually trying to hide the fact that this $40 million stock purchase was done entirely with debt—a major obstacle to winning Federal Reserve approval of any banking deal. Buying a bank with debt makes it harder to answer the question of who is actually in control of the bank: the buyer, or the buyer's creditors? It later came to light that Banca Unione had lent Sindona's Fasco A.G. all the capital for the purchase, to be repaid within a year.

This unorthodox arrangement by itself would have raised questions about Sindona's motivations and business ethics. Around the time the Fed and the Comptroller of the Currency began to study whether Sindona's Franklin purchase gave him control of the bank, an ABC radio reporter, Jack Begon, aired "Hot Dollars," a report suggesting that Sindona, as early as 1957, had ties to American and Italian crime syndicates.

Tisch's decision to bail out of Franklin was proving to be a lot more complicated than he had expected. He would face accusations that he failed to do his homework on Sindona, whose organized crime links were later proven. But, as Franklin's president, Paul Luftig, said, Tisch couldn't have known much about Sindona at the time. "There were a lot of rumors, but nothing specific," he said.

Even with the rumors about Sindona, it wasn't hard for Tisch to justify the sale. Sindona had agreed to pay $40 a share, or about 30 percent more than the stock's trading price before the sale rumors started. Not a bad price, considering that, about this time, the *Bank Stock Quarterly,* a publication of M.A. Shapiro stockbrokers, had just branded Franklin the worst of the 100 banks it covered. Tisch, who had bought his Franklin shares from Shapiro, could justify ignoring unfounded rumors about Sindona, whose credentials otherwise appeared "impeccable," as a Loews spokesman would later put it.

In the end, Tisch could easily argue that he had handled the Sindona affair in the most cost-effective manner. Ten years after the $40 million sale—which was a hefty $8.3 million above the stock's market value at the time of the sale—Tisch would agree to pay a relatively paltry $1.2 million to settle related lawsuits alleging he was negligent in selling out to Sindona without making sure the buyer wasn't a crook.

In the meantime, Tisch faced a storm of protest over the sale. Even as the cash was being readied for the sale, the former chairman of Franklin, Arthur T. Roth, a one-time teller who had built Franklin National to its pre-Gleason, pre-Sindona stature, urged New York bank regulators to determine that Sindona was "above reproach" before clearing the sale. In an open letter to Tisch, Roth asked, "Did you know enough about Michele Sindona to unconditionally recommend him as a person who will be good for the bank?"

Roth, the voice crying in the wilderness, asked the most obvious question: Why was Sindona willing to pay such a huge premium for a stake in a bank that was clearly in trouble? He faulted Tisch for failing to make sure other shareholders also would be able to get $40 a share. Roth sought a response from Tisch and from bank regulators, but received none, perhaps because Roth, whom Gleason had ousted, was viewed as a disgruntled ex-chairman.

Roth also raised questions about how well the Fed and the Comptroller of the Currency had done their homework to ascertain Sindona's suitability. Was Sindona helped by connections in the U.S. Treasury Department? Roth would later testify in Congressional hearings that "Sindona had entree" in the Treasury Department.

It later came to light that as the Fed was doing its review of Sindona's interest in Franklin, he attempted to make a secret $1 million donation to President Nixon's 1972 reelection campaign. Coincidentally, a unit of Sindona's Fasco A.G. owned the Watergate complex in Washington when burglars, just one month earlier, broke into Democratic headquarters there, causing the scandal that forced Nixon to resign.

For Tisch, the entire Franklin investment was a frustrating lesson. "It was one of those situations where we did nothing wrong," he said. "Kuhn Loeb brought in Sindona to us. I said to Al Freedman at Kuhn Loeb, a first-class investment banker, 'Have you checked this man out?' We had him checked out. Everybody thought Sindona was great. He was the banker for the pope. Everything was wonderful. In fact, the secretary of the Treasury, David Kennedy, when he left the Treasury, was his big supporter. . . . It was one of those situations where with hindsight everybody became a genius."

What irritated Tisch most was that although the Fed had run its own check on Sindona before approving him to control Franklin

National, the Fed wrung more than $1 million out of Tisch for failing to detect Sindona's intention to commit fraud.

"I like when the Federal Reserve Bank has the right to approve it, they approve it, and then it becomes my fault three years later," Tisch said.

In August 1972, Sindona and Carlo Bordoni, one of his key assistants, were named directors of Franklin. Credito Italiano immediately canceled a credit line to Franklin. Did the Italian lender know something about Sindona's character that his newfound admirers in the United States did not?

Roth would prove to be Sindona's nemesis, pressing him on the very issues that ultimately would lead to the failure and bankruptcy of Franklin National two years later. By March 1973, Franklin shares were trading at just $24 each, compared with the $40 Tisch got eight months earlier. An alarmed Roth met with Sindona. Why hadn't Sindona dumped Gleason, whom Roth blamed for the bank's costly interest-rate disparities? Why was the bank gambling in foreign exchange? Sindona's response: "Give me a year." Roth wanted a halt in currency speculation, as well as management changes and a reduction in problem loans. He got nowhere.

Tisch and Sindona had another, later encounter. In early 1973, they were bidding against each other for Talcott National, an unprofitable Chicago-based financing and factoring company. Franklin's senior officers opposed the move, but Sindona bulled ahead, unwilling to lose out to Tisch. Through Fasco, Sindona snapped up 50 percent of Talcott's 3.3 million shares outstanding, derailing Tisch's $16-a-share tender offer, then engineered Talcott's takeover by Franklin in a stock swap valued at $57 million, or about $17.27 a share. Sindona won the battle, but he was about to lose the war.

The man they called St. Peter's banker was as inept as he was corrupt. He was well on his way to reducing Franklin National's $3.4 billion of assets to just $1.7 billion in 1974. In May 1974, the SEC began an investigation of $37 million in unauthorized currency trading at Franklin National. The disclosure was followed quickly by a run on the bank and a scramble by the Fed to head off a full-scale banking crisis amid a deepening recession triggered by the October 1973 Arab oil embargo.

By the end of May 1974, the Federal Reserve would kick in a record $1.77 billion in an unsuccessful attempt to save the bank. Trading in its stock was halted. Sindona's desire for a respectable American bank began to look like nothing more than part of a scheme to prop up his already crumbling Italian empire. In October 1974, another bank took over the ruins of Franklin National, protecting all its remaining depositors from losses. Arthur Burns, Fed chairman at the time, attributed the successful management of the Franklin National crisis, then the nation's largest-ever bank failure, to "luck."

With his own luck running out, Sindona, in 1978, launched an ill-conceived preemptive first strike against Tisch. He sued him and several Loews units for $120 million for selling him the Franklin stake. The suit ultimately was thrown out as Sindona began to drown in his own considerably deeper legal morass, but Tisch still faced suits by the Federal Deposit Insurance Corporation (FDIC), filed two days after Sindona's, alleging breach of fiduciary duty in failing to check out Sindona sufficiently before the stock sale.

Specifically, the FDIC asserted that Sindona had paid a high premium for the Franklin shares as compensation for Tisch's aid in gaining management control over Franklin. When the suit was settled in 1982, Tisch denied any wrongdoing, saying he settled only to avoid enriching lawyers unnecessarily.

SINDONA'S DOWNFALL

When the FDIC filed its suit against Tisch in 1978, the government was clearly laying the groundwork for a case against Sindona. The day after the FDIC acted, federal prosecutors indicted three Franklin National officers, including Gleason and Luftig, alleging deliberate efforts to cover up the bank's precarious condition. They were convicted in 1979 of falsifying bank records to win loan extensions from another bank, and were sentenced to three-year jail terms. Each served one year.

In 1980, Sindona himself was convicted of 68 counts of fraud, misappropriation of bank funds, and perjury for looting Franklin National of $45 million and faking his own kidnapping to delay the trial. He was sentenced to 25 years in prison. Five years later, he was convicted in Italy for siphoning off an additional $225 million from his Banca Privata Italiana, which also collapsed in 1974.

Finally, in 1986, he was convicted of ordering the murder of a lawyer who had handled the liquidation of one of Sindona's banks. Four days after being sentenced to life in prison, Sindona, 65 years old, committed suicide by drinking cyanide with his breakfast coffee in an Italian prison.

Tisch summed up the Sindona affair: "That was a sad episode. Not for me [but for Sindona]." For Tisch, the expense was insignificant compared with the price Sindona paid and the impact on Franklin National.

In purely financial terms, however, the Franklin National debacle was hardly a blip on Tisch's radar screen. The Sindona affair offended Tisch's sense of fair play and confirmed the wisdom of always preparing for the worst. Tisch didn't miss a beat in his search for the next great bargain, but in that next venture, he wouldn't be so lucky financially.

After collecting $40 million from Franklin, $5.5 million from selling Reed Candy Co. and several other millions from hotel deals, Loews had a $500 million cash hoard in 1972. Tisch, 49, was ready for the next deal that made sense. It could be anything. He hadn't been shopping for a cigarette company when Lorillard happened along. As Tisch said a month after the Franklin sale, "The best things come in from left field."

The search for the next big acquisition would follow the insurance path, but it would include one major blunder. Tisch was about to flush $7.3 million down a black hole of an insurance company called Equity Funding.

6

Getting Burned in the Equity Funding Fraud and Bouncing Back

"It wasn't easy to tell a man he had paid $8 million a few hours earlier for something I considered worthless."

—Raymond L. Dirks, *The Great Wall Street Scandal*

By early 1973, Loews Corp.'s assets stood at about $1.3 billion, including an investment portfolio valued at nearly a half-billion dollars. About the only limit to what Loews could do in terms of acquisitions was the availability of an appropriate target. As always, the new venture had to be a fundamentally sound but underperforming business that would respond quickly to Tisch's aggressive management style.

"Insurance is one of the best businesses around," he said. "The assets are immediately convertible into capital." Tisch loved having capital; it beat having good credit. Asked whether any deals were imminent, he said, "There is always a chance. You can do anything in America."

Tisch was indeed more entrepreneur than professional manager. In business, nothing was carved in stone, except perhaps the responsibility to reward all investors. "If you are in business," he said, "you are involved in buying and selling every day. If someone came to our company and wanted to buy it all for a really high price, we would have to consider it for our shareholders."

Insurance, Tisch had decided, was the next land of opportunity. The business offered access to huge sums of capital and provided a vehicle for Tisch to exercise his considerable prowess in the stock and bond markets. Insurance also opened windows on other businesses. It was a natural for Tisch. Both life insurers and property/casualty insurers are by nature conservative investors, because their assets are pledged against future claims. The money can't be tied up in hard-to-liquidate or high-risk investments like real estate, below-investment-grade bonds, or volatile stocks.

Life insurers sell individuals the ultimate conservative investment: personal-wealth protection. They don't promise to make the policyholder rich, only to protect his or her wealth from the vagaries of inflation and taxes and to guard the family against ruin because of the sudden loss of its breadwinner. The appeal is to the security-conscious, not to the aggressive investor. Success depends on solid marketing and solid financial strength to ensure that the money will be there when policyholders cash in their policies or annuities.

Property/casualty insurers sell risk protection to businesses and individuals. They need to show superior financial strength to make sales, but their success depends on solid underwriting—that is, making sure the property or business being insured isn't exposed to inordinate risk of destruction or loss. Businesses and homeowners have to buy insurance; without it, they don't do business or borrow to buy a home. Underwriting commercial insurance requires understanding a business's vulnerabilities. Having that kind of insight on businesses appealed to Tisch.

By March 1973, Tisch had become a buyer of insurance stocks. One benefit of owning an insurance company was that it would give Tisch a vehicle in which he could maintain a hefty investment portfolio without being criticized for being too risk-averse. His strategy, however, put him on a collision course with Equity Funding Corp., an undervalued asset that turned out to be undervalued for a good reason.

THE BAIT AND THE HOOK

The story of Equity Funding and how Tisch got drawn in began on March 6, 1973, a Tuesday. Ronald H. Secrist, who had just been dismissed as an official of Equity Funding Life Insurance Co., called Raymond L. Dirks, an insurance industry analyst at stockbroker Delafield Childs, and made a startling assertion. Secrist told Dirks that about one-third of all the life insurance policies on the Illinois insurer's books were fake.

Dirks had no reason to believe Secrist, whom he had never met. Equity Funding Life was the main business of Equity Funding Corp. of America, based in Century City, California. At the time, Equity Funding's stock was trading at $28 a share and was getting positive reviews from several Wall Street firms. Still, something knowledgeable in Secrist's approach prevented Dirks from dismissing him as a crank. If Secrist was right and was prepared to prove it in public, then Equity Funding's days were numbered.

In fact, Secrist simultaneously told his story to the New York State Insurance Department. Within days, Illinois insurance regulators launched a surprise audit on Equity Funding that ultimately would uncover even more fraud than Secrist was alleging.

For now, however, Dirks was left to sort out Secrist's credibility on his own. Maybe Secrist was just a disgruntled ex-employee seeking revenge, but did that preclude the possibility he was telling the truth? The next day, Dirks met with Secrist, who described the whole process of inventing policyholders and policies. The allegations were too detailed and too provable to dismiss—and too outrageous and potentially devastating to the company to accept without proof. Secrist said he hadn't blown the whistle until now because he feared for his family.

Dirks decided to seek independent confirmation and confront the company and its auditors. The following Monday, he met with Equity Funding's chairman, Stanley Goldblum, a muscular former meat packer, and the company's auditors. Dirks repeated Secrist's accusation. "Preposterous," Goldblum said. The auditors expressed shock.

Dirks still had no solid confirmation of whether Secrist's information was accurate, but any analyst worth his salt would begin to worry about the impact of the rumor on the stock. Dirks decided to warn his clients. He had to give them the opportunity to protect themselves from a sudden sell-off.

Within a day of his meeting with Goldblum, Dirks decided to relay Secrist's story to Jerry Zukowski at Boston Co. Institutional Investors, which owned 5 percent of Equity Funding's stock outstanding. A fraud that extensive seemed highly unlikely, Zukowski reasoned. He was reluctant to sell at $28 a stock that had been trading at $35 two months earlier, on the basis of wild allegations by a single angry ex-employee, especially in view of Goldblum's confident, swift denial.

In the end, Boston Co. decided to take no chances. It sold its 400,000 Equity Funding shares, contributing to a sudden steep drop in the price. Within one week of Dirks's meeting with Goldblum, Equity Funding lost more than 25 percent of its market value.

CASTING THE ROD

Larry Tisch and other investors took notice. A desirable insurance stock had suddenly fallen into the undervalued category. As near as Tisch could tell, the decline wasn't related to any fundamental problem. At $20 a share, it was irresistible. Never mind that the New York Stock Exchange viewed the drop with sufficient alarm to begin an investigation of the trading in the stock that same Monday.

On Wednesday, March 21, Loews bought 220,000 shares of Equity Funding for $19.25 each, or $4.2 million, on the recommendations of three securities analysts. Two days later, the stock was holding even, but only because Tisch wasn't the only investor who figured the decline provided a buying opportunity. In fact, unbeknownst to Boston Co., another of its own affiliates, John W. Bristol & Co., had loaded up on Equity Funding stock, acquiring an even larger stake than the one Boston Co. had just dumped.

Tisch was aware of the rumors swirling around the slump in Equity Funding stock, and Goldblum, whom Tisch had met once socially, was aware that Tisch had bought a large block. Goldblum "offered to bring me up to date," Tisch said. Salomon Brothers arranged for them to meet for breakfast, along with Yura Arkus-Duntov, Equity's executive vice-president, investment management, in the dining room of Loews' Regency Hotel that Friday, March 23. In that 20-minute meeting, Goldblum satisfied Tisch that the steady decline in Equity's stock price had nothing to do with the company's condition.

The two men agreed it made sense to buy low and sell high. The company and its outlook were as strong as ever, Goldblum assured Tisch, despite vague rumors to the contrary. Tisch believed him. Later in the day, Loews bought 53,100 more shares at $19 to $19.75 each.

THE HOOKED FISHERMEN

Goldblum spent part of the rest of the day repeating his assurances to Big Board officials seeking an explanation of the unusual trading in Equity Funding stock. The following Monday and Tuesday, Goldblum and other Equity Funding insiders joined the selling spree.

Meanwhile, the Illinois regulators were hitting pay dirt, and the stock's newest converts were tracing unsettling rumors back to Dirks. On Monday, March 26, Bristol placed an order with Salomon Brothers to sell 446,000 Equity shares just before the Big Board's opening bell at 10 A.M. Salomon found a buyer for the entire block: Loews.

Later that day, Dirks learned of the purchase and got a message that Loews' portfolio manager, Wallace Bowman, was trying to reach him. Bowman wanted to hear about the fraud rumor. As with Bristol, Bowman was seeking intelligence after becoming a major holder. "This block was just trailing around the Street," Dirks said, "and I was getting a phone call every time it changed hands." Both Bristol and Loews had bet against the market, assuming the market was wrong. Dirks, who by now was getting feedback suggesting Secrist's story was solid, told Bowman everything he knew.

"It wasn't easy to tell a man he had paid $8 million a few hours earlier for something I considered worthless," Dirks said.

Bowman's response wasn't what Dirks expected.

"Well, I think it's absolutely hilarious," Bowman said. "Larry Tisch bought this stock, not me," he added. "I'll have to call Larry and tell him."

A month earlier, Tisch had appeared to take full credit for the success of the investment portfolio Bowman ran for Loews.[1] Bowman's amusement at Loews' misfortune came out in testimony before the Big Board. Later that year, Bowman left and was replaced by money manager Joseph Rosenberg.

Tisch insisted Bowman's departure had nothing to do with this incident. Bowman went to work for Tosco, a California company that claimed it was going to cash in on the energy crisis by developing an alternate energy source via oil shale.

Loews managed to unload 102,000 of its 490,000 Equity Funding shares at $17 each before the Big Board halted trading in the stock the next day. Dirks began four days of testimony before the SEC, providing the names of at least 30 employees who knew of the fraud Secrist had outlined.

On Wednesday, March 28, the SEC suspended trading in Equity Funding, thus slamming the door forever on Loews and everyone else who may have hoped for one last round in this Wall Street version of keep-away. It would soon come to light that fully $2 billion of Equity Funding's $3 billion face amount of policies was fake.

By the beginning of April 1973, less than a month after Secrist called Ray Dirks, it was clear that his allegations were a conservative representation of the truth. Illinois insurance officials discovered that the fake life insurance policies had been resold to reinsurers. California insurance officials seized the company's operations in that state. A class action lawsuit in Los Angeles federal court alleged that Equity's assets included $20 million in nonexistent bonds. The Federal Bureau of Investigation (FBI) later in the month called it a $120 million counterfeit securities operation involving two printing companies.

Goldblum quit and would later plead guilty to five federal felony counts. He spent four years in prison. He admitted that he had considered taking Equity Funding into bankruptcy court as early as 1969, but decided that somehow he would find a way to end the fraud before it could be discovered. To this day, he still faults Dirks for alerting his clients and sparking the sell-off rather than going straight to the Securities and Exchange Commission with Secrist. What was left of Equity Funding's assets later became the highly successful investment company Orion Capital Corp.

Loews, feeling suckered in, was forced to scramble to undo its Equity Funding trades. With 273,100 shares in hand, it told broker Goldman, Sachs & Co. to refuse delivery of an additional 216,900 shares and to refuse payment on sale by Loews of 102,000 shares.

On Friday, April 5, one month after Secrist's call to Dirks, Equity Funding Corp. filed for bankruptcy court protection in Los Angeles. The next day, California regulators discovered more than 56,000 fake insurance policies at Equity Funding and 35,000 real ones. It was becoming apparent that Equity Funding had been run as a criminal enterprise. Lawton General Corp., the portfolio management unit of Loews, joined the list of those suing Boston Co. in an effort to undo more than $9 million of Lawton's Equity share purchases. The allegation was that Boston, after six conversations with Dirks, was selling on the basis of inside information.

No one wanted to accept that the game was over. In early May, J. W. Bristol, Boston Co., and Boston Co. Institutional Investors Inc. countersued Salomon Brothers Inc., which had sued to break its agreement to buy 456,900 Equity Funding shares at $17.50 each, or nearly $8 million. Bristol and Boston Co. acknowledged that Dirks had warned them of trouble but denied they were selling on the news.

"FRAUD NEVER ENTERED OUR MINDS"

Tisch was undeterred by the Equity debacle. The hotel business continued to grow, and Tisch continued to look for deals on the Street.

Tisch viewed the Equity investment as a costly mistake for Loews, but not much of a reflection on Tisch's judgment. He should have waited a little longer to determine what was behind Equity's tumbling stock price, before deciding it was a buying opportunity. But the sellers of Equity weren't acting on inside information; they were selling on rumors, a staple of the Street.

The sellers and buyers weren't betting so much on whether the rumors were true as on how the stock would move after the rumors circulated. Besides, Graham and Dodd never wrote about how to detect criminal intent in a company's public disclosures.

"There are a lot of geniuses after the fact," Tisch said. "But there's no way to adjust for massive fraud in analyzing a stock. There's just no answer to it. Either you believe the whole system of investing is based on fraud or you do business on the basis of audits, insurance regulation, and other safeguards. The idea of massive fraud never entered our minds."

Perhaps it would have, were it not for an investment strategy that put so much emphasis on identifying stock-market buying opportunities by screening for low price/earnings ratios. The assumption is that if an investor can't identify a fundamental business reason—as opposed to something having to do with stock market dynamics—for a company's low stock price, then the stock is artificially depressed and is bound to recover to a more appropriate level.

The Equity Funding case was a perfect example of what this strategy fails to detect: that the sellers pounding a stock know something a value investor like Tisch doesn't know—something that doesn't amount to insider information. Indeed, it was rare that the market—the vast majority of investors not privy to inside information—knew something about a company he didn't know. Were Tisch more open to that possibility, he might not have gotten burned.

But it wasn't Tisch's nature to factor into his analysis the possibility of deliberate deception as the underlying reason for a bargain price. Besides, the sellers who brought down Equity Funding weren't selling on information; they were selling on rumors, betting that the rumors would be proven. As such, they were gambling as much as Tisch was.

Tisch had little patience for trying to sort out the difference between rumors started by desperate traders and rumors based on fact. He used his considerable mental powers in a search for opportunities that "made sense." Owning the stocks of strong companies in strong businesses made sense. Buying such stocks didn't make sense if they were expensive relative to the rest of the market. Knowing when to buy was as important as knowing what to buy, and knowing when was often a function of how well one understood the economic cycle rather than of one's ability to analyze rumors.

THE ECONOMIC CYCLE'S OWN CLUES

Tisch paid close attention to the economy's vital signs for clues to the fundamental reasons a company's stock was underperforming the market. In broad terms, the question with any stock-market dog was whether the price was low because of problems with the company, or problems with the economy, or both. Even a value investor can get burned buying an underperforming stock in a poor business environment.

In simple terms, understanding the economic cycle means understanding (1) whether interest rates are likely to go up, go down, or hold steady, and (2) that the direction in which rates are headed can make or break an investment. The economic cycle swings from periods of growth to periods of contraction or recession, with the Fed lowering interest rates during recession to stimulate growth and raising rates during boom times to stem inflation.

Tisch was disciplined in his approach to interest rates and the economy: these were investment variables he could analyze and adjust to. In the beginning of 1994, for example, when the Dow Jones Industrial Average was flirting with the 4000 level, Tisch was selling stocks and bonds and moving money into cash equivalents—short-term Treasury debt.

"If you look at the charts, you've entered that parabolic stage, the last hurrah," Tisch said, referring to statistical stock-market patterns.

"Does it stop at 4000, 4500? I don't know. You just go off to the sidelines. You keep selling into it and at some point say the hell with it, you're out. Cash. Short-term Treasurys. You pay a premium. You don't buy safety free. The question is: How much is the premium and how long do you have to pay it?"

Tisch would be criticized from time to time for being too cautious about the stock market, but his conservative nature wouldn't permit him to risk getting out too late to avoid a downdraft. "Everybody thinks they're going to get out in time," he said. The comment was as true about the market in general as it was about an individual company's stock like Equity Funding. Despite that misstep, Tisch was still cash rich, and the economy was about to create lots of stock market bargains.

In 1973, inflation was starting to pick up, and the stock market was beginning to sag. If the economic cycle was on schedule, the downside of expansion was about to take hold. Sometimes, an event will accelerate the process; for example, the demand for military hardware at the start of World War II lifted the country out of the Depression of the 1930s. Once again, war would play a role, but with the opposite economic effect.

On October 6, 1973, Israel's Arab neighbors attacked the Jewish nation. As Larry Tisch spearheaded a $25 million fund-raising drive to help Israel in what became known as the Yom Kippur War, President Nixon committed the United States' unqualified backing to Israel. For Nixon's transgression, the oil-exporting Arab nations in the Mideast launched a devastating economic war by imposing an oil embargo on the West.

The embargo was custom-made to accommodate the cyclical trend. It sent the price of a major inflation component soaring. Motorists lined up for hours at gas stations for the privilege of buying increasingly rare gallons of gasoline at two to three times the previous price. Consumer confidence was destroyed. Car sales plunged. Factories were shuttered. Unemployment climbed. Air went out of the stock market and its premium-priced Nifty Fifty. The inflation run-up forced interest rates higher. The first oil-shock recession was under way.

Anyone holding a lot of cash could find plenty of bargains in the stock market, and Larry Tisch had a lot of liquid assets. The situation was ideal for a bottom-feeder like Tisch.

OPEN SEASON ON CNA FINANCIAL CORP.

Loews was not immune to the negative circumstances that were depressing the economy and creating bargains. Soon after the embargo began, Loews posted lower profit and cut its dividend. It cited declines from selling hotels and hotel leases, and reduced returns on securities. In effect, Loews was paying the price for raising cash and reinvesting it with limited success. Still, Loews was beginning to see the benefits of diversification. While the country was mired in the energy crisis, Bob Tisch and other hoteliers noticed a rise in business for their big-city luxury hotels. Gas lines had taken the fun out of car travel. People were returning to the cities to escape the aggravation of commuting. The hotel business benefited.

Larry kept shopping. Despite the Equity Funding disaster, he was still in the market for an insurer. By March 1974, he had identified a desirable target, another stumbling insurance company—only this time, the stumbling wasn't obscured by fraud. By March 14, Tisch had publicly acknowledged, as required by law, that Loews held more than 5 percent of CNA Financial Corp. He wanted to own more, he said at the time, but he wasn't interested in launching a hostile tender offer.

The big Chicago insurer was a slumping business. CNA was on its way to posting a $208 million loss for 1974, and Tisch was discovering it wasn't just the fault of a rotten economy. CNA was suffering from poor management, poor underwriting, and poor diversification decisions. Tisch declared open season on CNA. He wasn't interested in having a stake in a mismanaged company any more than he was interested in taking a loss on another insurance stock.

There was just one problem: CNA's managers didn't want to work for Larry Tisch and company, let alone do things his way.

"It was one of those investments where he thought he was buying value," said John J. Gutfreund, former chairman of Salomon Brothers Inc. "As he looked at [CNA] more and more, he realized the management was not optimizing results for the shareholder and decided that a team under his stewardship would do a better job. The Chicago establishment at that time was not overly anxious to have Mr. Tisch."

As Warren Buffett would later observe, Tisch was bound to attract criticism, just as he would years later at CBS. "He changed the status quo in both places," Buffett noted. "Anyone who comes in as a big agent of change is going to catch a certain amount of criticism."

At CNA, an epic corporate battle tinged with animosity began. CNA's defense included a short-lived effort by the city of Chigago to enact a code barring nonresidents from buying local businesses. At one point, Lester Pollack, Loews' lawyer, stumbled across a CNA document characterizing the Tisches as the sons of a "garment manufacturer." The Tisches wondered if this was a thinly veiled effort to identify them as Jews.

The battle also entailed an obligatory effort by CNA to bring in a friendly suitor, much as Commercial Credit had done to successfully escape into the arms of Control Data. In this case, the designated white knight was a Swiss firm—Accident & Casualty Insurance Co. of Winterthur. Loews responded quickly.

In May, Loews went on the attack. It let it be known it was interested in acquiring a controlling interest in CNA, asked the Illinois Insurance Department for clearance to do so, and sued Winterthur, its bidding rival, for $120 million.

The lawsuit worked. A U.S. District Court judge, in July, barred Winterthur from offering to buy CNA stock because the Swiss company had failed to disclose (1) its longtime relationship with CNA through reinsurance agreements and (2) that the main purpose of its CNA purchases wasn't to buy the insurer but to keep others from doing so. Later that month, Illinois regulators gave Loews permission to proceed—despite testimony against the takeover by a familiar figure, Ray Dirks, the analyst who brought Equity Funding crashing to earth.

Dirks felt that the bid, a fraction of CNA's book value, was too low, and that Tisch had painted a far bleaker picture of CNA than was justified. "It was a steal," Dirks said. "The public was getting screwed." Nevertheless, Loews gained the upper hand.

That August, Loews offered $6 a share for a 51 percent stake in CNA, a few weeks after CNA had posted a huge second-quarter loss that it blamed on a slumping housing market. At the end of October, because of its worsening financials, CNA began to see the wisdom of working with Loews. It recommended that its board accept the Loews offer; but there was a hitch. CNA's results were rapidly deteriorating. Loews decided it had to rethink its bid and came back in November with a bid of $5 a share, citing CNA's $135 million third-quarter loss and the suspension of its dividend. For $100 million, Loews bought 20 million CNA shares, gaining control of a company that one day would have revenue of more than $10 billion a year.

The success of the CNA bid hinged largely on two factors: first, Tisch's appetite to take on an underperformer, fully confident in his ability to install strong enough management to turn it around, and second, Tisch's ability, through persistence, to turn many of his opponents on the board into supporters and to win over certain large holders.

One of those large holders was his good friend Gerald Tsai. A few years earlier, CNA had purchased Tsai Management & Research Co., whose main operation was the Manhattan Fund, for a large block of CNA stock. Like several other CNA diversification moves, this one proved to be a dog. The fund promptly turned in a dismal performance, investors bailed out, and Tsai himself quit. But he held his CNA stake and became a Tisch partisan along with other large holders.

Among the board members Tisch converted was Richard B. Oglivie, a former Illinois governor who stayed on for many years as a director despite his initial opposition to Tisch.

"We fought vigorously," Oglivie said in 1986. "We really weren't sure what he was going to do with it. But it was impossible to prevent them from getting control. Looking back now, I'm delighted. They brought in strong management, and now the company is doing very well."

Oglivie's comment was familiar. Repeatedly, Larry Tisch sparked dread among the managers of the companies he wanted to control—Loew's Theatres and Lorillard, for example. The arrival of his management team was something to fear. The weak would not survive. The strong, however, would be rewarded, not only with financial success but with the benefit of being exposed to a commonsense approach to frugal management. They would experience a success built on a strategy of carefully managed growth backed by a mountain of cash.

TURNING AROUND CNA

At CNA, the Tisches found lots of weaknesses. As with Loew's Theatres and Lorillard, both of which were hobbled by underperforming assets, the Tisches wasted no time identifying the problems and executing solutions. In December 1974, Bob Tisch went over CNA in search of waste. As Larry and Bob would at CBS years later, Bob found a company that seemed to have forgotten its obligation to shareholders.

For starters, CNA executives had recently rewarded themselves with an opulent skyscraper in downtown Chicago. The upper echelon gave themselves the top three floors. Each executive office had a private toilet. The chairman, Elmer L. Nicholson, occupied a suite with a spiral staircase to his private dining room. This was diametrically opposed to the corporate culture at Loews, where executives ate takeout lunches at their desks in modestly furnished offices and the decor bespoke practicality and economy.

Nicholson was ousted in a hurry. He didn't fit into Larry Tisch's philosophy of responsible corporate governance. Larry became chairman, Bob executive committee chairman, and Lester Pollack finance committee chairman. "One of the first things they did was to close down those overpretentious top floors," one Chicago businessman said. "The Tisch brothers and Pollack took 200-square-foot offices. If you're going to sit there and fire people, it isn't going to look good if you take a 3,000-square-foot office." Said one former CNA employee:

"It seemed cruel to let all those people go right before Christmas, but Loews couldn't afford to go slowly."

In the CNA overhaul, "the Loews people showed a callous disregard for people," according to one executive there at the time. "They did not trust anyone, and they meddled in every department."

Still, Tisch noted: "Everybody on the board after this bitter fight was kept on the board. When we took over, it was their board. But we said, 'What's the difference? We'll live with it. We'll do the right thing.' I always work on the theory that if you do the right thing, it will take care of itself. You do what's right for the shareholders and what's right for the business."

In less than two years, every CNA unit had been put under the microscope, not so much with the idea of reversing CNA's diversification but to identify weaknesses and cure them through a combination of cutbacks and sales. Its 55 nursing homes were sold for $22 million. A legal fight over capital commitments to a 45 percent-owned dental supply company was settled, clearing the way for future growth and the company's sale. Larwin Group Inc., a home builder, was slashed to a staff of 96 from 600 and moved to less-expensive Encino from Beverly Hills, California.

Edward J. Noha, former executive vice president of Allstate Insurance Co., was brought in as CNA's chairman and CEO, and the insurance operations were turned upside down in search of savings. Ultimately, the search cost 1,400 of CNA's 12,000 workers their jobs. Yet the acquisition of CNA by Loews resulted in the addition of just one person to Loews' headquarters staff in New York.

Soon after Noha's arrival, Tisch brought in Jay L. Kriegel, former chief of staff to ex-New York City Mayor John V. Lindsay. He was named director of special projects of CNA and would play an increasingly important role in shaping Loews' public image. For CNA, the turnaround was dramatic.

By year-end 1975, under the firm hand of Loews—and Noha's free hand—CNA posted a $110 million profit versus a loss a year earlier, of $207 million. Tisch would tell shareholders it was the year's "most satisfying accomplishment."

THE FRUITS OF FAST MANAGEMENT RESPONSE

By 1976, the Tisches owned 41 percent of Loews, which had grown to annual revenue of $2.7 billion from $166 million in just eight years. Yet management was concentrated in the hands of a few men. They included Larry, Bob, Pollack ("the third brother"[2]), and four divisional managers: Curtis Judge at Lorillard; Robert J. Hausman, president of Loew's Hotels, who built the Aunt Jemima pancake restaurant chain and sold it before moving to Loews in 1967; Bernard Myerson at Loew's Theatres; and Noha at CNA.

"Loews is entrepreneurial," Pollack said at the time, "[operated by] good businessmen who understand diverse industries and can apply management techniques to a varied group of companies."

The key to the Tisches' success was hands-on-management. As one former executive put it: "Loews people usually know within a week if anything happens in any of their companies. They have taken away all bureaucracy, all impedimenta."

As Tisch explained it, "We let people have authority, otherwise they lose their effectiveness." But the Tisches weren't known for patience. They did not wait for problems to solve themselves. "A decline of any kind concerns us," Bob said. "We go in immediately to see how we can do better."

No doubt, Bob's personal style contributed greatly to the family's ability to keep close tabs on operations. Bob "knows every towel and every doorknob in every hotel," a former executive said. "He also knows most of the people by their first name."

Increasingly, Pollack was the operations manager, along with Bob Tisch.

Lorillard was a case in point. In the first half of 1976, its share of the cigarette market had slipped to 8 percent from 9.3 percent, coming off several marketing failures, with cigarette brands named Zack, Maverick, Luke, and Redford. The Tisches detected this weakness quickly and gave Judge the mandate to move fast. The problem was that these new brands were all aimed at the so-called full-flavor market, but the growth was in low-tar cigarettes—14.8 percent of the market in 1976 versus 10.7 percent a year earlier. Before the year was out, Lorillard responded by producing Kent Golden Lights and True Fives and by successfully promoting a repackaged Newport.

When sick divisions resisted treatment, the Tisches weren't reluctant to act, as in the case of Loews J.H. Snyder homebuilding venture, which was phased out because of persistent losses. "They're not sentimental about keeping losers," one Loews alumnus observed.

Said Tisch: "Your constituents are very simple. In America today, you have the public, the employees, and the shareholders. Those are your three constituencies. And if you do the right thing, you never have a problem. From time to time, the outside perception of what's right may be different from mine. But I find that as long as I come to work in the morning and say I'm going to do the right thing, in the long run, my perception is the right thing. I can't go by what everybody is criticizing that day, because they have no vested interest."

Larry kept tabs on the empire's cash flow, spending most of his time in New York. The term "power breakfast" was coined to describe the frequent meetings of powerful businesspeople and investment bankers at Loew's Regency Hotel. "If somebody had to meet somebody uptown for breakfast," Tisch said, "they'd say, 'I'll meet you at the Regency,' and it's still that way."

This was one of the ways Tisch himself gathered the intelligence that gave him an edge in his pursuit of the well-rounded conglomerate. It wasn't foolproof, as Equity's Stanley Goldblum had shown, but Tisch used Loews' honey pot of liquid assets to attract investment ideas. The Regency became an informal forum in which such ideas coalesced long before the average investor would see their effect in the financial markets.

The Regency breakfasts exemplified the value the Tisches placed on personal contact in their approach to business. Besides the benefits of face-to-face interchange with investment types, the Tisches and Pollack used the breakfast forum to set the day's agenda for Loews.

Loews managed its way so successfully through the oil-shock recession that, by 1978, it had nearly tripled its profit—all in the wake of a wrenching economic slump and a costly encounter with Goldblum.

Because of Larry Tisch's adaptability to changing conditions and his ability to set aside ego considerations, he was able to survive the challenges of the Equity Funding and Franklin National scandals. His success in following through with his strategy by acquiring CNA and turning it around ultimately minimized the extent to which the business world even remembered bumps in his road to success.

Tisch's winning investments had more to do with day-to-day management of finances and operations than with economic foresight. In 1979, Tisch was asked what he would buy to hold for 20 years. Fourteen years later, many of his picks would look like dogs. For example, he liked savings-and-loan associations, which turned out to be one of the most prominent national economic disasters of the early 1990s, because of high-risk lending and investing. Federated Department Stores, another Tisch pick, would get gobbled up by a reckless Campeau Corp. in the late 1980s, only to be plunged into bankruptcy by too much debt. He liked Tosco, wrongly betting that its oil shale business would boom because of problems with the traditional sources of oil. Savin Business Machines would end up in bankruptcy court in 1992, Studebaker-Worthington Inc. would be bought out later that year by McGraw-Edison Co., and Northwest Industries was the subject of a crippling, debt-laden buyout in the mid-1980s.

But Tisch wasn't one to make bets himself on the basis of a 20-year forecast. "We're pragmatic," he said. "Our philosophy could change from one day to the next."

7

Philanthropist and Family Man

"I find business very relaxing."

—Larry Tisch

By 1977, Larry and Bob Tisch had built the well-rounded, risk-averse organization loosely envisioned in 1959 when the family started accumulating shares of Loew's Theatres. With CNA under control, Larry Tisch, at 54, was enjoying a low-profile business and personal life. For the next several years, however, his reputation for success in the world of business and finance would spread.

With his tight focus on shareholder value, Tisch would become an increasingly sought-after adviser in some of the major takeover plays of the 1980s, most notably Getty Oil and CBS. Tisch's shareholder focus was broad: a strategy that didn't benefit all shareholders was unacceptable. In this regard, he stood in sharp contrast to the likes of Carl Icahn, Victor Posner, T. Boone Pickens, and Saul Steinberg—all of whom would be identified with the questionable practice of accumulating a company's shares with the implied intent of taking over the company in order to force the target to put itself up for sale or buy back its shares from the unwanted suitor at a premium.

In the early 1980s, these men would come to be viewed as preda-tors—corporate raiders out to make a killing in the stock market as opposed to strengthening a company's fundamentals. They were dis-mantlers. In contrast, Tisch was a *builder* with little use for the vast fortunes that seemed to motivate the raiders.

After 30 years in business, Tisch's motivations were fairly simple. He took great pleasure in doing business, spending time with his fam-ily, and working for charitable causes.

As his empire grew, Tisch's philanthropic impulses became more pronounced. Both Larry and his wife, Billie, were active in Jewish char-ities—they paid $1 million to the estate of Israeli leader Moshe Dayan for a collection of antiquities valued at $2 million to $3 million and promptly donated them to the American Friends of Israel Museum.

A Tether of Loyalty

Tisch contributed greatly to his alma mater, New York University—$7.5 million would go to what is now known as the Tisch School of the Arts. As early as 1967, the Tisch Foundation had donated $2 mil-lion to NYU for a new Commerce School building, and Tisch soon after had been named a trustee, reflecting his interest in donating more than just money. Tens of millions more would flow to NYU over the years.

Tisch was also personally committed to NYU—so much so that, in June 1978, he was elected chairman of the school's board of trustees.

"If I called his office now and said, 'It's about NYU, he'd be back in touch in half an hour," said Leonard Stern, the chairman of the Hartz Group and another NYU graduate who would become a multimillion-dollar benefactor and for whom NYU's Stern School of Business is named. "If I said it was business, I'd go on his business schedule. . . . His brilliant, disciplined mind is a very important part of where the university is today."

Tisch's involvement, however, wasn't entirely free of controversy. He took a lot of heat for a financial decision that some viewed as costly for the university. He pulled a large chunk of the school's endowment fund out of stocks in the early 1980s, just as the bull market of that decade was taking off. About the same time, he lightened up on stocks in the Loews portfolio as well. Tisch's style was not to take profits at the top of a market; it was to seek a haven—high-yielding bonds—before the whole world decided to do the same thing. Tisch had not achieved success by running with the herd.

As for the impact of NYU's move out of stocks, Tisch and Stern were making a decision that went beyond a one-dimensional risk–reward investment strategy. To begin with, NYU as a nonprofit had greater flexibility than a for-profit business. It could still achieve decent returns on fixed-income bonds without the risk that Tisch perceived in the stock market. But there was another reason for cashing in stock profits.

"To build up the revenue of the university, we took several hundred million dollars of endowment money to finance the building of dormitories with 4,400 beds in the '80s," Stern said. "That has generated new revenue and brought in better students. How can you increase enrollment otherwise and draw students from all over the world?"

It was a smart business decision that achieved its goal. Tisch seemed to take even greater pleasure in such nonprofit successes than he did in his business dealings. In the end, money wasn't what drove Tisch.

In all his activities, business and nonbusiness, Tisch was never passive. He had "a tremendous sense of what is right and what is just," his son Andrew said. "He really believes he is the best judge of what's right. He did not want an asset to be misused."

This philosophy influenced some of his business dealings as well. For example, his loyalty to his Jewish heritage played a role in 1977–1978 when Loews sought to acquire three New York City hotels from Penn Central Corp.'s Penn Central Transportation Co. unit. In November 1977, Loews agreed to buy the Barclay, Biltmore, and Roosevelt hotels for $45 million. One of the three, the Biltmore, had been the site of a 1942 conference on establishing Israel. Penn

Central, then in bankruptcy proceedings, formally asked the court's permission to complete the sale the following April; soon after, a better offer surfaced from the other side of the world: an Arab group offered $50 million for the three hotels.

Within three weeks, Loews came back with a $55 million offer for the three hotels, outbidding the Mideast-bankrolled Halad International and Biltmore Hotel Associates. The bid was accepted, and Loews was rewarded almost immediately for its willingness to add $10 million to the price. By the end of the month, Loews sold the Barclay to Intercontinental Hotels Corp. and the Biltmore and Roosevelt hotels to developers Seymour and Paul Milstein, thus booking a $5 million profit in less than a month.

It would not be the last time Tisch's personal interests would influence an investment decision. His initial purchases of CBS stock were motivated in part by his interest in seeing CBS News remain free of owners with a political agenda. Similarly, the CBS investment nevertheless would prove to be hugely profitable.

Tisch enjoyed such quick-profit opportunities. They were ongoing business challenges and, usually, victories. The dollar amounts of the victories had become less important than the victories themselves. He had reached a level of success that, measured in dollars, is often linked to an obsession with wealth and to the tabloid notoriety of the broken families and moral bankruptcy of tycoons and would-be tycoons. The Tisches had never fit that mold, and, by the late 1970s, it was clear their success was more a function of disciplined work and intelligence than of any ambition to imitate or be ranked among the wealthiest.

"Wealth doesn't impress us," Billie Tisch said. "Larry and I are both very mindful of the things money cannot buy and the things it can buy. We always felt that we wanted the kids to be mindful of that. To be able to stand out as different in whichever community they chose to live in, we felt that you couldn't create an economy of scarcity where one didn't exist. We never made any pretense of not being able to afford things, nor did we see any value in extravagance. I think they know that."

"Larry has a wonderful relationship with them. While they don't discuss philosophy as such, they discuss enough of the daily business that the philosophy comes across in a hundred little ways."

A SOURCE OF VALUES

Despite their loyalty to Jewish interests and philanthropic support, Tisch and his family were never regulars in synagogue, but, beginning in 1977, as his philanthropy grew, he and his sons began weekly Talmudic study sessions that focused on business ethics in the context of Judaism. It had bothered Tisch that many successful Jewish business-people seemed to leave their roots behind. He once termed assimilation, the efforts made by Jews to blend in, "a disaster," a culturally self-destructive effort to gain acceptance.

Directing these early-morning meetings was Rabbi Nesson Scherman of Brooklyn, who had heard of Tisch's interest through a colleague, Joel Unger, a Denver-based Orthodox Jew. Larry had indicated to Unger that he was "curious about the Talmud," in response to a suggestion from his youngest son, Tommy. "So I went and we sat and schmoozed. We became very good personal friends," Scherman said. In the beginning, the group included Larry, Andy, and Jimmy; Tommy joined the group after graduating from college.

Such weekly study had always been the norm for Orthodox Jewish businessmen like the Reichmanns, the Toronto real-estate developers. The Tisches, however, weren't Orthodox. Larry, who had less religious training than his sons, was a Reform Jew, but seeking such instruction was becoming fashionable.

"For a time, we concentrated on the parts [of the Talmud] that deal with civil law and torts," Scherman said. "They would compare the legal system to the scriptures. About half of the time, we spent on text, the rest just visiting—an hour all together."

These weekly sessions became a steady feature—although Larry couldn't always attend—and would remain so during the relative lull between the hectic empire-building years through the mid-1970s and the volatile CBS years that began in 1985. During these years, the father and his sons cemented their already deep friendship and mutual loyalty.

HANDING DOWN VALUES

Larry's children, as they became adults, were becoming his best friends. Andrew and Jimmy, in particular, were ascending in the family conglomerate, along with Bob's son, Jonathan, who would rise to the top of the hotel division.

The relationship between the father and his sons was "warm and exciting," said Leonard Stern, the Hartz Group chairman and a friend. "Larry has no spoiled children."

"We've had a great relationship," Andrew Tisch said. "He always tells me exactly how he feels and vice versa. There are never long periods of disagreement. I never once doubted what he was saying to me was in my best interest. After all is said and done, the most important thing in the world to Larry is his family. We can disagree on business practices and the like, but at the end of every conversation, he'll say, 'How are the kids?' "

Even in the early years, when Larry was still putting in long days, he made sure he and his young sons had at least one block of time together every week. Friday night was boys' night—time for the family to pile into Larry's Mercedes two-seater, with all four sons jammed into the luggage space behind the seats, and head to the movies or a fair. And the dinner hour, always a semiformal affair, was dominated by talk of what the boys were doing, not of business.

Said Andrew's brother Jimmy: "He's not the father you would see in the advertisement with his arm over the shoulder of the nine-year-old son who just lost a baseball game. That's not to say he's a poor father at all. He just doesn't fit that particular mold. He's much more of an adult's father. His interest, first and foremost in his mind, was that everything be all right, that his sons be healthy and well. But he's not one who deals in details, and kids per se aren't his primary interest.

He developed that interest more as they got older. It's been the same with the grandchildren. He cares intensely about the grandchildren, but he's not the kind of guy to go goo-goo ga-ga with them. That's more Bob's style."

The Tisches' sons "all started to work early on in their careers, because work was considered fun in our house," Billie said.

Andrew, the oldest, remembered working during the summers as early as age 14 in the bowels of the Americana Hotel in New York and enjoying the work, even though his various unglamorous jobs included sorting dirty laundry. That early experience in the hustle and bustle of hotel operations led to his decision to study hotel management at Cornell University.

During Andrew's years at Cornell, the Tisches' values faced and survived the challenges posed by what Billie Tisch called "the Vietnam upheaval." Andrew, who graduated from Cornell in 1971, was there for the 1968 armed takeover of the student union building by African American students, and participated in an antiwar protest in Washington, against his parents' advice. Such experiences, however, failed to shake his respect for his father and the capitalistic environment in which he thrived.

"Cornell in that very short period of time was a seething place," Billie said. "It was *the* place. I remember Andy saying to us once, . . . we had talked him out of going to the first Washington march, and he called us one night in his senior year. It was a huge march. He said, 'I just called to tell you I'm going on the march and I don't want you to try to talk me out of it.' He said, 'You can't imagine what it's like unless you're here.' We said to him, 'Be careful.' . . . It was a terrible time."

None of the anti-big-business sentiment that characterized that time rubbed off indelibly on the Tisches' sons. All four sons gravitated to the business world during that period in the 1970s when, as youngest son Tommy put it, "there was a tremendous cynicism toward business. Whatever our feelings were then, we never responded to our father with a sense of moral judgmentalism."

As a father, "he never was so rigid or doctrinaire," Tommy said. "He was always willing to listen and concede the other side may be right.

He is a fascinating combination of a person who on one hand has very strongly held beliefs and at the same time sees that the world exists in various shades of gray. He tends to be a very good listener and at times a conciliator. He never pushed us. When any of us expressed a desire to do certain things, there was always an openness. There was always a sense that he was not a particularly judgmental man, and in that sense, it was very hard to rebel against him. He certainly is a strong figure in a number of ways. He would express his opinion, but it was always very clear he was not trying to impose his will on you."

Even the second-oldest son, Daniel, who adopted the counterculture look, remained tame by most radical standards of the time. His mother recalled a picture he had of himself while a student at Brown University. He was proudly sporting what he called his quarter coat, purchased at the Salvation Army for that amount of money. "He had the whole look that went with it," Billie said, but noted that none of her four sons had been "radicalized" during the counterculture revolution, although many of their friends "just never came back from that experience."

Billie theorized that the Tisch sons "saw Larry using the fruits of his labors to accomplish goals that they could buy into. The money, the resources didn't go for things that were discredited. I think that without our articulating it, that's what they knew. Working and having money was not a bad thing for them, because they knew it could create values that they believed in."

Daniel knew his father was successful, but even though Larry had a reputation as the quintessential conglomerateur, Daniel's perception of his father's business at the time was considerably less sweeping ("We were in the theater business") and their life-style was much less lavish than one might expect of a multimillionaire. "None of us liked to admit we were raised in Scarsdale," he said, because it is generally considered one of New York's most affluent suburbs.

"We were not raised to believe we were among great wealth," Daniel said. "We did not live in a flashy style. Our home was situated on less than an acre. We never had an alarm system. Our phone was always listed. We were not raised any different from anybody else. I'm a lucky sperm. That's about it. I was not special. I'm still not special.

That was part of the tone we were raised in. We believe in work, effort, honesty, the value of the dollar. We did not waste."

After attending public schools in Scarsdale, all four sons went to private boarding schools from 10th grade on. New York City was becoming the family's primary residence, and the boys didn't want to attend city high schools.

As the sons one by one graduated from college, their father's empire stood ready to include them, but only if they were so inclined. Larry Tisch had no grand vision of global corporate dominance, of establishing a powerful family dynasty, or of achieving fame to go along with his fortune. The opportunity later in life to work with his sons—to share the pleasure he took in his own enterprises—was an unexpected bonus.

Daniel was the one son who chose not to pursue a career in the family business. Andrew and Jimmy worked their way up in Lorillard and Loews, respectively, and Tommy took on the management of the family's money and philanthropy. Daniel carved out his own career on Wall Street, despite being the only one of the four sons who had never worked on the floor of the New York Stock Exchange.

The closest Daniel came to the family business was a summer job in the London hotel Loews owned. He was growing a beard, so he handled out-of-view jobs, such as sorting dirty laundry. "I learned that the hotel business wasn't for me," he said. Besides, he added, he was well aware of his father's strong personality and wanted to prove himself independently, adding that Larry never pressured any of his sons to join the family business. Daniel may have had only one summer on a Loews' payroll, but he played a pivotal role in Larry's move into CBS, and the arbitrage firm he set up in 1989 after leaving Salomon Brothers would be 25 percent funded by Tisch family money.

The strength of Larry Tisch's personality was obvious to his sons as they were growing up. "You knew you did not want to get him angry," Daniel said. "You never crossed him, though it wasn't as if he hit us or spanked us. After a while, you learned the limits of what you could or couldn't do. We were raised in a liberal household."

Besides his family, Larry Tisch most enjoyed tennis, skiing, bridge, business, and playing to win. As a tennis player and skier, he made up with tenacity what he lacked in form. He was goal-oriented in his approach to both business and pleasure, but he was not motivated by a desire simply to accumulate money. His wealth grew through masterful gamesmanship, through working the system and having fun at it.

"When you have the ability to keep the ball rolling," Billie observed, "that's what you do. We enjoy having the nice life and not having to worry and all of that, but that's not a driving force. We could be poor and it wouldn't make a bit of difference, and there's a great level of comfort in that. Clearly, our life-style has changed, but we just don't think in terms of having a lot of money."

Larry Tisch may have taken great joy in doing business, but he could be a brutally tough negotiator in pursuit of victory.

"He definitely has a temper," Rabbi Scherman conceded. "I've seen him lose his temper. But he gets angry for legitimate things."

Tisch disputed this often-repeated observation. "I'll fight for a cause, but I don't lose my temper over the cause," he asserted. "I just believe in fighting for a cause. I'll get exercised over a moral issue, never over a business issue. A business issue, you handle it. It's not that important. But a moral issue is something you've got to fight for."

The picture that emerges is that of a morally conscious individual whose primary goal was to play hard, to enjoy the play, to win, and to return value to family and community.

Andrew summed up his father's winning ways this way: "First, he has an uncanny ability to identify undervalued assets. He's very self-assured in his investment philosophy. Second, he can be a contrarian and really believe he is right. Third, he doesn't let money burn a hole in his pocket. He's content to let it sleep. He's willing to wait. And if there's no immediate return, he doesn't lose his convictions."

Larry passed this strength of character on to his sons. "He raised us to also believe in what you're doing, because you won't get credit for listening to everybody else."

As Larry's parents had believed in him and his brother, Larry believed in his sons, and he would be rewarded for his belief. Andrew, for example, had decided, by the time he finished at Cornell's hotel school, that the hospitality business wasn't for him. He went to work at Lorillard in 1971 as a brand manager for four years, took time out to get an MBA from Harvard, and returned to Loews as manager of operational analysis.

Larry Tisch's philosophy was based on adding value for the benefit of many and not allowing oneself to become too fascinated with wealth for the sake of wealth. Larry and Billie Tisch were content to drive Pontiacs. Their home in Rye, New York, and their apartment in New York would remain their only two personal residences.

8

Rabbi of Wall Street

By 1979, Larry Tisch's empire was reaching a plateau. Loews was one acquisition away from taking the form it would maintain for more than five years. The year marked the beginning of a lull in Tisch's career during which he would play the role of corporate elder statesman, advising other titans of industry.

The last significant acquisition target came into Loews' sights in January 1979. Loews—by then, an insurer, cigarette maker, and hotelier—added another capacity to its jack-of-all-trades description: watchmaker. For a mere $11.4 million, Loews bought 30.3 percent of Bulova Watch Co. from a single shareholder and quickly followed with an offer to buy the rest of the outstanding shares. It was a bargain-basement purchase, but with good reason. The watch market was buckling under the weight of a worldwide oversupply. With Japanese makers grabbing an ever widening share of the market, Bulova was in critical condition. Loews needed six years to squeeze a profit out of Bulova, which also made Accutron and Caravelle watches. In the meantime, the acquisition further diversified Loews' sources of revenue and helped to keep it out of the gunsights of industry analysts and stock market speculators.

Soon after gaining control of Bulova, the Tisches lost Lester Pollack, a pivotal member of a small core group of managers at Loews. He had been lured away by Seymour and Paul Milstein, the New York real estate developers, who had just taken control of United Brands Inc., a New York food company.

115

Pollack was one of the two most important people Loews had ever hired, Bob said. "I was sorry Lester decided to leave." Pollack remained a Loews board member.

One of Pollack's most important roles had been as communicator. Larry and Bob had a solid relationship but did not spend a lot of time talking things over. Similarly, Larry had good relationships with his sons with a minimum of communication.

Pollack's departure was an insult to Larry's sense of fair play and integrity. "The Milsteins wooed him away," he said. "They promised him the world. He was gone from there within a year." What irritated Tisch was that, just a few months earlier, Larry had used his influence to pave the way for the Milsteins to acquire then-embattled United Brands. "No good deed goes unpunished," he observed. To be fair, the Milsteins had helped Loews turn a quick profit on the three hotels Tisch had acquired by outbidding Arab investors two years earlier.

Gone was the benefit of Pollack's powerful management capabilities, in terms of both the breadth of what he oversaw and his skill in maintaining a steady balance between the Tisch brothers' own considerable talents. His departure, however, helped clear the way for Larry's sons Andrew and Jimmy to advance.

Ten days after Pollack resigned from Loews, Bob Tisch fired Sol E. Flick as Bulova's chief executive; four other top executives left under pressure—a management upgrade similar to those at CNA and Lorillard. Bob was named chairman of a six-member executive committee that included Larry and Larry's son Andrew, then 29 years old. Five months later, Andrew was named president of Bulova.

"I went there for 30 days," Andrew said, "and ended up spending 10 years there. It was the highlight of my career. It was a company that was so screwed up, no matter what you did was right. It was a case of taking something that was within 30 days of bankruptcy, turning it around, and making it into a viable entity."

What turned it around was the successful pursuit of defense contracts. This strategy, however, lost its effectiveness with the collapse of communism in the early 1990s and subsequent downward pressure on defense spending. Bulova once again began struggling for a share of the highly competitive watch market.

In 1979, when Andrew began to perform triage on Bulova, he wasn't fully ready to fill the vacuum left by Pollack, although Andrew's focus, unlike any of his brothers', was more on managing operations than on finances. Much of the void created by Pollack's departure would be filled by Larry's third son, Jimmy, a 1975 Cornell graduate with an MBA from the Wharton School. He had been working at Loews since 1977 and would be named a vice president in financial analysis in 1981.

Jimmy ultimately worked at least as closely with Larry as Bob did. Having inherited many of his father's intellectual powers in crunching numbers and managing money, Jimmy would be seen as Larry's most likely successor at Loews.

ABC

The numbers to crunch and the money to manage were ever mounting. By the end of 1980, Loews' annual revenue was $3 billion, 30 times what it had been a decade earlier.

Within the canyons of Wall Street, it was no longer "Larry Who?" His ownership of shares in a company was taken seriously, even by friends. In November 1980, Tisch, who had had a hand in the near-takeover of ABC by ITT in the late 1960s, himself began to accumulate ABC stock—an early indication of Tisch's serious interest in the network business.

"Larry and I often discussed broadcasting," said Leonard Goldenson. "He was always full of questions about the business, which he found glamorous and exciting."[1]

By January 1981, Tisch had spent $43.5 million for a 5.4 percent stake in ABC—a huge commitment, more cash than it took to acquire all of Bulova. He kept on buying shares through March, building the stake in Loews' name to 1.8 million shares, or 6.5 percent of the total outstanding. "I began to worry about that, because with 6.5 percent he owned more shares than did ABC's management," Goldenson wrote. Tisch insisted he wasn't contemplating a takeover, but Goldenson remained wary. "With little prodding," Goldenson convinced Tisch to sell the bulk of his shares—at a profit, naturally.

The brief encounter presaged ABC's ultimate acquisition by another company and Tisch's own future involvement in the media industry when he took over CBS.

THE PRICE OF CAUTION

Tisch's decision to sell his ABC stake in mid-1981 was a symptom of his growing nervousness about owning any stocks. A long, painful recession was beginning, and, by mid-1982, convinced that the stock market was vulnerable to collapse, he began to sell stocks in general and replace them with municipal bonds—both for Loews and for NYU. Why carry the risk of stocks when he could lock in high interest rates, protected from the dangers of investor stampedes?

The problem with this decision was that he guessed wrong about the stock market. Tisch was dumping stocks when the Dow Jones Industrial Average was within a few dozen points of its lowest ebb in the 1981–1982 recession. In August 1982, with the country a year into the slump, the Dow bottomed out at 777 and then suddenly turned, taking off on the longest, steadiest, steepest climb in its history. By the end of the recession, just three months later, the industrials had risen 33 percent, to 1039.

Three years later, Tisch's caution about the market was again ill-timed. Around the end of 1985, after Tisch had joined CBS's board, he learned that a majority of the company's pension fund had recently been invested to track the performance of the Dow industrials, racking up a 20 percent gain within a matter of months. With the Dow at 1500, Tisch suggested that the odds it would go a few hundred point higher were no better than the odds it would lose a few hundred points over the next few years. That day, the pension fund locked in most of its profits related to the strategy, just to be on the safe side. Within five months, the Dow would soar to 1700. Within eight years, it would double that level, without ever closing below 1700 in the interim.

Did Tisch feel foolish for poor market timing? No. He had no appetite for gambling and paid no attention to critics who had 20–20 hindsight. He didn't even like the idea of buying into hotels with casinos, where the profits depended partly on gamblers' being consistently unlucky. Not that Tisch was afraid of risk. He just preferred situations in which he could minimize risk, although he acknowledged the importance of luck in his own success. Bad luck, for example, was a key element in the loss he suffered in the Equity Funding investment.

Another reason for not feeling foolish about his apparent failures was that Tisch wasn't in business to impress anyone. He was in it for the fun—he probably had more fun making money than spending it. "I find business very relaxing," he once said. "I look forward every day to going to the office."

Perhaps one of Larry Tisch's most attractive qualities was that he was not trying to prove himself. Unlike many corporate overachievers, he wasn't driven to succeed by an unquenchable need to win the world's admiration—or to avoid its disapproval. He was raised by parents who believed in him, and so he believed in himself. The occasional failure seldom seemed to shake his self-confidence. By the age of 60, Tisch had little to regret—a few ill-timed investment decisions or awkwardly handled management moves were not enough to take the fun out of business.

GETTY OIL CO.

The fun included opportunities to take box seats in other businesses' board rooms. As his reputation grew, a headlining opportunity arose near the end of 1983, at the first light of the takeover-crazed 1980s. Tisch was at the center of the day's biggest and most controversial takeover: the $10 billion fight for Los Angeles-based Getty Oil Co. The way Tisch handled himself in this high-stakes game of black-gold poker illustrated the qualities that characterized many of his business deals: tough negotiating tactics, a commonsense approach to getting the best deal without becoming too greedy, and an uncanny ability to change to a course that would achieve the best outcome, and not be wedded to a set strategy.

By the summer of 1983, Gordon P. Getty's anxiety about Getty Oil's stock price and diversification moves had put him on a collision course with Sid Petersen, the company's chairman and chief executive. Until then, Petersen, J. Paul Getty's hand-picked successor, had viewed the late legendary founder's son as someone to be tolerated because of the 40 percent block of stock he controlled on behalf of Getty's heirs. Now, Gordon Getty was becoming alarmingly activist. He wanted to get more involved in management or sell out. Petersen was about as interested in sharing power with Getty as he was in losing it altogether.

Harold Williams, one-time SEC chairman under President Carter, had to watch this situation carefully. As president of the J. Paul Getty Museum in Santa Monica, California, Williams controlled 12 percent of Getty Oil through a trust. Williams had an obligation to the museum—just as Gordon Getty had to the heirs—to make sure Getty Oil stock was performing well compared with other investments. But no one seemed to think the company would be better off with Gordon Getty in charge. Williams, the top executive at Hunt Foods in the late 1960s, had to figure out whose side he was going to be on, Getty's or Petersen's.

To be fully prepared, Williams decided to hire Martin Lipton of the New York law firm Wachtell, Lipton, Rosen & Katz. Lipton (a close friend of Larry Tisch) was considered one of the top antitakeover lawyers in the country.

By early October, the battle lines had been drawn. While Gordon Getty tried unsuccessfully to induce Williams to join him in ousting Petersen's directors, Petersen proposed a plan to dilute Getty's stake and hire investment banker Geoffrey Boisi, of Goldman Sachs, to shop for a white knight.

Getty decided he needed his own mergers-and-acquisitions expert. He hired a friend of Lipton, Martin Siegel of Kidder, Peabody & Co. The friendship of Siegel and Lipton proved to be important in the outcome of the Getty battle. Even more important, however, would be the role of Larry Tisch.

In early December, Getty and Williams, angered at Petersen's effort to limit their power, agreed to vote their shares as a unified, 52 percent block. Together, they had neutralized Petersen. Getty and Petersen reached a temporary standstill agreement: Getty could name four of his own directors, but Petersen's directors were given what amounted to veto power during the standstill.

Gordon Getty's wife, Ann, did the research to find four board candidates: A. Alfred Taubman, the real estate developer and owner of A&W Root Beer; Graham Allison, dean of Harvard's John F. Kennedy School of Government; Warren Buffett; and Larry Tisch. Buffett declined because of a business-affiliation conflict. Getty and Buffett had interests in competing insurance companies.

Late in December, with minimal effort and persuasion, J. Hugh Liedtke, chairman of Pennzoil Co., got his board's approval to launch a bid for Getty Oil. Buying Getty was a cheap way to gain access to 1.9 billion barrels of proven worldwide oil reserves without having to prospect for them. The price Liedtke had in mind for buying part of Getty, in partnership with Gordon Getty, worked out to less than $5 a barrel at a time when crude oil was selling for $29. Liedtke was drilling for oil on Wall Street.

Liedtke, who got his start in the business with the help of J. Paul Getty, wanted to meet with Gordon Getty to explore the possibility of the two working together, but Siegel—who later achieved notoriety for insider trading with infamous arbitrageur Ivan Boesky—advised Getty to hold off.

Meanwhile, Texaco heard about Pennzoil's interest in Getty. John McKinley, Texaco's chief executive, had just learned that his own company's $100 million gamble in search of oil in an Alaskan prospect had come up dry, a total loss. Texaco, which was producing more oil than it was finding, already had been thinking about the virtues of prospecting for oil on Wall Street. On January 2, 1984—the day after McKinley learned of the Pennzoil bid for 60 percent of Getty—the Getty board voted the Pennzoil bid down. Tisch was one of the five directors who voted for accepting the $110-a-share bid; the others were: Harold Williams, A. Alfred Taubman, Gordon Getty, Graham Allison, and retired Getty chairman Harold Berg. Ten other directors opposed the acceptance.

The meeting went on until 1:35 A.M., and Tisch, whose reputation for integrity and Wall Street savvy had brought him to Getty's attention, began to wonder about Getty's focus. Getty had met Tisch just a few weeks earlier and had already begun to rely on his commonsense approach to the situation, but it quickly became clear that Tisch wasn't there to further Getty's agenda. As always, Tisch was there to do the right thing for all the shareholders.

The board reconvened at 1:45 A.M. Tisch told Getty he should demand that Pennzoil increase its bid to $120 a share. Pennzoil had to offer enough money to eliminate any lingering doubts about whether the price was a fair one. If the board approved a low bid, directors could face litigation by angry shareholders. On the other hand, Tisch saw no point to Sid Petersen's proposal that the Getty company should buy back its own shares.

"If we're voting for a self-tender just because we're upset at Pennzoil and Mr. Getty, that's not a valid reason," Tisch told the board. Addressing Getty, he said, "You may have suits if you do this by threat, and you should discuss this with your attorneys." The threat was that, once the standstill was over, Getty and Williams would vote out opposing directors, but the board couldn't take the legal risk of accepting a deal that Goldman Sachs hadn't deemed fair.

"If someone challenges this transaction," Tisch told him, "we will say you forced us, Mr. Getty."

"I have done nothing unethical!" Getty said.

"This is not ethics. You have not given the board the opportunity to seek a fair price," Tisch said. "A small ten-dollar sweetener. Something to satisfy this board."

Why was Getty's new friend being so hard on him? After all, hadn't the stock doubled to $100 a share since Gordon Getty had become the sole trustee of the Getty heirs' trust and had begun campaigning to enhance its value? Wasn't Pennzoil's $110-a-share bid, which Tisch had voted for earlier, fair enough?

"No," Tisch said. "Go back and bargain for more."

Harold Stuart, the board's senior outside director, grew suspicious. Why would Getty hesitate to demand a higher bid, especially in view of the fact that independent analysts were estimating the company had a breakup value of more than $150 a share? Surely Liedtke knew $110 was a bargain price, and if he couldn't pay more, how hard would it be to find someone who could? Under the circumstances, Getty seemed too anxious to accept Pennzoil's offer.

Stuart forced Gordon Getty's hand by asking whether he had any secret agreement with Pennzoil. Getty was caught. He admitted signing a letter to the Pennzoil chairman the day before, promising to do everything he could to either get the board to accept the deal or move to oust the opponents and replace them with Pennzoil-friendly directors. The letter was the brainchild of Liedtke's lawyer, Arthur Liman, another close friend of Tisch. Under the Pennzoil plan, Gordon Getty was to take over as chairman, with the Getty trust taking a 57 percent stake and Pennzoil 43 percent. An insurance unit, a 70 percent stake in ESPN Inc., and other noncore assets of Getty Oil would be sold.

THE SEARCH FOR A HIGHER BIDDER

The board's outrage over Gordon Getty's side deal with Pennzoil cleared the way for more aggressive bidding. Lipton, the museum's lawyer, suggested Getty request $120 per share, with $10 in the form of a bond. Tisch transmitted the request to Liman in the Pennzoil group. Liedtke decided to sleep on it.

The next day, Boisi, of Goldman Sachs, began to shop for other bidders. He contacted all the big oil giants (including Texaco) as well as General Electric Co. and the Saudi Arabian government. He was looking for bidders at $120 or better.

Liedtke told Liman he wanted to keep the price at $110 a share, but he was willing to add to the price, within five years, whichever was greater: a minimum of $3 a share or whatever amount over $1 billion he could get for Getty's ERC Corp. insurance unit. Goldman had estimated ERC would fetch $1.4 billion. An extra $400 million would work out to about $5 a share extra.

Lipton didn't like the idea. Figuring that $3 in five years was worth $1.50 in 1984 dollars, he demanded a guarantee of $5 in five years, giving the new bid a current value of $112.50 a share. Boisi, the company's investment banker, still wouldn't give the bid his blessing, and the board could not, in conscience, approve the bid without it.

Tisch, Lipton, and Williams (the Getty museum's president) began to pressure Boisi. What was his problem with the bid? Tisch lost his patience, noting that oil prices were starting to edge lower. (Within a year, oil would plunge to $18 a barrel from $29 and dip briefly below $10 later in 1986.) It was Tisch's habit *not* to hold out for the highest possible price. He preferred making an offer work rather than dithering around while market forces conspired to undercut the benefit of waiting for a higher bid.

But Boisi wasn't dithering. He warned the directors who hadn't been nominated by Gordon Getty that another bidder was likely to emerge, possibly Chevron or Texaco. If they accepted a deal that hadn't been deemed fair by the investment banker, they'd all face lawsuits. The directors' dilemma was: if they didn't accept the Pennzoil bid, Getty would fire them, the stock would plummet, and they'd face lawsuits anyway.

When the board meeting resumed, the revised Pennzoil offer was approved. Only one director voted against it, citing the lack of a fairness opinion. Although the offer was board-approved and was signed by Getty, Liedtke, and Williams, the agreement wasn't signed by the company. The approval document was so full of errors that, ultimately, a jury would decide whether a deal really had been made that January 3. In the legal wrangling that followed, "never . . . would so many handshakes be remembered only by one-half of the clasp," said one industry analyst.[2]

NOT YET A DONE DEAL: THE TEXACO TAKEOVER

Among the bits of information the jury would weigh as evidence of a done deal was Larry Tisch's meeting later that evening with Ann and Gordon Getty in the Gettys' Pierre Hotel suite. The purpose: to celebrate the deal with champagne.

Yet Tisch himself was equally instrumental in casting doubt on the finality of the Pennzoil deal and in garnering support for it.

The next day, January 4, a news release was issued describing the deal. Bruce Wasserstein, First Boston's star mergers-and-acquisitions lawyer, sensed problems with it—and therefore an opportunity. Perhaps there was still time to find another buyer—someone who would be willing to bid for the entire company, not just for a 60 percent portion.

He called Tisch and asked, "Is there a deal here?"

"No, not yet," Tisch said.

"Is there going to be a tender offer? A merger? What is the form of it?"

"Frankly," Tisch said, "I don't know if it's worked out yet."

Before the day was out, Texaco had hired Wasserstein to negotiate a friendly takeover of Getty. Wasserstein characterized Tisch as the "key director": he had voted for the Pennzoil deal but would look seriously at a better one. Wasserstein speculated that Gordon Getty could be converted into a seller of Getty shares at $125 each. The key would be buying out the museum's stake first.

The next day, Tisch assured McKinley, "The transaction is still open," and Petersen told him a bid would be welcome. With Wasserstein convinced that the company was worth $140 a share, Texaco's board agreed to offer $125. McKinley then met with Getty at the Pierre but got nowhere. Finally, Marty Siegel, Getty's investment banker, called Tisch at the restaurant Lutece, where he was celebrating a birthday party, and implored him to intercede.

While Pennzoil was hammering out the final details of its Getty offer, Tisch and Lipton worked on Gordon Getty for about a half hour. McKinley waited in the lobby. Tisch and Lipton then came down to invite McKinley to Getty's suite. On their way up, Lipton asked what Texaco was going to offer. McKinley said about $122.50. Lipton said it had to be $125. "At $125," Tisch added, "I can assure you, John, that the Getty board will wholeheartedly support the Texaco proposal and enter into a merger agreement with you."

By the time everyone was back in Getty's suite, Gordon Getty was ready to hear $125 and accept it. Getty would later claim that when he agreed to the Texaco offer, he did so with the knowledge that it was far from clear whether it was too late. He knew Pennzoil might be able to prove that its offer already had been irrevocably accepted.

For the moment, Texaco looked like a clear winner and Pennzoil the loser. Liedtke had a different view: he had made a deal, and Getty had broken the contract. Somebody was going to pay, and it wasn't going to be Pennzoil. "We're going to sue everyone in sight," Liedtke announced. What Pennzoil lost on Wall Street, it would more than recover through litigation that would result in the largest civil-suit judgment in history and the temporary bankruptcy of Texaco.

Because of his central role in the Getty sale, Tisch was compelled to testify in a Texas state court at the trial that decided Pennzoil's suit against Texaco. In testimony in October 1985, Tisch insisted the Getty board vote on the Pennzoil offer was nonbinding, and that his toast with the Gettys afterward wasn't to celebrate a done deal but "the acceptance of a price that could lead to the agreement on a contract"—kind of a mouthful for proposing a toast.

Joe Jamail, the feisty Texas Lawyer for Pennzoil, was good at making Tisch look bad.

"You're not friends with Gordon Getty?" he asked Tisch.

"No, sir."

"Did Gordon Getty think you were his friend?"

"Define 'friend' and I'll answer the question," Tisch said.

"Sir," Jamail replied, "I can't define the New York friendship"—a cheap shot that no doubt scored points with the Texas jury.

The jury sided with Pennzoil. It found Texaco guilty of fraudulently inducing Getty Oil to break a binding merger contract with Pennzoil. Judge Solomon Casseb, Jr. ordered Texaco to pay $11.12 billion, a record breaker. The award survived all kinds of court challenges and pushed Texaco into bankruptcy court, where it negotiated the penalty down to a mere $3 billion and settled with Pennzoil in December 1987.

The Getty episode showed Tisch's toughness and independence in high-stakes negotiations. He belonged to no one. His only loyalty was to all the shareholders, not just to Gordon Getty and the trust he controlled. Tisch showed the extent to which he was capable of changing roles to adapt to conditions—and of using semantics to keep his options open.

A 1986 article in *Fortune* asserted "that Tisch's unchallenged reputation as a man of his word depends partly on the lawyerly care with which he sometimes chooses his words. His commitments are often sharply limited. When he says he 'isn't considering' something, he is expressing only a transient state of mind subject to infinite later change."[3]

"The word 'forever' scares me," Tisch told Sherman. "I don't like to box myself in."

Tisch's central role in such a high-profile, high-stakes takeover deal showed that he had become one of Wall Street's leading power brokers. He had not sought this role and perhaps did not want it, but his reputation for Street smarts, board-room savvy, integrity, and contacts in key business positions made his name synonymous with informed, objective guidance and hands-on experience with the problems of business life. He had become a kind of rabbi of Wall Street.

PART TWO

ON TO
"BLACK ROCK"

9

The Road to CBS

William S. Paley and Larry Tisch were similar in two respects. First, they both had grandparents who joined the turn-of the-century exodus of Eastern European Jews to the United States; their fathers were born about 240 miles apart on the Dnepr River in Ukraine. Second, they both would play commanding roles at CBS. Otherwise, they were poles apart.

Paley was charming, but, unlike Tisch, he was vain and egotistical. He put his number-two executives through endless second-guessing, often humiliating them with back-stabbing efforts to undermine them when they seemed to be stealing the spotlight. Paley spent much of his life submerging his Jewish roots in an effort to be more acceptable to the blue bloods he envied, and he maintained a steady stream of extramarital affairs and was described as an indifferent father.

Paley and Tisch were brilliant businessmen who operated more by instinct than by strategic plan, but their styles were strikingly different. Paley basked in the limelight. He worked hard to establish a reputation as a founding father of the network radio and television industry, but that description more aptly described his hated rival,

RCA's David Sarnoff, founder of the National Broadcasting Company (NBC). Paley worked hard to ensure himself a place in history; Tisch worked hard for positive financial results. History would take care of itself.

Paley had bought 41 percent of the Columbia Phonograph Broadcasting System for $417,000 in 1928, became president, and renamed it the Columbia Broadcasting System Inc. He set up shop in the Paramount Building on Times Square and built CBS into a powerful competitor. His subsequent success was spectacular and came quickly, although in the retelling, he concealed his initial skepticism.

Success depended on delivering large audiences to advertisers, and that meant lining up as many affiliates as possible for the network. Part of Paley's success came from being in the industry during its infancy. To beat his sole competitor, Paley needed only to cut a better deal than NBC for affiliates, which he did. He took a similar approach to talent, luring away top performers like Jack Benny. Years later, Tisch employed the same approach in getting talk show phenomenon David Letterman to leave NBC.

CBS and NBC realized during their radio years a basic network maxim: the larger the audience, the bigger the ad dollar. CBS loaded its schedule with the stuff of vaudeville, introducing Benny, and George Burns and Gracie Allen. Soap operas and variety shows were other popular features. By 1936, Paley had driven CBS to solid success. In 1929, CBS's $4.8 million ad revenue, compared to NBC's $15.5 million, was less than one-third. Seven years later, CBS's revenue had nearly quadrupled to $18 million versus NBC's $26 million, and CBS outearned its older rival, $4.8 million to $3.5 million.

Throughout the 1950s and into the 1960s, CBS flourished at the expense of NBC and ABC. A large part of its success originated from Paley's focus on the network's content. He saw a clear connection between effective programming and profitability, and he was determined to provide the best news programming money could buy. This meant that, in the shared monopoly of network television, Paley could afford to make the cost of doing business a secondary concern to the pursuit of ratings.

A money-is-no-object orientation became deeply ingrained in CBS's corporate culture. Paul Kesten, Paley's promotional chief, had established the foundation of the "Tiffany image" at CBS. Sleekness was emphasized in every element of the company. A designer was hired to customize practically every fixture to conform to Kesten's vision of understated elegance vaguely in the tradition of Art Deco. Paley did his part on the programming side, spending liberally to attract top talent—from his competitors, if necessary.

Its image of quality was later viewed as CBS's most valuable corporate asset and—because it was so closely associated with Paley—its most vulnerable. The strong linkage between CBS's intangible value and its leadership made the arrival of an outsider like Tisch all the more threatening to the insiders. The Tiffany culture was far removed from Tisch's cost-accounting approach, but in the days before cable TV, Paley figured that as long as he maintained a large audience share, the money would roll in. And it did. By 1967, CBS's annual profit had climbed to $64 million on revenue of $814 million.

PALEY'S EXPANSION OF THE CBS EMPIRE

In the mid-1960s, Paley got the urge to make CBS a conglomerate, like Tisch's Loews and others that were already being created. But where Tisch looked for businesses with solid but generally unrecognized values, Paley acted on emotion and shied away from any entity whose success and value weren't already well known.

He bought the New York Yankees baseball team in 1964, when it was one of the winningest teams in the American League. Nine years later, he sold a lackluster, unprofitable Yankees organization, at a loss, to George Steinbrenner's group. The Fender electric guitar company was acquired by CBS in 1965, and Creative Playthings was added in 1966. In each case, the emphasis was on proven winners, as though past performance guaranteed high returns into the foreseeable future. Paley was like an art collector who paid top dollar for the prestige of owning famous names' works.

In 1967, CBS plunked down $280 million for publisher Holt, Rinehart & Winston Inc., in what was then the largest-ever acquisition of a publicly traded company. He probably overpaid, but as was often the case with Paley, he was unwilling to be outbid. He lacked Tisch's discipline for walking away from deals when they ceased to make sense financially. Holt's profitability failed to meet CBS's expectations.

A film-making venture established by Paley in 1967 was shut down in 1970 after racking up $30 million of losses on 27 films. Frank Stanton, CBS president, concluded that Paley's scattershot approach to diversification had hurt CBS's image as well as its bottom line. The relationship between the two had already been fraying, and Stanton's move from president to vice chairman in 1971 was merely an interim step on the way to retirement in 1973. His departure ushered in a succession of Paley understudies who quickly learned their boss had no intention of retiring.

The last in this line, before Tisch's arrival, was Thomas H. Wyman, vice chairman of Pillsbury Co., a job he held by virtue of having been CEO at Green Giant when Pillsbury acquired it. Wyman had the blue-blood pedigree Paley favored. He had attended prestigious Andover Academy and Amherst College, and spent years acquiring European polish as a corporate executive overseas.

In May 1980, Wyman was named president and chief executive officer, with the understanding that he would add the title of chairman a year later, when Paley, 78, promised to retire. The arrangement had the board's support. Wyman appeared poised to do what his three predecessors failed to do: get Paley out of CBS's way.

THE END OF LAVISH SPENDING

Almost as crippling as some of CBS's ill-starred diversification moves was a corporate spending style that had no place in the 1980s. Cable was altering the television landscape. No longer was success practically guaranteed to at least two of the only three broadcasters in the business. When offered more than three choices, viewers were start-ing to switch off the networks. The effect on the bottom line brought into sharp focus CBS's habitual lack of spending discipline.

The ultimate example of this out-of-control spending came in 1980. When competitive offers arrived from ABC and NBC to con-tract CBS's star news correspondent, Dan Rather, CBS drafted a 10-year contract that started at $2.5 million, escalated to $3.5 million, and guaranteed that Rather would succeed retiring anchor Walter Cronkite in 1981. The contract sharply inflated an already over-heated run-up in the salaries of on-air talent. Even more amazing, from CBS's perspective, was that CBS News president William Leonard could make such a massive spending commitment essentially on his own, especially after Paley had been led to believe that it might cost just $1 million a year to keep Rather.

Wyman may have recognized the importance of changing CBS's free-wheeling spending habits, but his ability to break or modify those habits quickly was limited.

Ted Turner saw CBS as a dinosaur and delighted in pointing this out to Leonard and Gene F. Jankowski, head of the broadcast division, in the spring of 1981, when the two flew to Atlanta to discuss buying at least 51 percent of CNN. Turner turned them down, saying he would never cede control, though two years later he would be forced to do just that to deal with a crushing load of debt taken on in his $1.5 billion acquisition of MGM/UA Entertainment. In 1981, how-ever, he was as cocky as ever.

"Someday I'm going to own you. You bet I am," he boasted. "Re-member I told you." As his visitors prepared to leave, he offered to buy their corporate jet, then waved off the idea. "What's the difference. I'll own it anyway, one of these days."

Instead of making a deal for CNN or any other similarly logical fit, CBS under Wyman seemed to drift further away from a coherent communications strategy, inadvertently providing much of the fodder for Tisch's later criticisms. In 1982, Wyman paid $57.5 million to add Ideal Toy Corp. to CBS Toys, which included Gabriel Toys, maker of such dependable lines as Tinkertoys. Ideal was known for fads. It was a riskier part of the toy business and would lead to the entire division's being unloaded at a loss.

Not until 1983 were Wyman and the board finally able to maneuver Paley out of the chairmanship, but this was not the end of Paley's own maneuvering. Paley, who still controlled about 7 percent of CBS's stock, quickly turned fiercely negative toward Wyman, viewing him as incapable of running a company that essentially markets raw creativity. Wyman seemed to have little respect for Paley and made merciless fun of him behind his back. Apparently, he viewed Paley as permanently out of the way, but Jankowski continued to seek Paley's advice on programming decisions.

Profits, however, were strong: by year-end 1983, they hit $187.2 million, up 26 percent from the previous year. The strength, fueled by economic recovery, perhaps caused CBS to take a less-than-cautious approach to outside opportunities. Along with Sears, Roebuck & Co. and IBM, it joined a venture called Trintex, a videotex at-home marketing project that later would be known as the Prodigy personal computer on-line service.

In November alone, as if in a rush to offset too much profit, CBS decided to spend $362.5 million for 12 consumer magazines from Ziff-Davis Publishing Co.—about $40 million more than the next nearest bidder was willing to pay. That deal alone would flatten 1985 profit growth. A week later, the company announced plans to spend $57 million for stakes in a collection of cable properties—four regional SportsChannel pay-TV services and two cultural channels.

Once again, CBS posted generally strong earnings, with profit up 13 percent at $212.4 million for 1984, although the toy division, which Wyman had expanded through acquisition, posted a $67 million loss. But Wyman had successfully unloaded some earlier underperforming acquisitions. The record division was rebounding, and two joint ventures—CBS–Fox Video and Tri-Star Pictures—looked promising.

Even as Wyman basked in his successes, a foreboding statistic emerged. The three networks' combined audience share, compared to a year earlier, had slumped 8 percent in the all-important "sweeps" rating period of November 1984. The industry's hopes that it could halt its losses to the cable channels by outprogramming them were punctured. The results also showed that NBC was eroding CBS's lock on first place.

Meanwhile, Paley, 83 years old, still couldn't let go. He couldn't accept Wyman's being in charge of the company he had built, and an employee roster that did not include the name of William S. Paley. If Wyman had any doubts about Paley's opinion of him, or about his ability to make his life difficult, they were about to be cleared up quickly.

ENTER LARRY TISCH

In January 1985, Republican Senator Jesse Helms's Fairness in Media organization announced it was launching a crusade to rid CBS News of what it perceived as its liberal bias. Helms sent out a letter urging conservatives to accumulate enough shares of CBS stock to start telling Dan Rather how to do his job. Wyman saw that CBS needed to line up some friends to offset this bizarre attack. He asked investment banker James D. Wolfensohn, a CBS director and friend of Larry Tisch, to look for vocal opposition to Helms in the Jewish community.

On a weekend morning later that month, the Helms letter came up in conversation between Wolfensohn and Tisch at the Century Country Club in Westchester. Tisch was outraged that Helms was blatantly declaring ideological war on CBS. He told Wolfensohn he was willing to offer whatever civic support he could to help ensure that Helms's attack would backfire. Wolfensohn said he might be hearing from Wyman on the matter.

Larry Tisch was a logical source for such support. Not only was he an active spokesman of mainstream Jewish causes, he was politically active in supporting Helms's traditional enemies. "I would call myself a liberal Republican or a conservative Democrat," Tisch said, although he figured he probably had voted for more Democrats than Republicans. As for Helms, "Jesse Helms was wrong," Tisch said. "I have nothing against Jesse Helms. He's entitled to his opinion, but to condemn CBS at the time was silly."

In February, a month after Tisch and Wolfensohn had spoken of the Helms stock purchase threat, Fairness in Media took its campaign one step further: it launched a proxy fight in a quixotic bid to get two representatives on the board. The effort clearly was doomed to be little more than a public relations battle, but Paley leapt at the opportunity to exploit the situation as a way to regain some of his power. Wyman had done little to placate Paley or make him feel important in his retirement. Now he would pay the price.

Paley asked Wolfensohn to explore the possibility of a management-led leveraged buyout of CBS. In March, Wolfensohn suggested a bid of $162 a share, giving the company a total value of $4.81 billion. At the time, the stock was trading above $100, up from $73 at the beginning of the year.

No one thought Helms's group posed a serious threat to CBS, but in the takeover-crazed mentality of the mid-1980s, any excuse was a good excuse for deciding that a company was "in play." Ivan Boesky already had made that decision. He quickly accumulated an 8.7 percent stake and was awaiting a bona fide offer from a purchaser. Boesky's buying helped fuel the run-up in CBS stock. Indeed, at the time—Boesky was still years away from pleading guilty to operating a hugely profitable insider-trading ring—a Boesky disclosure of a large position in a company was widely viewed as official notification that a company was ripe for takeover.

CBS's board rejected Paley's request for immediate authorization to take the company private without first getting its investment banker's opinion. Wyman refused to participate in any such effort, and decided it was time to feel out Tisch, through Wolfensohn, on something more than just vocal support. In effect, Paley himself was putting the company in play and pitting himself squarely against Wyman.

With rumors flying that Ted Turner was about to make a bid in league with the Helms contingent, Wyman understood that the threat to CBS's integrity was serious enough to require a comprehensive battle plan. Would Tisch be willing to enter the scenario as a friendly suitor? Tisch told Wolfensohn that, if necessary, CBS should consider Loews a possible white knight. Larry Tisch discussed with brother Bob the possibility of investing in CBS.

Turner "was a wild man, but brilliant," Larry said. "I just thought that this was a great institution and it should be preserved as an institution."

Adding fuel to the network takeover rumors was the announcement in mid-March that Capital Cities Communications, with help from Warren Buffett, was acquiring ABC for $3.5 billion in a friendly deal backed by Leonard Goldenson. The entire industry was under competitive pressure that wasn't going away. Profits no longer were automatic. The age of the open-ended expense account was over. RCA was beginning to feel pressure to sell off NBC or do something to head off the leveraged-buyout crusaders who were carving up oversized, lumbering corporations to realize hidden breakup values.

Toward the end of March, CBS started to look like it might escape that fate. About a week after Boesky disclosed his stake, Fairness in Media said it was dropping its proxy fight because it didn't have enough time to prepare for CBS's April 17 annual meeting.

CBS then lined up a $1.5 billion credit facility, but denied that it was for takeover protection or for a leveraged buyout. Boesky, meanwhile, worried that his CBS bet might not work out, began to pressure the company to talk to him about increasing shareholder value or buying him out. This thinly veiled threat blew up in his face. CBS sued Boesky, alleging that he had financed his CBS purchase with more than the margin allowed by the Federal Reserve. The lawsuit ultimately forced Boesky out of the game and briefly boosted Wyman's image as a tough Street fighter.

CBS stock plunged, putting a punishing squeeze on Boesky and anyone else who had gambled on a windfall from a CBS takeover. With Helms's group out of the way, Boesky discredited, and the Turner threat murky at best, it looked like CBS might defy the odds.

But Turner hadn't gone away, and the Tisches and Loews appeared to be raising cash. Loews was preparing to sell what was left of its theater division for $165 million to Hollywood investor A. Jerrold

Perenchio, co-owner of Embassy Communications Inc., and Bob and Larry Tisch sold 4 million shares of Loews to cut their stake to 36 percent.

On April 18, Turner made a bid for CBS that looked hopelessly jury-rigged. The offer was for 67 percent, and none of it was in cash. It was a combination of stock in Turner Broadcasting System Inc. and junk bonds that Turner claimed were worth $175 a share. Analysts said the bonds' value was more like $150. Once the 67 percent was acquired, holders of the remaining shares outstanding would get the same offer. If all went well, the entire company would cost Turner $5.41 billion. Essentially, he'd be borrowing the money from shareholders, then paying them off by selling CBS's radio stations, records, magazines, and toys and keeping only its television broadcasting operations.

No one seemed to think the deal would fly. "He had a good chance," Tisch said, "If he had had better investment banking advice, he could have been much more successful. I think it was just screwed up."

Investors—including Ivan Boesky—registered total disappointment, pushing CBS's stock price down $3.50 a share, to $106.25, on the day the Turner bid was announced. After all, how could Turner's company, with annual revenue of just $282 million, swallow one raking in $4.9 billion a year? Still, Wall Street analysts liked the basic concept of buying CBS and selling off all the nonbroadcasting assets. The following Tuesday, CBS's board rejected Turner's quirky bid and set the wheels in motion to permanently scare off the sharks.

Wyman weighed the idea of a merger with Gannett Co., the giant newspaper chain, but Gannett chairman Al Neuharth clearly intended to be the surviving postmerger chairman.

Wolfensohn, who still viewed a buyout as CBS's best defense, arranged for Wyman and Tisch to meet. Wyman called Tisch on May 2 and met with him that day. The discussion stayed away from any talk of Tisch as a potential investor. "Tom Wyman came to see me about building up support against Ted Turner and Jesse Helms in the Jewish community, and I said, 'This is not a Jewish issue.'"[1]

Instead, Wyman and Tisch focused on the need to line up federal regulatory opposition to a Turner–CBS deal. "The purpose of the meeting was to get them comfortable with each other," Wolfensohn said. Over time, they would get to know each other almost too well, eventually viewing each other at times with bitter disdain."

Gradually, it was becoming clear to Tisch and others that CBS wasn't an innocent victim. It was a valuable asset burdened by mismanagement. A handful of minor acquisitions were being undone. CBS News's sterling reputation was getting badly tarnished by a libel suit filed by General William C. Westmoreland over a 1982 documentary on the Vietnam War. The incident was further evidence that Van Gordon Sauter, Wyman's choice to succeed William Leonard in 1981, wasn't the right person to protect the legacy of Edward R. Murrow. Sauter, who had run CBS stations in Los Angeles and Chicago, had been criticized for overemphasizing entertainment values in news broadcasts.

In a move suggesting its recent magazine purchase was flawed, CBS demanded that Ziff-Davis refund part of its money, alleging Ziff had deliberately overstated the magazines' earnings. A lawsuit trying to accomplish the refund was later dismissed. The inescapable conclusion was that CBS hadn't done enough work to determine the right price to pay for Ziff.

The pattern of CBS's acquisitions and divestitures seemed to have no logic. When it bought the Ziff specialty magazines, it sold to Gannett a newspaper insert called *Family Weekly*, which John Backe, Wyman's predecessor, had purchased less than six years earlier. Next, CBS cut a deal to buy part of a company that specialized in making T-shirts for rock concerts.

To make matters worse, CBS was losing its status as the number-one network. At the end of May, the sweeps showed that NBC had taken the lead.

Tisch Buys In

On the morning of July 3, Daniel Tisch, then a managing director in risk arbitrage at Salomon Brothers, called his father at his 17th-floor office at Loews on Fifth Avenue. CBS had just announced plans to borrow nearly $1 billion for a $150-a-share buyback of 21 percent of its stock. The move was designed to load up CBS with so much debt that a Turner-type bid couldn't possibly succeed.

Any shares Tisch bought that day would essentially have at least a 21 percent discount built in, because after the buyback, he would still have the same percentage share of the company. Not only that, proceeds from the buyback, considered a dividend paid by one corporation to another, would be taxed at a mere 7 percent under the same tax-law provision Tisch had exploited in his run at Commercial Credit Co. 16 years earlier. Daniel believed it was a classic Tisch-style low-risk investment opportunity: the stock was trading at that moment at just $118 a share, and CBS still was considered a company in play. Larry gave the go-ahead and picked up 25,000 shares that day, the first of practically daily purchases throughout July.

Not everyone in the Tisch family saw the wisdom in buying CBS shares. "We really were a house divided on that," Jimmy Tisch said.[2] Jimmy, who worked closely with his father on investment strategy, felt that Larry's judgment was influenced uncharacteristically by noninvestment considerations.

Tisch had always been interested in media stocks, because their principal source of revenue—advertising—was relatively inflation-proof. The networks were among his top choices because he perceived that they enjoyed a near-monopoly—a monopoly, he would concede years later, facing extinction because of cable. Finally, Tisch the philanthropist was motivated to play a role. He saw CBS as a national institution—a vital public service that reached 75 million people every day—and its integrity was at peril. Jimmy queried: "Does it have to be preserved with our money?"

Jimmy believed that buying CBS stock in the heat of a takeover battle violated the Tisches' discipline of buying hidden value when it was cheap. Larry pressed on. Within three weeks, Loews would own more of CBS than Bill Paley.

Jimmy had a point. CBS seemed to have just passed a peak and was starting to slide. CBS News had been the top-rated prime-time news program for five years, but was starting to lose out to ABC. In 25 of the previous 30 years, it had been number one in prime-time entertainment ratings; now, NBC was gaining on it. On the other hand, CBS had assets—books, magazines, records, music, and toys—that could be sold to improve the parent's ability to reestablish its dominance in its core business.

Although Tisch bought shares in anticipation of benefiting from the buyback, he believed a restructuring that included asset sales was a better takeover defense. Piling on debt would only rob the company of its ability to restructure on its own terms. The company would be forced into a series of emergency cost-cutting moves focused more on dealing with a short-term financial squeeze than on streamlining the company for future success.

Turner all but admitted defeat in the face of CBS's buyback deal. At a National Press Club function in Washington, he offered some parting shots that even Larry Tisch ultimately would agree with. He said Wyman had admitted to him that CBS wasn't exactly a lean operation. "It's an admission that they're wasting money," Turner said. "There's no corporation in America that's as arrogant as CBS is."

Turner briefly but unsuccessfully tried to challenge the legality of CBS's buyback, arguing that the ploy was designed specifically to exclude him as a bidder. He also questioned whether the company could do the buyback without Federal Communications Commission approval, because it amounted to a change in control.

In mid-July, Tisch called Wyman to inform him that Loews was accumulating shares of CBS but had no hostile intentions. The message seemed logical; Tisch hadn't waged a hostile takeover since CNA in 1974.

At the end of July, Turner's bold gamble for CBS officially died in an Atlanta courtroom, after costing him $18 million in takeover fees. Loews, on the other hand, owned 9.9 percent of CBS. While Wyman and the board privately worried about how much control Tisch wanted, the company's rank-and-file accepted Wyman's outward characterization of Tisch as the ideal white knight.

But Tisch's true intentions were the subject of intense speculation. In a Securities and Exchange Commission (SEC) filing, Loews said it had offered to buy CBS in a friendly takeover but was rejected. *The*

Wall Street Journal, in reporting the Loews disclosure of its CBS stake, described the immediate strategy as a "complex arbitrage maneuver." Larry Tisch was facing an array of options, none of which he was willing to eliminate that early in the game.

Wyman, aware that Paley had it in for him, figured that, with Tisch, he would have a better shot at running the company without having to watch his back. Tisch, whose stake now was greater than Paley's post-buyback 8 percent, could become an ally against Paley. If Paley viewed Tisch as a threat, he might become distracted from interfering with Wyman. The third option—that Tisch and Paley could somehow become allies—didn't seem likely, given their obvious differences.

In August, Tisch joined Paley at his home for tea. Paley, with his keen eye for style and his studied elegance, surely noticed how little he had in common with Tisch, although both were sons of Russian Jewish immigrants. Afterward, Paley told Smith, his biographer: "I found him to be straightforward, seemingly decent and with integrity. He said he had no intention of buying CBS, but I know intentions can change."

Paley had zeroed in on a major element in Tisch's low-risk approach to business and investing: Always keep all the options open.

10

Conquest

"Did I know Wyman was the idiot of the century when I bought CBS stock? No. I found out later."

—Larry Tisch[1]

In August 1985, Larry Tisch began a gradual process of bringing to bear on CBS everything he had learned in business. On the day Daniel Tisch started buying CBS shares for his father, Daniel figured the purchase was going to be a short-term stock play. But a funny thing happened on the way to the broker. Larry Tisch seemed less interested in profiting from someone else's takeover attempt than he was in seeing to it that no such attempt materialized. He built his stake slowly, making it clear he had no interest in flipping it for a quick profit, yet almost no one trusted him. What loomed ahead to make Tisch a longer-term player was a leadership void at CBS—a vacuum he would be drawn into almost effortlessly.

Wyman and others on the CBS board worried about the parallels between CBS and CNA, in which marginal divisions were quickly shed. Was Tisch staging a sneak attack? What was to stop him from acquiring a controlling stake through daily incremental purchases? Was it possible he only wanted to be a passive investor? All their worry reflected, to some extent, a justified insecurity about their own abilities to lead the company.

Loews had built a one-million-share stake in ABC, hoping to profit from its impending takeover by Capital Cities, a deal Warren Buffett was participating in as an 18 percent friendly investor, to keep a bidding war from erupting. Buffett's agreement was that he would be named a director but would buy no more shares and wouldn't have voting control of the purchased shares for at least 10 years. Tisch saw a similar role for himself at CBS. As Paley noted, such a passive role may have been his initial intention, but an intention isn't a commitment.

Meanwhile, the cost of thwarting a hostile takeover was becoming painfully clear at CBS. The 1986 budget increase for CBS News was to be capped below 4 percent, by order of Gene Jankowski, the CBS Broadcast Group president. Accomplishing this would be next to impossible. Staffers categorized as "talent"—including on-air personalities—accounted for a whopping 29 percent of the total budget, and that portion had climbed 13.3 percent in 1985, largely because of salary jumps for superstars like Dan Rather, Morley Safer and Ed Bradley of "60 Minutes," and Charles Osgood of CBS News. "Of the 650 in the 'talent' category, 20 percent of them now earned 50 percent of that payroll," according to Edward Joyce, then CBS News president under Sauter.[2]

It meant layoffs, something newly acquired ABC was about to undergo at the hands of Capital Cities. NBC would not be far behind: it would soon be acquired, along with RCA, by General Electric (GE). Joyce conceded that CBS had plenty of fat to lose, but it seemed inevitable that the 1,300 employees of CBS News would feel picked on, because only their division was forced to cut costs through deep staff cuts. Jankowski knew the move would cause an uproar, but other divisions were instituting cost cuts in other ways. The entertainment division, for example, with just 400 employees, cut back on the number of pilots, which rippled through Hollywood production companies but cost no CBS employees their jobs.

Joyce detected in Sauter an extra sense of urgency about the layoffs. Sauter, Joyce said, indicated that Jankowski was under pressure to put on a show for Wall Street, to prove CBS was serious about cutting costs. Sauter speculated that the pressure was coming from Wyman. But Joyce was getting feedback that Wyman was responding, directly or indirectly, to Larry Tisch's questions about the body count.

In September 1985, CBS began a frantic effort to put a $300 million dent in its buyback debt. It put three book publishing units up for sale, shut down its hemorrhaging toy business—a year too late, Wyman conceded—shed its one-third stake in Tri-Star Pictures, and sold four musical-instrument properties, including prestigious Steinway & Sons.

A "for sale" sign was hung on one of its five owned and operated television stations, KMOX-TV in St. Louis, and CBS was about to sell, to partner Sony Corp., its half-interest in their Digital Audio Disk Corp. joint venture, the only U.S. maker of compact audio disks at the time.

CBS also launched an early retirement offer aimed at cutting 2,000 employees from its total payroll of 28,500. Finally, it fired 74 network-news employees in the course of eliminating a total of 125 positions.

Increasingly, CBS's antitakeover buyback was looking like a partial leveraged buyout, with assets being liquidated to pay the debt taken on to retire stock. The only problem was that CBS remained a publicly traded company and still owed a decent return to its shareholders, the largest of whom was Larry Tisch via his family's 34 percent-owned Loews. By the end of the month, Loews had raised its stake to 11.1 percent, Atlanta/Sosnoff Capital Corp. disclosed it held 5 percent of CBS, and takeover rumors flared anew.

TISCH JOINS THE CBS BOARD

At its October 9 meeting, the CBS board discussed at length how to deal with Tisch, given his expressed intention of increasing his stake. They couldn't brush him off; he had more of a right to a board seat than anyone else already there. His management and investment prowess was legendary, but he had no experience in the television business—nor, for that matter, in any of CBS's businesses. Despite his reputation for success in other businesses, it was feared that his involvement could cause further disruption. If he was kept off the board, he might get hostile. Better to bring him inside and keep him in plain view, where the evolution of his intentions could be influenced or at least closely monitored.

With the directors' blessing, Wyman walked to Tisch's office on Fifth Avenue and invited him to become CBS's 14th director. Tisch had already indicated he wasn't interested in owning more than 25 percent of the shares outstanding. As with Franklin National years earlier, CBS was federally regulated—in this case, by the FCC. Any perception of a change in control triggered potentially disruptive oversight. Tisch also wanted to avoid opening a golden-parachute clause in Wyman's contract that gave him the right to buy 62,500 shares at $79.50 each in the event of an outsider's acquiring 25 percent or more of the company.

Wyman and the board, however, were reluctant to take Tisch at his word on the 25 percent limit. Wyman gingerly raised the issue in conjunction with his invitation to Tisch. Wyman recalled telling Tisch: "There's been a lot of discussion in and outside of CBS about what Larry Tisch's intentions are. The board would like some level of assurance as to your intentions."[3] Wyman was feeling out Tisch. Would he be willing to play a role similar to the one Buffett had agreed to with ABC?

"I made it clear I wasn't interested in a stand-still agreement," Tisch said. He believed such an agreement would be viewed as proof that CBS didn't trust him. Besides, Tisch had nothing to gain by limiting his options.

The board wasn't the only constituency nervous about Tisch. Two days after the meeting between Tisch and Wyman, Don Hewitt of "60 Minutes" began to spread the word that he was interested in leading a management buyout of his program and the "CBS Evening News." Included in the group would be Diane Sawyer, Morley Safer, Mike Wallace, and Dan Rather. It was a thinly veiled vote of no-confidence in Jankowski, Sauter, and Joyce and the things they were doing to help foot the bill for management's costly anti-takeover moves.

Hewitt, whose credibility derived from his role as producer of CBS's "60 Minutes," had discussed the idea over lunch with Lew Wasserman, chairman of MCA Inc.

Wasserman said, "You're crazy. You'll look like a fool," Hewitt recalled.

"I'm going to to do it," Hewitt said.

"It's a stupid idea. Don't do it."

"I'm going to do it."

"Don't do it, but if you do do it, call me first," Wasserman said.

Paley and Tisch both rejected the idea. Within a week, it died without a single investment banker getting involved.

Wall Street, for its part, grasped at theories in an effort to deal with the unfolding reality that Tisch was settling in for the long haul at CBS. How would Loews integrate CBS into its current balance of tobacco—a strong, steady source of cash flow—and insurance, which provided alternating periods of good and bad years, with the bad ones providing tax relief for the rest of Loews' profitable businesses?

On a valuation basis, CBS's stock price was an overperformer. Relative to the rest of the market, it was clear from its price—then about $115 a share—that CBS had been driven higher by takeover talk. On the other hand, some analysts figured CBS's breakup value at the equivalent of about $200 a share, even with all the assets already being sold. A huge chunk of that value was locked up in CBS Records, conservatively valued at $1 billion. With the Tisches' reputation for turning around underachievers, perhaps CBS was on its way to being a better-run company.

At about the same time, CBS publicly announced it was inviting Tisch to join the board and to increase his stake to 25 percent. The announcement let some air out of the stock, as investors concluded CBS no longer was in play. Suddenly, the world was waking up to the reality that an industry outsider had quietly bored into the middle of CBS and stood an excellent chance of altering its course. It was time for Tisch and Paley to meet again.

THE TISCH FACTOR

Tisch indicated to Paley that he was troubled by CBS's top-heavy management. Coming from Loews, with its short, underpopulated chain of command, Tisch was astounded at CBS's army of top executives—42 presidents and vice presidents—and wondered how they avoided tripping over one another. Tisch was playing Paley's tune. These problems could be blamed on Wyman. Together, Paley and Tisch might have the power to oust Wyman. It gave Paley added enthusiasm for devising a plan to reclaim what, in his distorted view, Wyman had taken away from him.

Having too many executives, however, was the least of Paley's concerns. Paley knew profits flowed from top ratings. Focus on programming, and the profits will follow. Cutting costs was a secondary concern—a stopgap measure when programming wasn't doing the job. What rankled him more than evidence of wasteful spending was watching NBC displace CBS at the top of the ratings with the kind of high-quality fare usually associated with CBS. NBC was doing it with hits like "The Cosby Show," "Cheers," and "St. Elsewhere."

Tisch had a slightly different cause-and-effect view. He wondered how effective the company could be in generating competitive programming if it was run like a bureaucracy.

A Loews source at the time said that Larry Tisch would be "an interested director" at CBS but "is not going to tell CBS how to run its business."[4] It was true that Tisch preferred to have the right people running his business, rather than run them himself. Tisch said he liked "being far enough removed from daily operations to have an overall view that comes in handy in the decision process." He was happier managing money than managing people.

Now the question was: Was Wyman the best person to run CBS? In the past, Bob Tisch would take the hands-on approach in answering such management questions, but so far, CBS's board had made it clear they didn't want more than one Tisch involved at CBS. At the first board meeting he attended, in November, Tisch posed tough questions that tended to focus on Wyman's management skills.

Bob Tisch, 15, and Larry Tisch, 18, in 1941 at the Lincoln and Laurel summer camps their parents, Al and Sayde, bought in Blairstown, New Jersey, three years earlier. The Tisches' desire to get into the resort hotel business was an outgrowth of their success with the camps. Underlying that success was the pleasure the Tisches took in working closely in a family enterprise.

Bob and Larry Tisch already were a successful, time-tested team in 1960 when they took control of Loew's Theatres on their way to becoming one of New York's premier hotel developers. Among eight hotel projects in the city that came in rapid-fire succession was the construction of the 1,850-room, 50-floor Americana begun that summer—the tallest hotel in the world at the time—where this photo was taken.

Laurel-in-the-Pines, the neglected resort hotel in Lakewood, New Jersey, that Larry found for his parents' to buy in 1946 with proceeds from the sale of their summer camps. This venture embodied many of the prominent features of the Tisches' business strategy and management style. In Laurel-in-the-Pines, they recognized hidden value in a bargain-priced asset and used common sense and strict cost accounting to generate enough capital to build the foundation of a corporate empire.

Top: The Traymore Hotel, an Atlantic City, New Jersey, landmark built in 1915, was a chronic money-loser when the Tisches bought it in 1950. The first Jews to own a hotel in Atlantic City, the Tisches upgraded it, boosted prices, and, in the first five years, coaxed $5 million of net profit out of it—$500,000 more than they paid for it.

Left: Larry and his father, Al, in 1959 at the construction site of the Americana in Bal Harbour, Florida, the property that moved the Tisches into the ranks of the multimillionaires and on to the front pages of the national business press. Larry managed its construction, and by the time it opened in 1958—on time and without a mortgage—brother Bob had convinced NBC to stage its 30th anniversary there to coincide with the hotel's opening.

Below: The Grand Hotel, the Catskills property the Tisches bought in 1949 as a summer resort to complement Laurel-in-the-Pines, whose season ran from Thanksgiving through Easter/Passover. The Tisches were no longer running either property, when both were destroyed by fires in the mid-1960s.

Left: Larry Tisch and Steve Ross, a longtime friend of the family. Ross and Bob Tisch shared a desire to own a professional football team, a dream Bob realized in 1990 when he acquired a half-interest in the New York Giants. Ross, who went on to build the Time Warner media conglomerate from the foundation of a funeral business, was the undertaker for Larry's father when he died in 1960.

Right: William Paley, chairman and architect of CBS and its broadcast network, had worn down many a would-be successor, but in Larry Tisch, he met his match: a no-nonsense manager, a compelling leader, and by the end of 1985, a bigger owner of CBS stock than Paley himself. Assuming the helm at CBS thrust Tisch into the harsh glare of the public eye.

Left: Larry Tisch and Michael Eisner, chairman of Walt Disney Co., at an entertainment industry luncheon in California in the late 1980s. Disney was a perennially rumored—and consistently denied—suitor for CBS.

Top: Larry Tisch with (left to right) Donald R. Keough, retired president and chief operating officer of Coca-Cola Co.; Warren Buffett and Wyndham Robertson, vice-president of communications at the University of North Carolina on one of Buffett's biennial getaways—this one in held 1991 in Victoria, British Columbia—for prominent investors, media executives and others. Tisch was an early investor with Buffett before the Omaha, Nebraska, native formed his own quasi-conglomerate, Berkshire Hathaway, and became one of the two richest Americans.

Below: The "four lucky fellows" after whom a family investment vehicle, FLF, is named are left to right (from oldest to youngest), Andrew, Daniel, James, and Thomas Tisch. Andrew and Jimmy are directly involved in Loews Corp. businesses, while Tom manages the family's personal investments and philanthropy and Daniel runs his own money management firm. Jimmy is viewed as the most likely to succeed Larry as Loews' top executive.

Right: The Tisch family with Golda Meir during a visit in the early 1970s at the Tisches' Fifth Avenue apartment in New York. The Tisches' activism in Jewish causes earned both Larry and wife Billie leadership roles in the American Jewish community.

Right: Tisch with Moshe Dayan, whose estate Tisch paid $1 million for a collection of antiquities, which was immediately donated to the American Friends of Israel Museum.

Left: Shimon Peres with Larry Tisch. A host of Israeli leaders over the past three decades have sought out Tisch's counsel as a powerful spokesman for the mainstream American Jewish community.

Top: The "60 Minutes" crew is feted at the program's 20th anniversary in 1988: (left to right) Morley Safer, Ed Bradley, Howard Stringer, Mike Wallace, Gene Jankowski, Larry Tisch, Dan Rather, Harry Reasoner, Andy Rooney, and Don Hewitt. Rumors flew that Tisch on occasion tried to influence news judgment at "60 Minutes" on coverage of Israel. Tisch denied any such effort to impose any political agenda on the news division, and program content tended not to reflect a sensitivity to Tisch's political views.

Below: Howard Stringer, CBS Broadcast Group president, and Billie and Larry Tisch meet with Pope John Paul II during one of Tisch's 1986 tour of CBS News' bureaus throughout the world.

Top: CBS and Tisch in 1993 announce the network has hired David Letterman away from NBC, claiming for the first time not only a presence but the lead in the late-night ratings race. For Tisch, it was a classic case of trusting his lieutenant, Howard Stringer, CBS Broadcast Group president, and his own instincts on an expensive investment—a three-year, $42 million contract—that essentially paid for itself within a year in terms of advertising profits.

Below: Barry Diller, architect of the Fox Network and head of QVC home shopping, appeared with Larry Tisch in early 1994 when it was announced that Diller would succeed Tisch as head of CBS as part of a deal to sell part of Loews' CBS stake to Diller. The deal, however, was pre-empted by a counteroffer from Comcast, a QVC part-owner. Tisch immediately backed off, already irritated by some of Diller's demands.

Top: Tisch, far right, meets with Vice President Al Gore and other media representatives on the future of the information superhighway envisioned under Bill Clinton's Democratic administration.

Below: Larry and Billie Tisch watching a "60 Minutes" segment in 1986 in their Fifth Avenue apartment. What attracted Billie to Larry back in 1948 was that "Larry was a grown-up person. He was not a boy. I liked his values. I liked his intelligence. I liked his sense of direction."

Many of CBS's problems had stemmed from moves approved by Paley, but it was Wyman's job to solve them. Ever since hearing how poorly Wyman had handled the Ziff-Davis purchase, Paley was developing a case against him.

Wyman sounded defensive in an interview in *The Wall Street Journal* two weeks before the November 13 meeting. *New York* magazine had just published a highly critical piece on him that appeared to have been engineered by Paley. Wyman detected the danger that Tisch was more aligned with Paley than with him. The turmoil, Wyman promised, was over. Tisch, he said was "the most important thing that happened to us in 1985." As for Tisch's refusal to put his self-imposed 25 percent limit in writing, Wyman repeated Tisch's own logic for not doing so, adding: "When Larry Tisch looks you in the eye and says 'I am your friend; . . . you either believe that or you don't. I do."

The suggestion that Paley was plotting his ouster, he said, was a "crazy idea." He conceded, however, that the firings at CBS News had been handled badly, hastening to add that Joyce and Sauter's jobs were secure.

Joyce and Sauter, however, were the embodiment of CBS's problem with layered management. These two men were doing the job of one predecessor, William Leonard, because of an inability to strike a compromise between Jankowski, who liked Joyce, and Wyman, who wanted Sauter. Paley had said use them both, but the result was that Joyce reported to Sauter, who reported to Jankowski, who reported to Wyman. Yet, despite all that bureaucracy, each could sign off on multimillion-dollar employment contracts without board approval, a fact that astonished Tisch.

After reading Wyman's comments in *The Wall Street Journal*, Joyce began to feel vulnerable about just how passive Tisch was going to be. Sauter only deepened his unease with news that Jankowski was collecting, for Tisch, information on what everyone did in the news department. Tisch suspected there were plenty of people producing little of value. Why, for example, couldn't the news president report directly to the broadcast group president? Why was there an executive vice president intermediary?

Joyce was homing in on what he called "the Tisch factor." It worked like this: Tisch wasn't telling anyone what to do. He was merely asking questions, but the questions clearly indicated disapproval. Who were all these people and what were they doing besides wasting money? Wyman and Jankowski saw which way Tisch was moving and sought to anticipate and please him. They had to figure that getting along with Tisch would enhance their own security. In that evolving environment, lower-level positions like Joyce's had no more security than a summer job.

CBS's stock gained, on mistaken rumors that other bidders were emerging, and despite the news that federal regulators had cleared Tisch to acquire as much as 25 percent of CBS. General Electric was among those thought to be interested, but in fact, GE was about to get in bed with RCA and its NBC unit.

At the November 1985 board meeting, Tisch clarified his position. Taking note of the media criticism being heaped on Wyman, he wondered whether it was time to slice a management layer out of CBS. At the same time, he had to be noticing the sharp contrasts between the ambiance of the CBS executive dining room—decorated, staffed, and operated in the manner of a four-star restaurant—and that of the industrially furnished conference room at Loews, where meeting participants were treated to takeout from one of the Loew's hotels.

The meeting took place against a background of published rumors about disarray at CBS News. Board member Walter Cronkite complained that the division had lost its hard-news edge. In its place were segments dripping with entertainment values—elements designed less to inform than to stimulate emotional reactions. Tisch wondered aloud if executive overpopulation wasn't part of the problem. Wyman was sure that it was.

Tisch expressed shock that the board had had no say on Dan Rather's contract or on those for Don Hewitt and Mike Wallace; each had a multimillion-dollar deal.

Tisch was still maintaining the demeanor of an observer: asking questions, expressing puzzlement, and challenging old assumptions, but not telling anyone what to do. He made it clear, however, that CBS's culture was alien to him. His presence was a reminder that things had to change. The company's fine reputation no longer guaranteed its success, especially not in a currently weak advertising market.

On December 5, Ed Joyce's worst fears were realized. Wyman, after gaining Tisch's blessing during dinner a few nights earlier, ousted Joyce as CBS News president. He banished him to a non-news executive job, which Joyce would quit two months later, and Sauter added the news president title. The process of thinning out the management ranks had begun, Wyman declared.[5]

CBS may have escaped being taken over, but for all the anxieties management now faced by enlisting Larry Tisch to its anti-takeover strategy, the effect was the same. Suddenly, a major investor with easy access to huge sums of money had to be placated. What if he didn't like what was happening? He could buy more shares, or sell his entire stake to a more voracious investor.

Besides, Tisch had credibility as a corporate strategist. Everything he and his family controlled was solidly profitable. In 1985, Loews earned $589 million, up 79 percent from a year earlier, on revenue of $6.7 billion. Earlier takeovers were prominent among the main sources of profit: CNA, $272 million; Lorillard, $137 million; Bulova, $17 million; and Loew's Hotels, $11 million. Tisch himself was an asset to be exploited.

CBS was in need of such expertise. In the course of the year, CBS profit plunged to $27.4 million from $212.4 million a year earlier; the company posted its first quarterly loss ever. Revenue totaled $4.76 billion, and profits in broadcasting, records, and publishing all declined. Wyman saw the wisdom of involving Tisch in the management process.

During the next seven months, Loews would steadily increase its CBS stake to 24.9 percent. Throughout this period, Larry Tisch would analyze the industry and CBS's operations and managers in much the same way he and his brother had evaluated the other companies they ended up running. What he learned only confirmed suspicions that began during the first board meeting he attended: the place wasn't being run like a business. Independent of Paley's own discontent with

Wyman, Tisch was finding plenty of hard evidence that the current chief executive at times seemed to enjoy the palatial trappings of executive prestige more than making the tough decisions necessary to build a powerfully profitable business.

When Tisch was only about halfway to the 25 percent mark, Wyman still faced one last bidder. Marvin Davis, the Denver oil investor and former owner of Twentieth Century Fox Film Corp., made what was viewed as a less-than-serious $160-a-share friendly offer to take CBS private. Wyman was said to have met with Davis several times, but talked with Tisch before rejecting the bid in late March.

Tisch then did his part. A week later, Larry's son Daniel, at Salomon Brothers, told Larry that Lawrence and Zachary Fisher, reclusive New York real estate investors, wanted to unload the million shares of CBS they had accumulated the previous fall in hopes of forming their own group to acquire CBS. Loews bought the brothers' stake, giving them a decent profit and boosting the Loews' stake to 16.7 percent. The move had a double benefit: It eliminated the Fishers as a potential takeover threat and reinforced the notion that Larry Tisch wasn't looking for a selling opportunity.

Wyman's decision to consult with Tisch on the Davis offer was consistent with other efforts to gain his confidence. He made sure Tisch met with Jankowski, Publishing Group president Peter A. Derow, and Records Group president Walter R. Yetnikoff. Tisch, in turn, introduced them all to brother Bob, whose mission clearly was to size them up as business managers.

Bob Tisch was beginning to fill at CBS the role he had always played in the Tisch family's approach to business. He debriefed CBS's senior vice president of finance, Fred J. Meyer, as part of the effort to identify CBS's true strengths and weaknesses. What he saw were appalling examples of business decisions divorced from business realities. One glaring example: Wyman had approved the conversion of a restaurant in the headquarters building to an employee cafeteria, thus forfeiting $500,000 of annual lease income while spending $1 million to convert space in the building to a non-revenue-producing purpose. The company's whole approach to real estate seemed wasteful; it owned a huge office building, yet was spending tens of millions of dollars to lease space elsewhere in the city.

As part of his continuing education on the business, Larry Tisch traveled to Hollywood to meet the industry's most successful entertainment executives—Michael Eisner of Walt Disney Co., Barry Diller, then CEO and chairman of Fox Inc., and Robert Daly, then chairman and chief executive of Warner Brothers Inc. These were the people who packaged and produced the programs that formed a network's lifeblood. CBS, he recognized, needed the equivalent of a Grant Tinker and a Brandon Tartikoff. Tartikoff had developed the idea of "The Cosby Show," which at that point was a major reason for NBC's passing CBS in the ratings. Tisch wanted to know how they did it. He asked everyone who ought to know, unconcerned about the possibility of sounding ignorant.

Tisch wasn't just trying to learn the business; he was gauging Hollywood's opinion of CBS's executives and scouting for candidates who could do better. Eventually, Tisch would try (unsuccessfully) to hire Tinker, who at the end of 1985 had informed NBC of his desire to quit the network and confine himself to producing shows on the West Coast.

In March 1986, cracks began to appear in the relationship between Tisch and Wyman. After Wyman met with Wall Street analysts in mid-March, Tisch was unimpressed. Wyman had trumpeted, among other things, his success in cutting annual costs by $20 million. In a company the size of CBS, the amount was practically negligible. Wyman's projections seemed to ignore the existence of a worst-case scenario.

Meantime, CBS's board was growing nervous about the presence of Bob Tisch, who was as much an owner of CBS stock as Larry. That fact probably contributed to Bob's lack of hesitation in airing his views on the company in a March 24 interview in *USA Today*. "The eventual goal," he told the newspaper, "is to control CBS and operate it as a first-class broadcasting company the way it was and the way it can and should be."

The comment seemed innocuous enough—the sort of thing he might have said about any company the Tisches were in the process of taking over. That was the problem. Board members who already were suspicious of the Tisches' intentions now became even more reluctant to trust them. For Paley, it reinforced the depressing prospect that the Tisches would end up owning his company. Bob Tisch conceded he should have kept quiet.

Larry Tisch agreed that Bob's published remarks were unfortunate, but he refused to publicly refute them. Indeed, CBS directors recognized that what Bob said wasn't necessarily what Larry thought, although, in reality, sentiment was growing within the family that Larry should be running the company, not Wyman. The incident forced Bob Tisch to take a less active role in the Tisches' CBS dealings.

Also, in late March 1986, Diller and News Corp.'s Rupert Murdoch, who had taken Fox private the previous year, toasted the creation of a fourth TV network, Fox Broadcasting Co. It opened another front in the assault on the already embattled networks. Diller was a formidable programming force. He had worked at ABC and at Paramount Pictures with Michael Eisner before joining Fox in 1984. Tisch would grow envious of the Fox network's rapid rise on a shoestring budget. Diller would claim he managed it with a staff of just 50 people.

Events were conspiring to hurt Wyman further in Tisch's eyes. Just one week after the board in April rewarded Wyman with an 11 percent raise and a $293,859 bonus, A. C. Nielsen Co. reported that, for the 1985–1986 season, NBC was the most-watched of the three networks for the first time in 30 years. NBC had gained 27 percent of the audience, compared to CBS's 26 percent and ABC's 23 percent. Two days later, CBS programming chief Harvey Shepherd quit and went to work for Robert Daly at Warner Brothers. About the same time, Dan Rather's "CBS Evening News" was losing ground to Tom Brokaw on NBC.

Board member Franklin Thomas defended the decision to fatten Wyman's compensation, despite plunging earnings: "He had to keep the troops' spirits up, he had to keep the wolves at bay, he had a board to deal with, he had a founder to keep happy, he had to deal with wild swings in the stock market."

A glaring omission in Thomas's list: shareholders. What was Wyman doing for shareholders? That was Tisch's question.

As depressed as Paley may have been about the seemingly unstoppable advance of the Tisches, he was undeterred in his desire to oust Wyman, the man who had stripped him not only of his title but of many corporate perks as well. Paley, apparently with Tisch's approval, invited Robert Daly to his Manhattan apartment to discuss the possibility of replacing Wyman. Published reports of the meeting and its purpose embarrassed Wyman. The message went out that his boardroom support was eroding.

The incident brought into focus Wyman's frustration over Tisch's role. The more he helped Tisch learn about the company's operations, the more Tisch seemed to work against him. Then, inexplicably, Bob Tisch was quoted in *The Washington Post* as saying Loew's intended to boost its stake to 35 percent, not 25 percent. With mixed signals from the Tisches and with Paley pulling strings behind the scenes, Wyman began his own maneuvering. Those who supported him on the board suggested he look for a whiter white knight to head off Tisch. The main motivation, however, seemed less to enrich shareholders than to protect Wyman and his team—just the sort of management focus Tisch found loathsome.

Toward the end of May 1986, Wyman held a secret strategy session with several CBS executives on how to neutralize Tisch—a task that was beginning to look harder than heading off Ted Turner. It had been easy to paint Turner as too reckless and too thinly capitalized to manage CBS. Tisch, however, had all the qualities that appeal to shareholders, the ultimate voters in any boardroom struggle. He had management credibility and he had cash. How was Wyman to convince the world that Tisch was a bad influence and deserved to be reined in?

Moreover, assuming Wyman could gain support for sidelining Tisch, how could it be done? About the only option was to somehow get Tisch to sign a stand-still agreement. At risk was the destruction of whatever working relationship existed between Wyman and Tisch.

Tisch learned of the secret meeting and its intent before any proposal could be formulated. The hostilities had begun.

In *The Wall Street Journal* a few days before the June CBS board meeting, Tisch declined to comment on rumors that he wanted Wyman out, but he also turned down the opportunity to say that he supported Wyman.

A close friend of Tisch told Smith, Paley's biographer, that Wyman "knew he had an enemy, and could never have a relationship of trust or confidence. Taking on Larry Tisch was like closing an umbrella in the rain. It was the beginning of the end."

Before the board meeting, Wyman met with Tisch at his Loews office in an effort to make peace. Tisch responded by suggesting that Wyman resign. He wasn't the right man to run the company, Tisch told him.

Soon after, CBS board member Roswell Gilpatrick relayed Wyman's request that Tisch sign a stand-still agreement. Tisch angrily refused, saying his word should be good enough. Gilpatrick fought back, arguing that a standstill agreement was necessary to remove investor uncertainty. Underlying the push for a standstill was the directors' fear that shareholders would sue them for rejecting attractive takeover offers and then letting the Tisches gain control without paying a premium.

At the June 11 meeting, the standstill was pressed again. Tisch again refused, but, apparently in an effort to appease the board, he agreed under pressure to sign a letter of support for Wyman. Citing press reports about the rift, Tisch's brief June 12 letter to Wyman said, "I want to reiterate to you that I continue to have full confidence in you and your management." Tisch justified the insincerity as necessary to avoid the public impression that CBS was in disarray. The letter added that Loews' "intentions" not to acquire more than 25 percent of CBS hadn't changed. Wyman chose, however, not to publicize the letter. Wyman knew better than anyone that it lacked candor.

A week after the board meeting, three directors—Roswell Gilpatrick, James D. Wolfensohn and Franklin Thomas—called on Tisch at his Loews office in one more bid for a standstill. Tisch was losing patience with their argument that such an agreement was necessary to protect shareholders from being cheated out of a potentially lucrative takeover offer. After all, hadn't he come in to help avoid a takeover by parties who might corrupt CBS's purpose? Besides, what CBS really owed its shareholders was decent management, and Wyman wasn't delivering. CBS, he told them, needed a tougher leader to trim the management ranks back to a high-quality, hard-working core. Peter Derow he branded a do-nothing, and Gene Jankowski, little more than an administrator.

Tisch had professed willingness to work with Wyman, but the rift between them was deepening. Wyman was finding it increasingly hard to manage without Tisch's unqualified support. One of them had to go; of the two, Tisch, by virtue of his now close to 20 percent holding, had the real power. Wyman had only a title and a negligible number of shares.

Only one option remained for Wyman to regain the upper hand: with Paley's support, find a merger partner. Both Wyman and Wolfensohn recognized the risk in such a quest. It would be hard to pull off without sparking a bidding war, although ABC and NBC had avoided that fate. Even if it succeeded, Wyman's job would still be at risk. In any case, the key was Paley's support. Wyman hoped that Paley's anxiety about the Tisches' controlling CBS would be greater than his desire to punish Wyman for past slights.

The same three directors who had sought the standstill agreement—Gilpatrick, Wolfensohn, and Thomas—then approached Paley for his support in pursuing a merger. Paley wasn't interested. He was now getting advice from lawyer Arthur L. Liman, a resident of the exclusive Manursing Island community in Rye, New York, where the Tisches lived. At that point, the directors and Wyman realized Paley was closer to Tisch's camp than to theirs. In fact, Liman was in the process of forging an alliance between Tisch and Paley.

In the days leading up to the July board meeting, Tisch would be heard at different parties describing Wyman and Jankowski as "nice" men, but lacking the necessary talent to run a company like CBS. At the same time, the Loews stake was rapidly closing in on 25 percent. The closer it came to the threshold, the more anxious board members grew about whether Tisch would keep his word.

As the board hunkered down for a fight to defend Wyman, a different dynamic was evolving in the news division. As the evening news program sank further in the ratings, morale was tumbling and Sauter, viewed as Wyman's man, was getting the blame. Continuing waves of layoffs in the Broadcast Group added to the discontent; 700 job cuts were announced in the first week of July, including 90 in News. The sense was that cutting costs had become more important than covering news.

Indeed, covering news seemed less important to Sauter than titillating viewers with arresting visuals and the kind of segments associated with celebrity news programs like "Entertainment Tonight." A few weeks earlier, on the day Chief Justice Warren Burger announced his retirement and President Reagan named Justice William Rehnquist to succeed him and Antonin Scalia to succeed Rehnquist—moves that had sweeping implications about the high court's future—"CBS Evening News" headlined its newscast with the death of Kate Smith.

Was the ratings slump a proof that this kind of news judgment wasn't working? For any network, it was important to draw a big audience to the evening news program, the lead-in to the all-important prime-time schedule. If the news was strong, it gave the network a head start on the rest of the schedule, because many viewers will stick with a station throughout an evening. But by the end of June 1986, CBS News, including the "CBS Morning News," had sunk into third place. The "CBS Evening News" had not occupied last place among the three major networks since 1981.

Based on what had been written about Tisch, news division employees believed he was involved in CBS largely because he cared about the news product and wanted to protect it from the Ted Turners of the world. They had read that news was one of the main things he watched on television and that he believed it was more important to maintain the integrity of the news operation than to make it profitable. They did not associate the latest layoffs with Tisch. Sauter already had a reputation for viewing the operation more as a business than a public trust.

SHOWDOWN

The July 9 board meeting developed into another volatile showdown. In the executive session afterward, the standstill agreement was again demanded. When Tisch again refused to sign such a thing, the board issued Tisch a threat: sign the standstill or face the possibility of a "poison pill"—a special dividend triggered when a single shareholder hits a certain threshold of ownership. The aim of the dividend, then gaining popularity as a takeover defense, would be to render the company impossibly expensive for the would-be acquirer. Tisch was furious at what he called this "declaration of war," especially because it followed a graphic example of how out-of-touch Wyman and Jankowski were with financial realities.

Jankowski, at the board meeting before the executive session, projected year-end Broadcast Group earnings of $334 million. The only trouble was, Tisch remembered that, just one month earlier, that same estimate had been $36 million higher. Besides, the new projection included a $112 million one-time gain from selling the St. Louis TV station. The revised projection called into question Wyman and Jankowski's other upbeat projection of presold ad time—the so-called upfront market.

Within weeks, Wyman had to admit that, because of heavy discounting and ad spending cuts at many companies, upfront sales would be $100 million less than projected, further knocking down the earnings outlook. Tisch's view was confirmed; Wyman wasn't a businessman and didn't understand what was going on. "By that time I realized these guys didn't know what they were doing," Tisch said. "They were always optimistic."

The incident caused other board members—Wyman's traditional supporters—to have second thoughts. With the bad news piling up, it was becoming increasingly difficult to back Wyman, and the embattled chairman knew it. To make matters worse, by August 1986, the network's prime-time ratings had sunk to their lowest level ever.

Tisch and Paley began a series of lunch meetings, with Liman mediating, on replacing Wyman. Paley wanted to be chairman, but he didn't want Tisch as CEO. He talked about bringing back Stanton, who said he would do it, but only reluctantly. Liman eventually persuaded Paley to go with Tisch.

August and September would prove to be the melt-down months for Wyman and his managers. Everything they did played into Tisch and Paley's hands. After a scathing editorial attack on Sauter in *TV Guide*, Sauter boasted to bureau chiefs in a speech in Park City, Utah, that he would survive. Wyman showed up, apparently to show his support for Sauter, and casually suggested that if Tisch ended up owning the network, the news content might be forced to reflect his loyalty to Israel. Word of this apparent fear-mongering quickly got back to Tisch, and the chasm between the two men widened.

Tisch visited Grant Tinker at his home in Los Angeles, in an attempt to recruit him to succeed Wyman. Tinker wasn't interested; he'd had his fill of the network business in general and was about to accept a $40 million investment from Gannett Co. to form his own studio, GTG Entertainment. It opened up shop a month later, with a 10-series commitment from CBS.

On August 11, 1986, Loews disclosed it now owned 24.9 percent of CBS stock; the average cost of acquiring the entire stake worked out to $127 a share. In league with Paley and a handful of small holders, Tisch was now part of a block that controlled slightly more than one-third of CBS's total shares outstanding. Because of a new New York State law that required two-thirds shareholder approval for a change in ownership, the Tisch group now had veto power over any outside takeover attempts.

Wyman, holding out hope against a Tisch–Paley partnership, made a last-ditch attempt to find a new suitor to oppose Tisch. His best hope was Coca-Cola Co., a candidate he had considered early in the battle to fend off Turner. At the same time, several board members were initiating discussions among themselves on a future course that probably wouldn't include Wyman. Prime considerations were: (1) avoiding a bidding war, and (2) keeping Tisch from cheating shareholders out of a lucrative buyout and dismantling the company. Wyman assumed that these talks, which didn't include him, gave top priority to walling off Tisch.

The turmoil was palpable, and nowhere was it more obvious than in CBS News. Starting on Labor Day, newscaster Dan Rather, for one week, signed off each night with the word, "Courage." Speculators said that it was a rallying cry in the wake of a decision to move the "CBS Morning News" out of the province of the News division and put it under Entertainment. Rather's unauthorized sign-off rattled the publicity department. He explained the word was one of his two favorites, the other being "meadow." Rival anchor Peter Jennings at ABC made fun of it, saying he almost signed off his own newscast with "meadow," but didn't have the courage.

Was it a response to a CBS rumor mill gone wild? Was Sauter in trouble? Was Tisch about to take over? Would Wyman succeed in attracting more takeover sharks to feed on the company?

During that week, Wyman lunched with a friend: Francis T. Vincent, Jr., chairman and CEO of Coca-Cola's Columbia Pictures unit. Wyman came away from the meeting thinking there was a good chance a CBS–Coca-Cola merger could happen and asked Wolfensohn to work up a scenario of how the two would fit. The tentative price was $170 a share. Wyman, meanwhile, discussed the deal with eight board members who he thought would back it. Wyman calculated that the deal might appeal to Paley, if he could be persuaded that it would ensure CBS's independence more so than under Tisch. Wyman was certain that Tisch was staging a slow-motion coup at the expense of minority shareholders. It was worth a try to stop him, even though Wyman was sure to lose his job.

What he didn't know, however, was that Coca-Cola already saw major stumbling blocks to acquiring CBS. The main obstacle: because of the cross-ownership of a network and a studio, the merger probably wouldn't pass regulatory hurdles unless some major assets were sacrificed.

On Sunday, September 7, *Newsweek* released advance copies of a cover story by Jonathan Alter entitled: "Civil War at CBS: The Struggle for the Soul of a Legendary Network." It was a detailed account of the turmoil rippling through the company, an epic family squabble gone public. It portrayed a company coming apart at the seams, wracked by insecurity and disloyalty, and torn by factions fighting for control and individuals fighting for their jobs. Most important of all, it indicated that Wyman had already effectively lost control of the company. His own people seemed to be questioning his leadership openly and with impunity.

Tisch was infuriated by quoted complaints from Jankowski and Sauter about "the distraction Tisch has created." Sauter said CBS's problems "are compounded by the nagging question of who will own this company and who will run it." In Tisch's view, these men already were distracted. Otherwise, they would have been dealing with the fundamental business problems that had made CBS vulnerable in the first place. The real issue wasn't who would own the company, but what was to be done to ensure it was a company worth owning.

The *Newsweek* article concluded: "From the start Tisch and Wyman were an unlikely pair: Wyman, the Midwestern Wasp, an intelligent and polished executive; Tisch, the New York-born Jew, a modest, brilliant entrepreneur who built an empire of his own. Their marriage of convenience has collapsed . . . ." A sidebar on Tisch concluded, "Larry Tisch, the investor, isn't interested in noble causes that don't pay their way." At the time, *Newsweek* noted, CBS News was the subject of 11 books.

"Executive vice president Howard Stringer, once a popular and talented producer," *Newsweek* wrote, "has been practically despondent in recent weeks while caught between management and his old colleagues. During one recent five-hour meeting, he stayed completely silent—unheard of for the normally gregarious Stringer."

Perhaps the unkindest cut of all was a contribution from Bill Moyers, who had decided to let his contract expire in November 1986. His parting shot, filled with venom, was aimed squarely at Jankowski and Sauter. "Once you decide to titillate instead of illuminate," Moyers wrote, "you become a video version of the drug culture, and your viewers become junkies. If you look at news as the conversation of democracy, you act one way. If you believe the mission is, instead, the small talk of diversion, you act another way."

In negotiating with Paley to gain management control of CBS, Tisch had defended his decision to abandon his original comment that he wasn't interested in running the company. "I lived up to everything I said. Did I know Wyman was the idiot of the century when I bought CBS stock? No. I found out later."[6]

A few days before the September board meeting, Wyman learned from Paley that Paley and Tisch were solidly in league. He then got a call from Wolfensohn that the board planned to meet without Wyman and Tisch present. The next call came from Michael Eisner: How about a CBS–Disney merger? Wyman waved him off. He decided he would propose his Coca-Cola idea at the September 10 meeting.

At a 7 P.M. meeting—the one excluding Tisch and Wyman—at the Ritz-Carlton the night before their September meeting, board members learned for the first time that Paley and Tisch had formed a coalition to oust Wyman. Until that moment, many of the directors still favored keeping Wyman, although they were opposed to the idea of proceeding with Coca-Cola for fear that it would necessitate an auction and would result in a less desirable merger partner. When it was clear, however, that Paley and Tisch were committed to firing Wyman, the other directors concluded that his leadership was hopelessly crippled.

The following day, at an 11-hour meeting, Wyman proposed the Coca-Cola merger.

"It's all wrong," Tisch shouted. "I'm 100 percent against it. My stock's not for sale at any price. What right do you have to offer this company for sale on your own?"

Paley concurred. End of discussion.

"It was a complete surprise to me," Tisch said at the time. "Eventually, I said that when I bought stock in this company it was with the intention of maintaining CBS as a completely independent company. I said that the CBS stock of Loews Corp. was not for sale. It was very upsetting."[7]

Wyman was fired. Paley, then about to turn 85, nominated himself chairman and Tisch chairman of an executive search committee, thus going back on his word that Tisch would be named CEO. On its own, however, the board named Tisch acting CEO and Paley acting chairman. Wyman was to get a $4.3 million settlement plus $400,000 a year for life. Tisch vehemently opposed the settlement, which he saw as assuaging directors' guilt about having let Wyman down. The up-front money was, instead, added to the annual payment.

Wyman's firing was settled in time for Dan Rather to announce it on the "CBS Evening News." The reaction was unqualified elation. The troops had felt the tension of a developing leadership vacuum for nearly a year.

"To have the man who built the thing in the first place back in charge, everyone will welcome that," Mike Wallace said of Paley's return. When Tisch arrived at a private party that night for Wallace and his new wife, the guests, mostly CBS News staffers, reacted as though the Messiah had just arrived.

Don Hewitt, one of the guests, said "I can't see any way that CBS will not recapture all that it once was."[8]

But as one board member put it (anonymously), "The news people are saying we're going back to the good old days. That's probably not true. All the pressures to cut costs remain. Larry is someone who knows how to cut costs, and it will be quite uncomfortable for those who are now overjoyed at the change."[9]

11

The Honeymoon

"I hope I'm connected to CBS for the rest of my life."

—Larry Tisch

On September 11, 1986, Larry Tisch's first day on the job as acting chief executive of CBS, he moved fast to clear the air of turmoil and uncertainty. He fired Van Gordon Sauter and officially yanked CBS off the auction block, telling Coca-Cola Chairman Roberto Goizueta the company wasn't for sale.

Although he was bottom-line-oriented, Sauter had to go because too much opposition to him had built up among his staff. It didn't help that, a month earlier, Sauter had defended Wyman against Tisch at the bureau chiefs' meeting in Utah. Still, it wasn't Tisch's style to fire people merely for disagreeing with him. Sauter, like his boss, Jankowski, was viewed as spending too much time trying to please his superiors and not enough time cultivating his own staff's support. His ouster was intended to eliminate a leader who was losing his employees' loyalty. They disagreed with his emphasis on appealing to viewers' emotions in the effort to inform.

Jankowski later defended Sauter's news judgment. Sauter's decision to put its chronically third-place "CBS Morning News" under the auspices of the Entertainment division was motivated, Jankowski argued,

167

not by a desire to make the show more entertainment-oriented, but to relieve the news division of having to provide that kind of material.

To replace Sauter, Tisch ignored Paley's suggestions of Bud Benjamin, the retired news producer, or Bill Moyers. Instead, he named Howard Stringer, Sauter's second-in-command. Benjamin or Moyers surely would have electrified the division with a sense of renewed commitment to pure journalism, but Tisch also needed a businessman. Naming someone already on the team was seen as less disruptive at a time when the division needed no more disruption.

Being number two under Sauter wasn't Stringer's only qualification. His credibility as a broadcast journalist was steeped in the traditions of "CBS Reports," the showcase of the network's news documentaries. Their popular format had been established by Edward R. Murrow, who at CBS in the 1940s, set the standard for broadcast journalism and became its patron saint. Stringer, a tall, curly-haired Welshman who had attended Oxford University, was admired for his intelligence, charm, and self-effacing wit. He had started at WCBS-TV, New York, in his mid-20s as a clerk. He became a researcher at "CBS Reports" in 1968, an assistant producer in the early 1970s, and an executive producer working with Bill Moyers on what would come to be viewed as the program's best documentaries. He had also spent time as executive producer of "CBS Evening News" and had developed "48 Hours on Crack Street," a documentary on drugs that would give birth to a successful weekly news feature.

Stringer, 44, represented a link between the News division's past glory and a hopefully hipper future to be determined by younger news executives like himself, although his ties to Sauter tainted him in the eyes of some staffers.

At the August bureau chiefs' meeting in Utah, Sauter had uttered what turned out to be possibly his most appropriate parting shot: "You can change the players, but let me assure you, you don't change the rules"—meaning the rules Larry Tisch obeyed. The ambitious Stringer showed a willingness to play by those rules, helping to execute many of the cuts ordered by his boss. Ironically, Sauter's departure would be costly; he had just signed a five-year contract at

$350,000 a year. In Tisch's view, it was far better for CBS News to pay Sauter to leave than it was to pay him to stay.

At the end of October, Tisch took the "acting" off Stringer's title as CBS News president, with the blessing of Dan Rather and Bud Benjamin, who had been Paley's first choice for the job. Stringer was the third president in less than a year.

One of Stringer's first acts as division head was to sign Diane Sawyer to a four-year, $1.2 million-a-year contract. The deal, a 50 percent raise from her $800,000 annual salary, came amid rumors of an even bigger offer from NBC. Under her contract, she was Dan Rather's backup in addition to her continuing work on "60 Minutes." What she really wanted, however, was a network anchor job, and her new contract included a clause that freed her if another network offered her such a job.

Sauter wasn't the only executive shown the door after Tisch took control. His first memo as CEO was intended to assure everyone of his "complete confidence" in the head of the company's three operating divisions—Jankowski, Peter A. Derow of Publishing, and Walter Yetnikoff of Records. Yet, less than four weeks later, he fired Derow and 14 of his staffers, having determined that they represented a costly management layer. Jankowski and Yetnikoff didn't last long either, although their departures were more on their own terms.

Expressions of "confidence" from Tisch were beginning to look like the kiss of death. Tisch himself asked rhetorically, "What is a vote of confidence?" The answer was open to interpretation. Did it mean he was confident of someone's ability to continue doing what he or she had always done? It was surely not to be confused with an unqualified endorsement of the way things had always been done, nor with a lifetime guarantee of employment.

SELF-EDUCATION

Tisch began to make the rounds in this new, unfamiliar business. He was relishing the access he now had to the studios where images were crafted and fed to millions of viewers. After visiting the set of "CBS

Morning News" as an observer, he remarked, "I've always wanted to do that." The environment of television—a marketplace of entertainment, information, ideas, talent, images, and fame—fascinated Tisch. It was unlike any other business he had taken on. But his fascination appeared to have had no mellowing effect on his business judgment.

As part of his on-the-job education, Tisch learned, from managers working for Jankowski, that of 500 or so people who were supposed to have been laid off, only 150 were actually gone. No one, it seemed, was holding anyone to a timetable. Tisch may have been viewed as a savior, but he was no less determined to wring at least $40 million of annual savings out of the budget. To Tisch, CBS was no different than CNA or Lorillard or Bulova in terms of the need to cut waste. In Tisch's view, a rush job in any business was to eliminate waste the moment it was identified. But this was CBS, the corporate equivalent of the British royal family in terms of how much attention the media paid to it. Tisch was determined to ignore the media coverage his every move would now attract. He aimed to enrich shareholders, not please reporters.

Still, Tisch's tour of the CBS empire reassured the rank and file that the new boss was going to restore the network's dignity. They believed their jobs were more secure, and Tisch fostered that impression with a natural friendliness. He wasn't there to warn or intimidate. He was there to offer support. His lack of overbearing ego was noted wherever he went.

For example, on a visit to WCAU-TV in Philadelphia, the place where CBS began, he walked into a studio, tripped over a tangle of cables during a videotaping, and fell flat on his face. He reacted with bravado, recalled Neal Zoren, a former public relations staffer at CBS-owned stations. "I'm all right, I'm okay," Tisch said as he brushed himself off. "What am I going to do, sue myself?"

Even Dan Rather found Tisch's demeanor reassuring. "I like the look in his eye, the warmth of his handshake, and I like what he says about news," he said at a Los Angeles news conference in 1986. "In a rough-and-tumble business the first thing anyone says about Larry Tisch is that he's trustworthy."

Still, the issue of trust was spawning an undercurrent. Vague but re-assuring expressions of confidence, of present intentions, continued to appear, but they were being interpreted as firm commitments by a staff hungry for the parental protection it once had enjoyed under Paley. Some who lost their jobs in the wake of Tisch's arrival realized it was an oversimplification to view Loews as a corporate Trojan horse or to brand Tisch as a traitor.

"When Tisch came in, everyone on every level was concerned, mainly for their own survival," said Neil E. Derrough, who was fired as president of the CBS-owned stations a month after Tisch succeeded Wyman. "It wasn't clear what Tisch was going to do, who he would keep, who he wouldn't. As a result, not everybody was at their best."

Perhaps in the rush to please Tisch, Derrough was sacrificed. As with other firings, the decision wasn't made by Tisch; it was made by Jankowski. Underlying such preemptive moves was an awareness that Tisch saw too many managers running around. For such managers, it was a matter of self-preservation to decimate the next-lower manage-ment layer before Tisch zeroed in on one's own layer.

Despite his forced departure, Derrough had no quarrel with Tisch's agenda. "A lot of his criticisms were right," he said. "I came from a different world. I had spent my life on the station side, where everyone had a bottom line and you had to explain it."

Costs at News and Entertainment had gotten out of control. In keeping with the Paley concept, the presidents of those divisions were charged with achieving and maintaining a number-one rating for CBS programs. Jankowski's job was to watch the budget; the division heads had much less of a cost-control mandate. In contrast, each sta-tion had to account for every dollar of cash flow; converting waste into profit at the stations was a part of their routine.

"The stations were more manageable and accountable," Derrough said, "but we got lumped in with the whole company" in a kind of cor-porate guilt-by-association. Broadly speaking, "everybody played their own game with attrition, but by the end of each year, they never quite reached the target. When Tisch arrived, he demanded that it really happen."

Still, Tisch was enjoying a honeymoon of sorts, in return for having chased off Wyman and Sauter. It helped that he was a genuine fan of the news operation and of such stars as Diane Sawyer and Dan Rather. It also helped that Wall Street, which bets on substance over style, loved Tisch's fast, no-nonsense approach. "He didn't come in as a polished refined manager," Derrough said, "but they could have done a lot worse."

THE FACILITATORS

Within weeks of assuming the helm, Tisch had hired Coopers & Lybrand as management consultants to enforce a cost-cutting regimen. They set up shop in the company's Manhattan headquarters—known as Black Rock—on the 20th floor, near Personnel. They were to make a weekly verbal report to Tisch on who should be cut and where. By the end of their one-month assignment, under the direction of Thomas C. Flanagan, Coopers & Lybrand had shown how it was to be done. Under a "no more Mr. Nice Guy" approach, more than 200 people lost their jobs—a greater number than Jankowski had managed to ease out since announcing, three months earlier, that 700 jobs would be eliminated.

Cuts were implemented in the personnel, research, broadcast standards, and public relations departments; all outside consultants were gone, including Coopers & Lybrand. A minority development program was scrapped, and a company store where employees could buy CBS paraphernalia was closed. Publications, personal photocopiers, limousines, first-class air travel, messenger services, executive kitchens and dining rooms, new furniture, rented typewriters, in-house medical care, and corporate philanthropy were all cut back.

The Tisch-endorsed Coopers & Lybrand approach was to set the standard for ruthlessness in cost cutting at CBS. Stringer, for his part, already understood what Tisch wanted and strove to show that he could deliver. A week after Tisch became CEO, Stringer took Tisch to Washington by train to see "CBS Evening News" in action. On the way down, Stringer briefed his new boss on where the News bodies were, what they did, and how much they cost. He was testing Tisch's appetite for detail while at the same time demonstrating his own capacity for dispassionate cost analysis. Stringer's point was: he knew how to lay the groundwork for mastering the budget.

Comments Tisch made during dinner with the Washington staff that evening were interpreted as assurances there would be no layoffs. Tisch, however, never specifically promised no layoffs.[1] His essential message was that he would cut fat, not meat. What or who was considered fat was open to interpretation, depending on circumstances.

To anyone who interviewed him at the time, Tisch's mission was stated as balancing public service with bottom-line responsibility. "I'm really wearing two hats," he said.[2] "My first obligation is to do what's best for the network and ensure quality programming. My secondary role is as a businessman to manage the company in a way that is right for the employees and the shareholders."

A HARSH NETWORK ENVIRONMENT

Two harsh realities faced CBS: (1) it was losing its share of a shrinking market (from 1980 to 1986, the networks' prime-time audience tumbled to 76 percent from 90 percent because of losses to cable), and (2) NBC, the number one network at the time, was clobbering CBS and ABC in the ratings, forcing both to cut ad rates as much as 5 percent. CBS's prime-time audience fell to 26 percent in the 1985–1986 season, down from 29 percent three years earlier. Any turnaround would take years to pull off. In the meantime, costs had to come down to fatten the bottom line. Wall Street analysts didn't view CBS as financially troubled; they saw it as a company full of untapped potential for even greater profitability.

At the heart of a conflict between Larry Tisch and some CBS journalists was a lack of understanding regarding why CBS needed to be more profitable than it was. Why tamper with something that seemed to be making "enough" money, despite its extravagances? The answer was numerical: Tisch's goal for CBS was a 12 percent return on assets. Under Wyman, the return never exceeded 6 percent. In Tisch's view, an investor had no incentive for bankrolling a company that couldn't produce a better yield than government bonds, which carried none of the risk of investing in a company's stock.

For Tisch and his fans on Wall Street, a corporate extravagance represented a waste of money that rightfully belonged to shareholders. If money wasn't being reinvested to further enhance profitability, then it should, at the very least, be paid to investors in the form of a dividend. Tisch's mission was to change the culture of rationalizing waste, although, as of September 1986, he didn't see himself as a permanent CEO who would instill a new discipline. Still, as an investor, he was involved for the long haul. "I hope I'm connected to CBS for the rest of my life," he said.[3]

BACK TO BASICS

Tisch's strategy of focusing on the broadcast business, the core of CBS, helped protect him from criticism in the media. He enjoyed a relatively free hand to start doing what Ted Turner would have been forced to do immediately, had his bid succeeded: put huge chunks of the company up for sale. Tisch wanted to keep what he viewed as the inflation-proof part of the business and convert the rest of the company's assets into cash. The process unfolded with lightning speed.

Even before October, Tisch was getting feelers for the CBS magazines division, publisher of *Woman's Day* and *Modern Bride*. He figured he could get $600 million for the division. Soon after, Nelson Peltz, head of Triangle Industries, a beverage can producer, contacted Tisch about buying CBS Records, the leader in its industry. Tisch figured the price at $1.25 billion, or 16 times the division's average annual earnings over the previous five years.

Yetnikoff, president of CBS Records, learned of this inquiry when an investment banker called to arrange for Peltz to discuss the financials. Yetnikoff, enraged, called Tisch and vented his spleen. Hadn't

Tisch promised him a role in any sale proposal? Tisch's response: Find your own buyer.

Yetnikoff wasn't the only insider distressed to learn Tisch was giving Peltz a peek at CBS Records. Paley, for one, was against selling the division, mainly because it was one of his biggest successes. He took it on in the 1930s when it was the struggling Columbia Phonograph Co., then built it into a trailblazer and an industry leader. It also did not go unnoticed that Tisch was contemplating doing what the company had spent so much money to avoid under Turner. Yet even Paley recognized that CBS Records, as a mature business, was ripe for divestiture.

Tisch decided to put the brakes on a CBS Records sale, but Yetnikoff already was shopping the division, along with himself, to Sony Corp., a company known for giving its division managers autonomy.

It wasn't the first time Tisch and Yetnikoff clashed. Their styles were vastly different, though they were both tough fighters. Tisch may have had a warm, engaging manner in non-negotiating situations, but as a boss, he was relentless and forceful in challenging his division managers. He wanted to be confident that their assumptions were conservative, that their projections weren't overly optimistic. As Tom Tisch put it, "If you worry about the downside, the upside tends to take care of itself."

Yetnikoff, however, was unintimidated by Tisch. As the architect of CBS Records' current prowess, he was in a position of strength. Tisch needed Yetnikoff's cooperation to get top dollar in any sale of the division because of Yetnikoff's singular skill in identifying and signing up top talent, and they both knew it. Yetnikoff played it to the hilt. When Tisch demanded that CBS Records shoulder its fair share of the corporate cost-cutting burden, Yetnikoff simply refused. Tisch's laser-guided intelligence met its match in the volatile, fast-talking Yetnikoff. Out of a payroll of 11,000, Yetnikoff agreed to cut a mere 40 people and, after much wrangling, prevailed in his refusal to shut his own dining room.

Yetnikoff noted how much more concerned Tisch seemed to be about cutting costs at CBS Records than about making sure the division maintained its powerful lineup of talent.

Yetnikoff continued to work on getting CBS Records out from under the conservative influence of Larry Tisch. Yetnikoff's opinion of Tisch wasn't improving. In an uncomplimentary narrative, he described how he and Tisch, during a trip to visit Barry Diller in Hollywood, bickered over such trivialities as what to eat for breakfast, whose car they would drive, who would drive it, and how they'd get where they were going. Tisch would eventually lose respect for Yetnikoff, whom he had once seen as a "very honorable fellow." Later, he referred to him at one point as "an animal" after Yetnikoff openly attacked Tisch's character at a CBS board meeting.

At about this time, Tisch got a taste of the harsh criticism to come. The October 13 issue of *Fortune* carried a short, biting analysis of Tisch, portraying him almost as untrustworthy. The article depicted Tisch as someone deliberately misrepresenting himself and his intentions, lulling CBS staffers into a false sense of security. "Don't be fooled," the article advised, describing Tisch's physical stature in less than flattering terms. Clearly, the media were turning on Tisch.

The article then went on to note that nowhere had Tisch promised that he would *not* buy more than 25 percent of CBS or sell his stake for a quick profit. Although the writer, Stratford Sherman, proved to be unnecessarily skeptical of Tisch, he was prescient in describing CBS's immediate future. It was struggling in the worst TV advertising market in 15 years. "CBS is in the middle of a slide that is still gaining momentum," Sherman noted, echoing the reason Tisch wanted to raise cash. He was preparing CBS for the worst, and he saw no reason to take his time about it.

The speed with which Tisch dispatched Derow and his crew was a case in point. On October 16, Tisch summoned Derow to his office and informed him of the decision. Derow asked if it couldn't wait for the budget process to unfold, noting that Coopers & Lybrand had yet to make its own recommendations for the division. It couldn't, Tisch said, ordering Derow and the others to be out by the next day. For

Tisch, there was nothing to negotiate. He knew what he wanted. Why wait?

"I think that Larry feels the entire corporation is overstaffed," Derow observed at the time.

In this rare instance, Tisch actually did the face-to-face job of firing someone. In the past, Bob Tisch was more likely to handle such tasks. Bob, however, was growing increasingly independent of Larry. Toward the end of the year, Bob would be nominated to become the new postmaster general. His decision to take the post was seen as the beginning of an effort to establish an identity separate from Larry. "He felt he needed that," said a family friend, "but it bothered the boys that he felt he was not enough of his own man on his own even though they felt he was."

A few days after Derow was fired, Tri-Star Pictures, the film venture CBS had recently abandoned, bought Loew's Theatre Management Corp. from Jerrold Perenchio for nearly twice what he had paid Loews a year earlier. Tisch's critics later pointed to the deal as evidence that he frequently sold assets too cheaply. But whether selling stocks or corporate assets, it wasn't Tisch's aim necessarily to make a killing—he just wanted at least a return that made the investment sufficiently profitable. Better to sell something that turns out to be even more valuable than to have a buyer who ends up feeling cheated.

Later in October, Tisch received a $500 million take-it-or-leave-it bid from Harcourt Brace Jovanovich Inc. for CBS Educational & Professional Publishing. Tisch took it, despite having said a few weeks earlier that he wasn't planning on selling the division to pay debt. The board approved the sale on October 24, along with the $125 million sale of CBS Songs, a music publisher, to SBK Entertainment World. Enhanced by its new owners, CBS Songs was resold in less than three years to Thorn EMI for $337 million.

A few weeks after the publishing sales, Tisch decided to yank CBS out of the Prodigy computer-database venture with IBM and Sears, soon after indicating in a *Broadcasting* magazine interview that he intended to stay in.

Cost Cutting at All Levels

While Stringer, with Tisch's approval, was prolonging the runaway inflation in salaries for on-air personalities, Tisch was shaking down department heads for savings of every magnitude, from multimillion-dollar line items to an employee newsletter.

One expense Tisch and the other networks' new owners wanted to cut was payment of roughly $150 million per year per network to affiliates for carrying network programs. A network needs affiliates to be a network, and anything that alienates them threatens the network, but Tisch felt that if CBS was making less money, then its affiliates should make less money. CBS could not unilaterally cut their compensation without running the risk of driving them into a rival network. But Tisch seemed willing to play hardball with a partner the business couldn't live without any more than a magazine could live without the post office and newsstands. It was an attitude that ultimately may have influenced the willingness in 1994 of eight important affiliates to abandon CBS to join the Fox network.

Local television stations distributed the CBS network's product, and Tisch seemed defiantly determined to have the stations share in the bad times as well as the good. Anthony C. Malara, CBS Television Network president, was given two months to find $50 million in savings. Despite Malara's arguments against such a move, Tisch wanted to cut stations' compensation. Doing so would become a whole lot harder a few months later, when NBC, looking for insurance to help keep it in first place, announced it would increase compensation to its affiliates.

In December, a sweeping reorganization aimed at erasing a management layer between Jankowski and broadcast division managers cost Malara his job; he became a senior vice president in the division. Thomas F. Leahy, whom Malara had reported to, was taking on Malara's former role. One of the three executive vice presidents being eliminated (Neil Derrough and Neal H. Pilson were the other two), Leahy was now president of the CBS Television Network, responsible for four divisions: Entertainment, headed by B. Donald "Bud" Grant;

News, headed by Howard Stringer; Sports and Broadcast operations, headed by Neal Pilson; and Television Stations, headed by Peter Lund.

Tisch had no patience for bureaucracy. He wasn't interested in written reports or organizational charts. Most of all, he wasn't interested in endless meetings and analysis. It didn't take long for him to figure out what made sense, and, in his view, it shouldn't take long for others to implement it.

FILLING A VOID

Tisch's savior status had barely begun to fade among Broadcast Division staffers, but the CBS directors never completely lost their skepticism about his intentions. He had resisted all their efforts to draw from him any promises about the future. They were expecting a betrayal, and they had begun to see what they viewed as signs of it. He seemed to lack a coherent long-term plan. What he really lacked was the patience to do a lot of hand-holding on how he was formulating a strategy.

Around the time Tisch was named acting CEO, Roger B. Minkoff, a real estate investor from St. Croix who owned a mere 12 shares of CBS, sued the board and Wyman. Minkoff accused them of letting Loews get control without paying a premium for the stock and offering it to all holders. This was the sort of lawsuit the board was hoping to avoid by demanding that Tisch sign a stock-purchase standstill agreement. Ultimately, CBS settled the suit after narrowing its focus to a dispute over CBS's having paid $40 million too much for the Ziff-Davis magazines.

Whatever the directors feared, Tisch wasn't interested in running CBS or any other company all by himself, nor was he a short-term investor. He wanted to establish a culture of frugality and the best possible team of managers to strengthen the company in a hostile economic environment. Tisch wanted to be free of the day-to-day.

Still, the board's anxiety bubbled to the surface at the November board meeting. Tisch mentioned he could get $600 million for the magazines division and $1.25 billion from Sony for CBS Records. But hadn't Tisch said he wouldn't break up the company? Did it make sense to cut CBS down to a single business when rivals seemed to be doing the opposite? Tisch's modus operandi was to *not* follow the herd. He did what made sense, regardless of what was in fashion. To him, it made sense to close some of these asset sales now, before the end of the year, and take advantage of tax benefits that were set to expire at year-end under the Reagan Administration's tax reform act.

It galled Tisch that several directors had counseled among themselves, before the meeting, on how best to contain him. Even his friend James Wolfensohn seemed to be aligned with those who viewed Tisch as dangerous. Their paranoia may have been a sign of the times: corporate raiders were routinely taking huge positions in companies in order to liquidate them piecemeal.

It seemed inconceivable to CBS's directors that Larry saw himself as an owner with healthy parental instincts, not a modern-day speculator. He was there to improve his new property's value. No amount of indignation, however angrily expressed, helped Tisch's cause. In the end, the board cleared Tisch only to quit the Prodigy venture, which already had cost CBS $40 million and was years away from financial success.

Having muscled his way into CBS by virtue of sheer financial power, Tisch faced a board that was tolerating him because it had no choice. The directors didn't trust him. Unchecked, he would suck CBS dry, they feared, despite the lack of evidence that he had ever taken that approach to any previous investment. His critics frequently cited the Loews reversal of CNA's diversification as evidence of Tisch's destructiveness. They failed to note how the insurer had prospered as a result and had remained a Loews unit.

At the December board meeting, the hostilities continued. Wolfensohn vented his anger at being accused of conspiring against Tisch, who was challenged for not doing enough to find Wyman's permanent successor. Tisch responded by naming potential insiders who might make good CEOs: Neal Pilson, Peter Lund, and Howard Stringer.

Over Christmas and New Year's, Tisch and Stringer traveled to Europe with their wives. They met with the news crew in Rome, where bureau chief Peter Schweitzer arranged for an audience with Pope John Paul II, and then went on to CBS's London and Moscow bureaus. Stringer had hoped that cost-conscious Tisch would gain a better sense of what CBS was getting for its money. He did, but it wasn't favorable.

Tisch saw evidence of out-of-control spending—more than a dozen idle staffers in Rome, and thoughtless waste in London, where the staff numbered 80. By contrast, the four-person Moscow bureau produced more material, even though the bureau's economy was imposed on it by the Soviets. Moscow was, arguably, the single most-important international beat. It was becoming increasingly difficult for Stringer to justify not cutting back on some of these operations. To even attempt to do so would be to risk losing Tisch's support.

To Tisch, protecting CBS's prestigious reputation in news did not mean he had to protect its culture of privilege. Where was the payback for keeping large staffs on fat expense accounts? Wasn't there a more cost-effective way to cover the world without viewers and advertisers perceiving a difference? Did CBS have to have so many of its own full-time camera crews? Why couldn't it use free-lancers? These were the kinds of questions Tisch was asking, and Stringer was hard put to answer.

Tisch was starting to change the corporate culture by asking questions about possible alternatives, not by issuing directives. By virtue of his 25 percent stake, CBS really was *his* company. He was the owner-operator, and his staff would have to adopt his priorities if they wanted to stay with CBS.

In the back of everyone's mind—not just Tisch's—in the broadcast division was an awareness that Turner's Cable Network News (CNN) was doing the job on a 24-hour basis for a fraction of what it cost any of the networks. At the same time, Barry Diller was running an equally lean network operation for Fox. It was becoming increasingly hard to tell what the networks were getting for outspending their startup rivals.

Despite the Fox challenge, which would return to haunt him in 1994, Tisch had little appetite for defending his own network at any cost. Tisch imposed his investment portfolio management discipline on CBS in his decision, for example, to let General Electric outbid him for Wometco Broadcasting's WTVJ-TV in Miami, a CBS affiliate.

The decision was especially surprising because it was the first time a network had bought another's affiliate. But Tisch didn't focus on the idea that CBS was giving up a chunk of viewers to a rival. He focused on the price. What was the chance that by topping NBC's whopping $270 million bid he could get a better return on the investment than by investing in U.S. Treasury debt, which carries no risk? Less important to him was that CBS-owned television stations now reached only 19 percent of the U.S. market, compared with 22 percent for NBC and 25 percent for ABC.

Tisch's firm focus on financial risk–reward balances was beginning to worry not just the directors but the troops as well. He seemed to look at even the tiniest expenses and ask, "What's the payback?" He wanted to see clearly how an expense enhanced the net income line on the balance sheet. The worry at CBS was that this kind of pressure to eliminate every such unjustifiable expense would hurt the company's ability to produce the programs that attract viewers and advertisers.

Tisch, however, found what he considered to be layer upon layer of waste. CBS was so out of control, it had lost touch with any semblance of a commonsense approach to living within one's means. He couldn't accept the premise that the creative people who produced television programming would somehow be stifled if they had to adhere to a tight budget—as if creativity weren't essential in businesses outside the entertainment industry.

The notion gaining currency was that Tisch, Tom Murphy of Capital Cities, and Jack Welch of GE were experts at cost effectiveness and therefore enemies of creativity, the lifeblood of the television business. Writers, actors, directors, journalists, and producers supposedly were incapable of doing good work unless they never had to think about the cost.

Much of the waste Tisch was seeing in CBS News's $300 million budget—nearly triple CNN's budget,—appeared frivolous. He wanted Stringer to attack the problem with urgency, but Stringer was bumping up against people like Dan Rather, who believed any further cuts would damage quality and hurt ratings. Stringer's effort to reconcile the company's journalistic interests and its financial interests was proving to be fruitless. He had already seen the futility of trying to convince Tisch that further cuts should be avoided.

Indeed, Stringer found it difficult to defend the news department's spending habits. His only hope was to get Rather and other news staffers to see the inevitability of a tighter budget and the merits of adapting to it rather than fighting it. His effort to do so included having Rather and Tisch meet; the aim was to bring Rather more into the Stringer-Tisch camp, or at least establish some personal contact that might smooth the way to compromise later. It would soon become clear that this strategy had failed.

TISCH INHERITS PALEY'S MANTLE

By the January 13 CBS board meeting, Wolfensohn and Tisch had buried the hatchet, after a conciliatory call from Tisch. The CBS directors voted to make Paley and Tisch's titles permanent, having never seriously considered other candidates. In fact, director Harold Brown's executive search committee had never even met. Tisch agreed not to seek the ouster of those on the board who had so distrusted him just a few months earlier.

The board had good reasons to endorse Tisch, other than to protect their own positions. Tisch thoroughly understood the company, was improving its efficiency, and, unlike any CEO before him, had neutralized Paley. Even if the network was in decline, it made sense to keep at the helm someone whose forte seemed to be the ability to steer through rough economic weather by building a cash hoard and retiring debt. Paley may have still held out hope that Tisch wouldn't want to stay in charge for long, but the rest of the board knew Tisch was there to stay and to control.

12

Tisch as Villain: Waning Popularity at CBS

"I own that company, Tisch does not own that company, that's the way I feel."

—Andy Rooney, *The New York Times*, March 9, 1987

Larry Tisch had been chief executive of CBS Inc. just six months when the media caught a whiff of blood and started circling for the kill. He had run dozens of enterprises over the previous 40 years—and presided over wholesale firings when deemed necessary. Nothing in that experience, however, prepared the Brooklyn-born billionaire for the ferocity of public reaction to a wave of layoffs ordered up at his newest company. To the press, this wasn't just any company. This was CBS, a media empire—one of its own.

March 5, 1987—coincidentally, Tisch's 64th birthday—marked the beginning of a kind of purgatory for this unpretentious, universally respected corporate leader. In this kind of purgatory, you know you're right but nobody else does. For nearly four years, he would endure regular doses of public ridicule, if not flat-out condemnation; his decades of stunning successes had rarely captured the public's imagination. On March 5, Howard Stringer, whom Tisch had elevated to president of CBS News, announced the dismissal of 215 staffers, including 14 on-air reporters.

Practically overnight, Tisch the savior became Tisch the callous cost cutter, a madman with a knife slashing away at fat and supposedly destroying muscle in the process.

A month before, the word had gone out that Tisch wanted CBS's $300 million budget to shrink by $50 million. Stringer was quick to defend the goal, adding that he didn't take his job to "preside over the destruction of CBS News."[1] In a memo to his staff just before the actual cuts were announced, Stringer said cost cutting was necessary. "Be patient," he told them, "and continue as I know you will even under this latest cloud to put on the best broadcast in journalism."

Stringer's layoffs were announced on a Thursday. The 15 percent staff cut was meant to save $33 million, well short of Tisch's target of $50 million. This third cut in 18 months was considerably larger than Wyman's earlier, half-hearted efforts. News bureaus in Warsaw and Bangkok were shut down, as was the Seattle bureau, opened just two years earlier at a cost of $1 million. The Chicago bureau was trimmed to two staffers. Paris was left with one correspondent.

The media had a field day covering the carnage. It portrayed Ike Pappas, a 22-year CBS on-air reporter, almost as a martyr, although technically, Pappas wasn't canned. He had a year left on his contract, for which CBS paid him. Measured by the scant air time he had been getting in recent years, the decision not to renew his contract wasn't a tough one.

Larry Pintak, the Mideast correspondent, also was let go. In Germany, only a camera crew remained. Richard Cohen, who had cheered Sauter's demise, no longer was cheering. "It is inevitable," he predicted, "that we are going to cover less news."

Rage over the firings was close to the surface. CBS newswriters were on strike at the company's 57th Street broadcast center, prompting one news staffer to observe, "It's the only place in journalism where you have to cross a picket line to get fired."

Former CBS News president William Leonard was shocked. "They're destroying the fucking place," he said. "It is heartbreaking.

It's not just the news division. The company, the company is destroyed. Its soul . . . never mind its soul, the BODY is gone out of it. My grand illusion in life was CBS. I had an illusion about it, not entirely based on nonsense. It was a place. A place worth wanting to be at. It isn't a place to want to be at anymore."[2]

The free-spending days at CBS were numbered by the time Tisch became CEO. Wyman had been taking steps, but not urgently enough for Tisch's goals. Now Tisch all too easily filled the staff's need for a scapegoat. Peter Boyer, the *New York Times* reporter covering CBS, provided Tisch the public forum in which to hang himself.

Boyer reached Tisch at his home in Rye, New York, a day or so after the latest layoffs were announced March 6. What came out in print on Monday, March 9—in a story headlined "Sadness Turns to Anger Over CBS Dismissals"[3]—would take Tisch years to live down.

Tisch scoffed at Boyer's suggestion that CBS News staffers felt betrayed. "A lot of people are lucky to be laid off right now because there are other jobs available in broadcasting," he reasoned. In print and out of context, the remark seemed insensitive at best. It was one of many examples of Tisch speaking without fear of distortion.

"When the media first started to pay attention to [the Tisch brothers] Larry would think that he could say whatever he really believed and people would understand," said his wife, Billie. "But sometimes people don't want to. Sometimes they have their own agenda."

Not that Tisch was naive. A friend was present at Larry's office at Loews Corp. when a reporter arrived for an interview concerning his CBS investment. Tisch readily answered all her questions. The friend was taken aback.

"Why do you talk to reporters?" the visitor asked. "Aren't you afraid they'll get it wrong?"

"They always get it wrong," Tisch replied, "but this way maybe she'll get it less wrong."

Big Business (Larry Tisch) exploiting the public's airwaves was an irresistible theme to journalists and a fairly easy one to portray. Tisch's remark about the benefits of being laid off made the job even easier.

The portrayal of Tisch as greedy and insensitive, however, was a gross oversimplification.

"I never said news staffers were lucky to be losing their jobs," Tisch asserted. "If you have to lose your job, you're better off losing it in 1986 or '87 than in 1991. If there are a lot of jobs available, losing your job is terrible but not a disaster, compared to losing it when there are no jobs available."

What was the real impact of the staff cuts? "With the severance, the way we treated these people was way beyond the call of any other company," Tisch said. "We didn't put anybody out on the street. Everybody got very handsome severance packages. There's no good way to let people go. But there are bad and worse, and if you try to treat people decently with decent financial packages, that's the best you can do."

THE DEMISE OF THE "CIVIL BROADCASTING SERVICE"

The process was painful and wrenching. It has stuck in Stringer's memory as a series of agonizing meetings in which longtime veterans were told to leave. The process not only reduced costs but also changed the culture of the entire company from one of rewarding loyalty to one of rewarding performance. The change was brought on less by Larry Tisch than by the changing realities of an increasingly competitive business environment—an environment in which the ambitious, imaginative, hard-charging types were displacing the civil-servant types accustomed to earning promotions by virtue of longevity.

"It was very difficult, very emotional," Stringer said in a recent interview, "but television was changing and everything that's happened since indicates that indeed television has changed whether for the better or for the good. The competitive framework is changing all the time, and the consequence of failing in ratings terms or financial terms is much more severe than it used to be. You can't recover in the speed you used to 10, 20 years ago."

In the days before cable and VCRs and upstart networks, a network could simply jack up the advertising rates to cover a multitude of sins. Programs could fail, and still rates went up. By the time Larry Tisch arrived, all that was changing. CBS, it used to be said, stood for the Civil Broadcasting Service.

Said Stringer: "The truth is that it was very fair; those early monopolies—like many governments, like IBM, and all the others—all believed in a sort of cradle-to-grave security, which was admirable. People expected to retire at CBS. The world has absolutely changed since that period, and to a certain extent one can mourn its passing." The change, however agonizing, was inevitable.

Stringer knew the culture wasn't changing fast enough, but he had grown up in that more comfortable environment. When he joined CBS in the 1960s, people expected to be a producer in their 40s, a senior producer in their 50s, and an executive producer or vice president in their 60s—a slow, measured pace toward retirement, with the realization of one's full potential occurring in one's 50s or 60s. Now the producer ranks of even the best news magazine programs are filled with people in their 20s.

"It's not about security," Stringer said. "It is about all those who want to compete in a more dynamic, competitive society in this industry than has ever been true. . . . What I stress today . . . is that there is zero complacency. We work harder, longer hours probably than any of our predecessors. It's more Darwinian, but it's also livelier. And the price of failure is so high, as we saw two or three years ago when we were in third place and McKinsey [management consultants] came in and it looked like we could lose $400 million; that was the abyss. So now we went to the edge of that precipice. We looked down and none of us liked it very much and we're now fighting for our lives. That is dramatic and exciting and opportunistic and so forth, so it's different. Is it worse? Is it better? It's certainly less comfortable and sometimes less reflective."

Stringer saw a parallel in the baseball business. In the old days, managers were tough on their players, but the environment was one of mutual respect and fierce team loyalty. Today, with free agency, the loyalty is gone, but players are paid a lot more. The same change was happening at CBS. "While people mourn the passing of the loyalty," he said, "individually many people have benefited. One of the reasons we got into trouble in the 1980s was that correspondent salaries went from $100,000 average to $300,000 average. So even while they were saying it's not the same anymore, people were getting very, very wealthy."

While salaries were going up and driving costs higher and higher, the news division was losing more and more money at a time when audiences were dwindling. Tisch, coming in as an outsider, had no trouble seeing the urgency of halting this dangerous trend. Unlike Stringer, Tisch wasn't a recent convert to the survival-of-the-fittest school of business. From the beginning of his career in business, success was defined by performance, results, and return on investment—not mere loyalty. CBS was in danger of strangling itself with its die-hard tradition of rewarding loyalty regardless of performance. Radical surgery was called for.

Cultural changes were already under way when Tisch took charge, but the changes were far from done. It was one thing for Tisch to come in from the outside and demand rapid change. Stringer, on the other hand, had to undergo the transformation himself and impose it on a staff far less prepared for it than he was. The media homed in on the pain of those less able to adapt—and Tisch's "lucky to be laid off" comment in the *Times* was especially inflammatory for those feeling the pain. But in terms of Tisch's standing at CBS, the comment wasn't nearly as damaging as Boyer's description of Tisch trying to give Stringer most of the responsibility for the layoffs. The message was that Tisch approved the cuts but they were Stringer's idea. Indeed, Tisch cast himself as the voice of moderation who kept Stringer from going overboard.

"I never said to Howard, 'We have to cut the budget at the news division,'" Tisch told Boyer. "That's the truth. Howard called me a month ago and said, 'Larry, I've got some ideas on restructuring the news division. It'll take me about 30 days to put them together.' I said, 'Fine, Howard, I'll be happy to go over them with you.'" Tisch said he even removed the names of six correspondents from Stringer's hit list—including minorities. For Boyer's story, Stringer had no comment on the notion that he was the chief proponent of cost cuts.

Stringer was enraged, but not so much over Tisch's apparent effort to give him sole responsibility for the cuts. What angered him more was the failure of the entertainment division to deliver similar cuts simultaneously, which would have sent the message that the cuts were companywide. The day Boyer's story ran, Stringer headed to CBS headquarters from the broadcast center on West 57th Street to make it clear to Tisch just how distraught he was. He said he did not, as reports suggested at the time, threaten to quit.

The problem was clear. Stringer was doing his best to follow the general's marching orders. Tisch, the shareholders' champion, wanted to bring to a screeching halt the notion that CBS News was exempt from the rules of capitalism. The division couldn't continue to spend more than it made, expecting some other part of the company to make up the difference. In the end, Tisch would insist he wasn't trying to weasel his way out of taking the heat from the backlash to this approach; in his awkward way, he only wanted to send the message that Stringer was in charge and not just being a yes-man to the new boss.

Because of the carelessness of Tisch's remarks, Boyer's story failed to make that point at all. Instead, to CBS insiders, it appeared Tisch was taking liberties with the truth. The rumor mill at CBS had been working overtime to spread the word that Tisch was demanding substantial cost reductions at every level, and that he wanted managers in place who could deliver them. Wyman's fall from grace was related to Tisch's impatience with the way he handled layoffs. It was assumed that Stringer intended to give Tisch substantially what he wanted rather than try to get away with some token amount, which would only alienate Tisch.

"It is absolutely true that he believed he was doing me a favor by giving me responsibility for what he thought was a sound business decision and not sabotaging me publicly," Stringer said, "but the way it came out was that here we were in the middle of a raging storm of agony and despair in the news division and that I had gone it alone and wreaked havoc for my own personal benefit. So it did feel very lonely that morning."

In the end, after meeting first with Jankowski, the CBS Broadcast Group president, and then Tisch, Stringer felt misled by Jankowski, not Tisch. While Jankowski seemed evasive, "Larry was very straightforward about it, and we worked it out," said Stringer, whose sensitivity was perhaps heightened by the knowledge that his two most recent predecessors in that position—Van Gordon Sauter and Ed Joyce—had been in effect run out as a consequence of layoffs. "We were once on the front page of the *New York Times* with 24 layoffs," Stringer recalled. "The irony is that we were simply at the vanguard of corporate change across the spectrum. . . . but journalists writing about other journalists get very protective and that's sort of what happened."

On the Monday when Boyer's story appeared, while Stringer met with Jankowski, Mike Wallace and Don Hewitt, executive producer of "60 Minutes," the network's single most profitable program, met with Tisch. Wallace and Hewitt urged Tisch to clarify publicly who initiated the layoffs. By the time Stringer met with him, Tisch was ready to go public with the statement: "The cuts were instigated by me."

Moving quickly to limit the damage, Tisch put out the statement to bolster the idea that, although Stringer was acting decisively, he was hardly acting on his own. The statement stopped short of noting that Stringer's cuts didn't go as deep as Tisch initially suggested they should go. It pointed out that Stringer's cost-cutting strategy was devised as an alternative to letting it be done by Coopers & Lybrand, whose management consultants Tisch had hired five months earlier to help streamline the slash-and-burn process. Many of the Coopers suggestions already had been put in place, although the consultant often appeared merely to be implementing cuts in areas Tisch already had identified as top-heavy—including personnel and public relations.

CBS wasn't alone among the networks in this cost-cutting drive, but it suddenly was moving faster than the others. Tisch's impatience gave it a decidedly urgent, if not adversarial, tone—more so than at NBC, which from the outset sought consensus on cutbacks, and at

ABC, where Thomas S. Murphy, the chairman of the parent company, successfully employed a certain charisma to win cooperation.

Tisch's rushed approach had more to do with Wyman's failure to execute the deep cuts he had promised the board months earlier than with Tisch's own sense of urgency to do something. At the time, however, no one saw Tisch as simply trying to follow through on what Wyman was supposed to have done already. Instead, Tisch was viewed as the sole villain. Alienation spread from the victims to the managers who had failed to implement what essentially was Wyman's cost-cutting mandate. One month after taking over, Tisch had fired Derrough, president of CBS-owned television stations, and added his duties to those of Pilson, an executive vice president. Soon after, Derow, and his Publishing Group staff were given notice.

Tisch was determined to quickly rid CBS of anyone who was slow to recognize the company was bleeding and stanch the flow. Now, however, with a push from the page-one story in the *Times*, Tisch was getting full blame for what originally was Tom Wyman's tough, but never fully implemented decision. The layoffs touched off a firestorm of rage, and CBS insiders like Andy Rooney and Dan Rather eagerly fanned the flames in public. Broadcast center staffers had nicknamed Tisch "Short, Bald, and Greedy."

Rooney, the "60 Minutes" commentator and veteran CBS journalist who began his career there under the tutelage of the legendary Edward R. Murrow and had earned a reputation as a curmudgeon, was startlingly unrestrained in his criticism: "This guy Tisch put his money in this company, but I put my life into the company, and so did [CBS broadcast veteran] Ike Pappas, and so did a lot of other people. I own that company, Tisch does not own that company, that's the way I feel. It's Ike's company more than it is Tisch's company."[4]

Rooney exemplified, perhaps better than anyone ever had, what Tisch viewed as a sense of independence gone dangerously awry. At no other company would a chief executive feel compelled to tolerate the heresy that somehow everyone in that company ultimately wasn't working for the benefit of the owners as well as themselves. Rooney's outburst raised the specter of rebellion. It would prove to be one of the first stunning examples of disarray in the ranks at CBS in the wake of the *Times* layoff story.

The second blow came the same day Boyer's story ran, when the *New York Times* received journalistic manna from heaven on the controversy: a defiantly anti-Tisch opinion piece signed by Richard Cohen and Dan Rather, the "CBS Evening News" anchor and therefore the most visible of its celebrity newscasters. The piece, titled "From Murrow to Mediocrity," appeared the next day on the *Times* op-ed page. "CBS Inc. is not a chronically weak company fighting to survive," they wrote. "But 215 people lost their jobs so that the stockholders would have even more money in their pockets."[5]

The biggest of these stockholders, Larry Tisch, surely wouldn't disagree. If CBS were chronically weak, he probably wouldn't have become a shareholder. And if 215 people were toiling with no hope of adding to the bottom line, then it would be irresponsible to keep paying them. In Tisch's view, CBS no longer could afford to be a 24-hour news service covering the world with its own full-time reporters and camera crews. It was going to have to cut these costly luxuries and find less expensive ways to remain a competitive news organization. This, however, wasn't the message in the Cohen–Rather piece.

Boyer apparently got the message and adopted it as his own. In his book, prematurely titled *Who Killed CBS?*, he wrote: "CBS News, as conceived by [former CBS News president Richard] Salant and [former anchor Walter] Cronkite, was dead. It had been mortally wounded by the abandonment of values and the absence of corporate will to maintain a serious and independent worldwide news-gathering organization no matter what the cost, to repay the public for the use of the airwaves, even at a loss. What had replaced it was a corporate view that began with Wyman and Jankowski, was exacerbated by the economic storms that buffeted network television, and culminated in the arrival of Larry Tisch."[6]

A third blow came when Walter Cronkite, whom Dan Rather had succeeded in the news anchor position, threatened to quit his post as a CBS director because of the layoff decision. Tisch declined his request for an audience before the next day's monthly board meeting, but scheduled an hour of meeting time to allow Cronkite to vent his anger.

Adding to Tisch's sense of being under siege was Rather's appearance on a picket line with striking CBS writers, coupled with reports of Rather's apparently casual offer to take a pay cut if it would save some jobs. Meanwhile, TV writer Tom Shales of the *Washington Post* wrote that Tisch had ruined morale at CBS News.

Tisch scoffed at Rather's pay-cut offer; no such offer had been formally made. As for Andy Rooney's interpretation of who owned the company, Tisch called him "an old blowhard who makes $400,000 a year for two minutes a week."

"THE BIGGEST BUNCH OF LIARS"

Author Ken Auletta visited Tisch at his office on the day the *Washington Post* reported on the layoffs. The embattled executive was blunt. He fumed over published comments from CBS staffers in Washington who claimed he had lied to them about his intention to lay off no one. "I feel hurt because it's a lot of nonsense," Tisch told Auletta. "These are the biggest bunch of liars I've ever seen in my life." Said Tisch of one of those staffers, congressional correspondent Lem Tucker, whose name he said he had struck from Stringer's hit list: "He's a son of a bitch. . . . Wait till I tell him what I think of him." Tucker's transgression was telling Shales in the *Washington Post*: "What hurts the most is that he looked us all in the eye and obviously lied when he said this wasn't going to happen."

Tisch was outraged by the bashing he was suffering at the hands of his own people. They shouldn't have been so naive as to view his reassurances as solemn vows. A well-known trait of Tisch's management style was that he reserved the right to change his mind. He had reversed his decision about being CEO at CBS and had, many times in the past, become a seller rather than a buyer of a particular company's stock. In all his business dealings, Tisch wasn't in the habit of making promises; he merely let people know his present intentions, which were always subject to change as new information was received.

What irritated Tisch more than anything was the implication throughout the media that week that Larry Tisch was singlehandedly corrupting the network's otherwise pristine reputation. In fact, Tom Wyman and Gene Jankowski had done plenty of damage in their pre-Tisch days, with questionable personnel moves that altered the network's focus and with their own waves of demoralizing cutbacks. Under Wyman and Jankowski, Van Gordon Sauter sought to imbue CBS News with entertainment values, thus alienating the hard-core news staffers. Sauter had named Phyllis George, a former Miss America, to cohost "CBS Morning News," a move viewed as a vote for style over substance.

Tisch briefly considered launching an editorial counterattack in the *Times*, but Stringer advised him to keep a low profile, unless he was prepared to promise no more layoffs.

The next day, at CBS's monthly board meeting, Walter Cronkite, once dubbed the most trusted man in America, took Tisch up on his offer for some meeting time. For two hours, Cronkite lectured on the risks of running a lean network operation. "My God, you can go by any fire station in town and look in and see these guys playing checkers and say, 'God damn it, why do I have to pay 10 guys in there to sit playing checkers all day?'" Cronkite told the board. "But when the fire comes, you'll wish you had 30 in there."

He urged Tisch to establish a team of quality watchdogs—old-timers, some legendary, such as retired news producer Burton R. "Bud" Benjamin, Bill Leonard, Frank Stanton, and Richard Salant. It was a nice idea, Tisch said, but when Tisch said something, or someone, was "nice," it wasn't an expression of support. The corporate battlefields where Tisch had triumphed were littered with the bodies of "nice" men. Cronkite's proposal went nowhere.

It didn't take long for Tisch to publicly apologize for the way he had handled the CBS News layoffs. Three days after Boyer reported Tisch's explanation of the layoffs, Tisch was publicly admitting to having exhibited some "insensitivity." Privately, he was seething.

Why were the media focusing all this attention on a handful of layoffs at a multibillion-dollar company?

At an informal meeting at *The Wall Street Journal*, Tisch, accompanied by Stringer, questioned then-managing editor Norman Pearlstine's news judgment. Why did 215 layoffs at CBS warrant more extensive coverage in the *Journal* than 27,000 layoffs at General Motors? Pearlstine defended the *Journal* by saying that the layoffs amounted to 1 in 5 at CBS News, while 27,000 at GM was 1 in 32 (for the entire company). Besides, Pearlstine later proved, the GM layoffs got as much coverage as the CBS layoffs. Tisch conceded the point but still felt strongly that the coverage of CBS was far more critical than that of other companies, and Pearlstine knew there was some truth to that.

"It's a business with a very high profile," he said. "If you wrote about something strictly on the basis of the number of shareholders affected, all you'd write about would be utilities and the like. I always felt it was easier to get good play in the paper for a story on the auto industry than on the steel industry, because millions of people drive cars. So it's interesting to millions of people more than just the stockholders and suppliers and all the other constituents of the company. Similarly, millions of people watch CBS. The business is a national and indeed a global phenomenon. It's not just shareholders, it's all these other constituents."

CBS wasn't the only network cutting costs, but it seemed to get more media coverage than its rivals because of the apparent willingness of CBS insiders to publicly criticize their new boss.

In the end, Tisch knew he deserved some criticism on the way the layoffs were managed. "I should have done more of it by attrition," he would concede years later. "It was a fiasco, one of those things that just got out of control."

Within 10 days of the Boyer layoff story that had sparked all the rancor, Tisch had hired famed public relations consultant John Scanlon to go on the offensive in the damage-control effort. That move did little in the short run to improve his image. Ultimately, only one thing could vindicate Tisch: success. But success was still years away.

Tisch could not afford to let CBS air its internal squabbles publicly. No benefit would come from Tisch and CBS's angry employees sniping at each other on the pages of the *New York Times, The Wall Street Journal, Washington Post,* and news magazines. The sniping was all the more destructive to CBS's image because no such public bickering accompanied the similar cost-cutting moves being taken at ABC and NBC.

This was one public-relations disaster Larry Tisch couldn't handle himself. He resorted to hiring Scanlon and other professional spin doctors who were more common in the realm of politics. Tisch's problem was his flagging reputation among CBS's employees. They believed he was a liar and were willing to say so publicly.

He had said he wasn't interested in being named permanent CEO, yet he accepted the position gratefully. He had said he was "confident" about CBS's top managers, yet he ousted many of them anyway. He had said he wouldn't seek major cuts in CBS News, but he did. He had said the cuts were Stringer's idea, but failed to mention that he had initiated them. To counter the employees' attacks, Tisch argued that, in every case, he was telling what was true for the moment, but circumstances later changed. Much of his trouble, he asserted, resulted from being misquoted, misinterpreted, or quoted out of context.

It was hard to fault Tisch for having changed his mind. On Tisch's watch, from 1986 to 1988, the company's annual costs were trimmed by as much as $100 million. The payroll, excluding employees attached to divisions being sold off, had shrunk by about 2,000, to 20,000. Wall Street liked those kinds of numbers and had pushed CBS's stock price into the range of $160 a share from $115 a share.

"The most important thing to me is my integrity," Tisch told *The Wall Street Journal* in a carefully managed interview two weeks after the fiasco over Stringer's layoff announcement, "and everything I've said has been true [at the time]." He added, "I've lost a certain confidence in the press, I must say."

Now he was taking advice from the combative Scanlon, the public-relations pro who had helped New York City deal with its fiscal crisis in the 1970s. Scanlon had managed CBS's public relations counteroffensive when General William C. Westmoreland (Ret.) sued the network for allegedly libeling him in the 1982 documentary "The Un-counted Enemy: A Vietnam Deception." Westmoreland dropped the suit just days before it was to go to trial in February 1985, perhaps re-flecting how thoroughly successful Scanlon had been at getting the case tried in the court of public opinion. Scanlon's main admonition to Tisch: Don't talk off-the-cuff so much.

Tisch's effort to cast himself as a media victim did little to reverse the tide of internal distrust. CBS News staffers seemed to be looking for evidence they could use to prove the inadvisability of the deep staff cuts. When the competition beat CBS on a story during Pope John Paul II's visit to Chile less than a month after the news cutbacks, the scoop was blamed on the decision to cover the trip with just one reporter.

Increasingly, Jay Kriegel, the political strategist who had joined the Tisch team at CNA in 1975, was building a reputation as Tisch's "*consiglieri*," helping to manage simmering intramural hostilities and relentlessly aggressive media coverage. Indeed, the damage control ef-fort appeared to be bearing some fruit: the press became a little less noisy in its coverage. But the notion that Tisch was sure to deliver the final blow to CBS's Tiffany image—and that he was slippery—would die hard.

Two days after Tisch's defensive interview appeared in *The Wall Street Journal*, Tisch suffered yet another embarrassment. Peter Lund—one of the three men at CBS Tisch had mentioned as a poten-tial successor—quit as president of CBS's shrinking stations division to become president of Multimedia Inc.'s Multimedia Entertainment unit, which syndicated the Phil Donahue talk show. Although Lund denied that the move was related to the cutbacks, Tisch was criticized for losing someone whose leadership potential he clearly valued.

The loss proved to be temporary. Lund returned three years later as Stringer's number-two person, possibly re-entering the succession pic-ture. Lund's successor as president of the TV stations, Eric Ober, proved to be a key figure in the long-term succession scenario.

Tisch continued to face more unwanted publicity. On March 25, 1987, Larry and Bob Tisch were named, along with several other un-witting celebrities, as investors in a tax-shelter scheme involving bogus trading in government securities. Their involvement had been noted in the past, but the context this time was an ironclad federal indictment against the scheme's operator, Charles Agee Atkins. Generating $1.3 billion in fraudulent losses and interest expenses and $350 million in false tax deductions for about 100 investors, Atkins' tax fraud was one of the largest cases ever. Atkins was convicted later that year.

Andy Rooney, the "60 Minutes" commentator, had boldly asserted Tisch's stock ownership of CBS would never confer on him the kind of ownership that comes from dedicating one's own time and talent. Now Rooney was refusing to work because of a writers' guild strike. His pay was suspended as a result. The *New York Times* cited a letter Rooney had written to Tisch saying that CBS News "has been turned into primarily a business enterprise and the moral enterprise has been lost."

Tisch had no shortage of vocal in-house critics. In the fall of 1987, *Broadcasting* magazine quoted Los Angeles bureau chief Jennifer Siebens on the state of morale at CBS. Her candor was unrestrained: "The only thing I think can turn [the low morale] around is some believable signal from Tisch he really is not interested in dismantling the organization. My desire would be to have him state what his vision of a network news division is. . . . he seems to be caught between a purported desire for excellence and a proven desire to make money."

Her published comments got Tisch's attention. Perhaps at Scanlon's suggestion, he called Siebens and challenged her to show where he ever said CBS News had to make money. His agenda wasn't for the division to make money but to stop wasting it.

Nor was his agenda to punish Siebens or anyone else for openly criticizing him. He was casting about for ways to silence the public dissension, but this was television—the window tens of millions of people every day stared at for hours in their own homes for glimpses of the world's heros and villains, real and imagined. Stories about the medium could be just as titillating in *The Wall Street Journal* as they were in the *National Enquirer*. To stop the flow of undermining commentary, Tisch would have to overcome what had become almost a hallmark of CBS's culture: a staff eager to debate with its leadership in the press. And he faced a celebrity journalist—Dan Rather—who seemed compelled at times to go beyond merely reporting events and become news himself.

A STRING OF SETBACKS

Bad publicity and angry insiders weren't all Tisch had to worry about. CBS's business was in turmoil, and every move Tisch made to achieve stability seemed doomed to create even more chaos, at least in the short run. Inside and outside critics joined in a chorus of dire predictions.

Paley was starting to view Tisch as simply another Wyman who was trying to solve profitability problems with numerical solutions that didn't apply to the broadcasting business. Paley's nagging suspicion was that Tisch was not a builder but an opportunist: Someone who sought bargains to be traded for a profit, not hidden potential to be nurtured. Paley believed the key to profitability in broadcasting wasn't so much in controlling costs but in successful programming: bank-rolling blockbuster TV shows and scheduling around them to keep audiences locked in.

Tisch was only beginning to get a handle on the programming side of the business. His goal was to first stop the waste, then figure out how to invest the savings to the network's best advantage.

The numbers themselves seemed to validate Paley's assessment that Tisch hadn't gotten it right. For the second year in a row, NBC won the prime-time season ratings and CBS turned in its worst showing ever. Worse, for the first time in 20 years, CBS News wasn't the top-rated newscast—more evidence, it would be argued, of damage incurred under Tisch. Finally, it was becoming increasingly clear that the three major networks were fighting over pieces of a shrinking pie. Faced with competition from cable as well as from independent TV stations and videocassettes, their combined share of the 1986–1987 prime-time audience dropped to 75.7 percent from 77 percent the previous season, and their share at the end of the season had slumped to 72 percent.

The networks were like the U.S. auto makers at the time: The Japanese were nibbling away at their market share, no matter how hard they tried to stop the slide. In both industries, TV and autos, the question was: Where will it end?

Tisch knew that any solution predicated on the concept of simply spending more money was a recipe for ever-widening losses. He would not allow Paley to advance any programming strategy that amounted to a large bet. Tisch wanted to try programming strategies that wouldn't be so expensive if they failed—opting, for example, to cut back on miniseries and movies of the week and buy more regular series, which were less expensive.

In his continuing education on the fundamentals of the entertainment side of the programming business, Tisch was quickly learning that raw talent was the essential element. CBS had only one major hit program, "Murder, She Wrote." Brandon Tartikoff at NBC had spawned numerous hits: "The Cosby Show," "Family Ties" with Michael J. Fox, "Miami Vice" with Don Johnson, "Golden Girls" with Bea Arthur, "ALF," "Cheers," "L.A. Law," "St. Elsewhere," "Hill Street Blues," and "The A-Team." Many of Tartikoff's hits were products of his own ideas, born of a genuine love of the medium. He was perhaps one of television's most avid viewers.

The success of a good idea depended on the creative talents of writers, directors, producers, and actors. Certain teams did it consistently better than the rest. Tartikoff's strategy was to lock up the best teams with long-term commitments. In the past, the common approach had been scatter shot, contracting for dozens of pilots, hoping to hit on a handful of winners. The new way carried its own risks. It provided exclusive access to the proven winners, but past performance didn't guarantee future success. Audiences can be fickle. Creative people can hit dry spells.

The business concept was ultimately not unlike what Tisch had experienced in the equity markets. A profitable company can become a dog in the stock market for reasons unrelated to the company's performance: shifting investor moods, or changes in asset allocation trends. In the long term, however, investors recognize and gravitate to the true winners. Television audiences are the same. It took a long time for the ratings to validate many of Tartikoff's best bets. Tartikoff's success only deepened Tisch's gloom about Bud Grant's lack of high-ratings products.

Two months after the layoff fiasco, in May 1987, Tisch chaired his first CBS annual meeting. It was a circus, a veritable convention of corporate gadflies, with the legendary Evelyn Y. Davis, initiator of countless stockholders' resolutions at several major companies, leading the pack.

Davis wanted to know whether Larry's nephew Jonathan's engagement to Laura Steinberg, daughter of investor Saul Steinberg, was arranged to keep Steinberg from thinking about launching a bid for CBS.

Another perennial annual-meeting denizen, John Gilbert, piped up: "I think the daughter will learn a lot from this marriage."

Not to be upstaged, Davis pressed on, but Tisch had had it. "There is a limit to what this meeting can handle as far as nonsense," he said. "I think this is enough."

"When I say it's enough, it's enough!" Davis snapped.

(Soon after, Larry and Bob Tisch donated $10 million for new gallery space at the Metropolitan Museum of Art. There, Jonathan Tisch and Laura Steinberg celebrated their marriage with a multi-million-dollar reception in which the Steinbergs' appetite for lavishness clearly triumphed over the Tisches' instinct for fiscal restraint.)

Even with Davis's bizarre anti-takeover theory for the marriage, the 1987 annual meeting would seem tame compared with the events of the following year's meeting (described later in this chapter).

Tisch faced a steady stream of criticism, both publicly and in the board room. The board, in a split decision, approved his proposal to sell CBS's 21 consumer magazines, including for $650 million to Diamandis Communications, formed by Peter Diamandis, head of the CBS magazine group. A mounting concern was that Tisch was liquidating assets without any idea what to do with the money. The sale brought CBS's cash on hand to $1.6 billion. Why was Tisch so intent on amassing so much capital? Why rush to sell assets?

Indeed, Diamandis, bankrolled by Prudential Insurance Co. of America for 70 percent, would resell the assets—including *Woman's Day* and *Car & Driver*—for $947 billion in less than a year. Most of it went to Hachette S.A., the big French publisher, which had bid $570 million for the division before Diamandis staged his management buy-out. Diamandis and his Prudential partners would book a $300 million profit in record time.

Diamandis, admittedly another of Tisch's satisfied customers, understood Tisch wasn't to be faulted for failing to make the sale himself at $1 billion. "He got the highest multiples in the history of the magazine business," he noted.

It's unlikely that Tisch spent much time feeling defensive about this deal. It was consistent with his discipline of selling for the right price as opposed to holding out for the highest possible price. Diamandis was lucky in his timing: his window of opportunity to make that kind of a killing didn't stay open long. Soon after Hachette bought its $712 million chunk, the magazine advertising market sank into a deep, painful slump.

Some directors failed to see any strategy in Tisch's decisions, but he was doing what the Tisches had always done: he was strengthening CBS's finances so the company could survive in any kind of weather, and he was building a war chest that could be cracked open when assets that made sense for CBS could be had for bargain prices. In the meantime, the cash was invested for a safe, respectable yield. Tisch knew that, ultimately, as in any other business, CBS's appeal to the smartest investors would be an asset valuation that exceeded the company's stock-market value.

Converting into cash what was left of CBS's publishing business made it easier for Wall Street to quantify the value of the company's assets.

To turn around the News division, CBS sought ways to get Dan Rather and his newscast out of third place. Stringer wanted Rather to project a gentler image. Tisch was lobbying to give Diane Sawyer more newscast exposure. Air time, however, was an anchor's lifeblood. Even the relaxed, grandfatherly Cronkite was acutely sensitive to any reductions in the precise number of seconds he was on camera and talking. Anything that meant reducing Rather's exposure would surely face strong opposition.

One hope was that a change in the way A. C. Nielsen gauged viewership would favor Rather. Neilsen had introduced the people-meter, which required viewers to push buttons instead of writing in a diary what they watched and when.

Rather's apparent concern about his ratings backfired on the network on September 11, a Friday. The start of the newscast—originating from Miami to cover a visit by Pope John Paul II—was delayed three minutes by the completion of a U.S. Open semifinal tennis match between Steffi Graf and Lori McNeil that went overtime. Rather, anxious about the impact of the just-expanded people-meter rating system, left the studio. For more than six minutes, the network went black while he stood on a balcony overlooking Miami. "It was the single most embarrassing moment at CBS," said Marty Koughan, a former CBS News producer.

CBS tried to portray the incident as an accident, suggesting that Rather didn't know he was causing a blackout.

Phil Jones, chairman of CBS's affiliate board and chairman of KCTV in Kansas City, Missouri, demanded that Rather apologize. Two days after the incident, Rather called Tisch, apparently to explain himself. Tisch later indicated he understood Rather's anger, adding, "The only thing I can say to you is that this is something that's never going to happen again."

Perhaps it didn't happen again, but it came back to haunt the network four months later in an episode that would cause almost as much embarrassment. Rather earned an uncomplimentary *Time* magazine cover story, and inadvertently helped Vice President George Bush erase the wimp image then plaguing his first presidential bid.

In a live interview on January 25, 1988, Rather was attempting to put the vice president on the spot about his role in the Iran–Contra arms-for-hostages deal. Bush, following a carefully planned strategy, went on the offensive to brush aside the issue, to which the network had devoted half the broadcast.

"It's not fair to judge my whole career by a rehash of Iran," Bush snapped at Rather. "How would you like it if I judged your career by those seven minutes when you walked off the set?"

Incredibly, Bush was the one who looked like the winner. He evaded the questions and said, in effect, that even if he did somehow err in the Iran–Contra deal, he shouldn't be judged by that alone. "What everybody missed at the time was that Rather was right on Bush's knowledge of the Iran–Contra deal," said Tisch.

More than anything, what made Bush look good was Rather's increasingly shrill demeanor. "You made us hypocrites in the eyes of the world," he told Bush. With such accusatory comments, Rather abandoned all pretense to objectivity. His conduct of the interview was viewed widely as a black eye for journalism as well as for CBS, despite the legitimacy of the report. The newscast, which had recovered some ratings ground in the wake of the people-meter, slipped back to second place. *Time*'s cover headline was "The Ambush That Failed." The confrontation went a long way toward strengthening Bush's image and perhaps even helped keep the arms-for-hostage controversy from derailing his ultimately successful campaign.

Time said it all by not focusing attention on CBS's careful examination of Bush's involvement in the controversy. Instead, it zeroed in on the confrontation as the latest in a series of strange incidents involving the anchorman, including the six-minute blackout.

What was Rather really saying in these network embarrassments? "CBS News is not just another division of another corporation," he had stated. Perhaps he was rebelling against those who, despite their public protestations to the contrary, seemed by their actions to want to treat it that way—Larry Tisch, for instance. In Rather's view, CBS News was first and foremost a public service, not a business. Yet, more and more under Tisch, it was being run like a business, with purchases and salaries being eliminated because they failed to contribute to the bottom line.

On September 9, 1987, two days before Dan Rather's six-minute network blackout, Tisch told CBS's board that Sony was willing to pay $2 billion for CBS Records. Tisch had been interested in selling

CBS Records since October 1986, when he had first been contacted by Triangle Industries and since Walter Yetnikoff had sought out Sony as a buyer. Having $2 billion in cash appealed to Tisch a lot more than having a record company that appeared to have reached its peak in earnings potential. Its talent pipeline, including the likes of Michael Jackson, Bruce Springsteen, and Barbra Streisand, was mature. Little had been accomplished in recent years to rejuvenate it with budding talent.

Being rid of the eccentric Yetnikoff also appealed to Tisch, and freedom from Tisch and CBS's financial bureaucracy appealed to Yetnikoff. But at the September 1987 board meeting, Paley and other directors balked. Tisch controlled the stock, but he still didn't control the board or the employees. He lacked his brother's unique ability to nurture a family feeling among nonfamily employees—to use his charm to rally support and build loyalty. Most often, Larry Tisch had succeeded by virtue of sheer intellectual brawn combined with cash-power. When he failed to persuade by these means, he resorted to intimidation by combative anger.

In this regard, Yetnikoff may have had more in common with Tisch than appeared on the surface. The two clashed fiercely as they sought to separate their destinies. Despite the board's hesitation, the time was right. The records division was on its way to posting its most profitable year ever, earning $75 million on sales of $525 million. But much of that volume was coming from sales of hot releases from Springsteen, who wouldn't stay hot forever. Under Sony management, Yetnikoff figured he would be free to spend the money needed to get executives who could replenish the talent pipeline. Of CBS, Yetnikoff once said, "One guy [Larry Tisch] was too cheap to spend any money and his predecessor [Tom Wyman] was too stupid to know how to spend money."[7]

Paley, agonizing over his rapidly shrinking empire, made one last bid to reassert some authority, at least in programming: In October 1987, Bud Grant was sent packing as entertainment head. His deputy, Earl H. "Kim" LeMasters III, wanted the job, but Paley wanted Steven Bochco, producer of the hits "Hill Street Blues" and "L.A. Law."

Tisch, his wife Billie, and son Tom met with Bochco for dinner. Bochco appeared inclined to take the job.

Nevertheless, Bochco turned it down, apparently not wanting to give up his freedom or the right to collect lucrative syndication payments from shows he produced. Instead, he signed an agreement to provide 10 new series for ABC, which, like CBS, was scrambling to line up top talent as a ladder out of a ratings hole. Tisch's failure to sign Bochco, even for series development, served only to remind Paley how little influence he had anymore.

Events were conspiring to guarantee that CBS Records would be traded away for a pile of cash. In addition to Sony, two other potential buyers were pursuing the division. Triangle Industries, source of the inquiry a year earlier that had inspired Yetnikoff to talk to Sony, was still interested. The other seeker was SBK Entertainment World Inc., which had bought CBS's music publishing division.

While the board hemmed and hawed over what to do with this highly cyclical but currently profitable business that had no connection to the network business, the stock market did what Larry Tisch had been expecting it to do for years: it crashed with a mighty roar. During the summer, the Dow industrials had surged to 2700 in a sharp, ever-steepening run-up. The prices of stocks were so high that the dividends they paid became a relatively puny reward for holding them. The yield on the U.S. Government's 30-year bonds was higher, and carried none of the risk of owning stocks.

Just before Labor Day, Alan Greenspan, a close friend of Larry Tisch, and the recently appointed Federal Reserve chairman, decided to exercise his authority to push interest rates higher. His aim was to combat inflation. Higher interest rates would rein in a rapidly expanding economy by making it more expensive, and therefore less desirable, for companies to borrow money to keep expanding. For stock investors, it was time to get out, time to lock in profits by selling overpriced stocks and reinvesting the cash in safe, steady, high-yielding bonds.

It took about a month and a half for the handful of investors quietly leaving the market to grow into a dangerous, frightened herd trampling one another in a stampede to get out all at once through a tiny opening. That tiny opening was October 19, 1987. In a single day, the industrials plunged 508 points, or 23 percent, just one trading day after losing 108 points. The volume of trading was so heavy, the New York Stock Exchange's reporting system couldn't keep up and nearly failed.

The immediate impact was to bring to a screeching halt the leveraged buyout craze that had helped drive stock prices to record highs in the mid-1980s. Deals that were in the works at the time of the crash were put on hold or canceled. Individual investors as well as institutional investors such as pension plans became extremely cautious, having just incurred huge paper losses. All the pessimism engendered by these losses raised the specter of recession. On the day after, the big question was: Is 1929 happening all over again? Was the new Great Depression about to follow?

Tisch had asked a similar question about stocks—and answered it with eerie precision—a little over a year earlier: "The question on the table is whether it is 1926, 1927, 1928, or 1929. At the rate we're going, at the pace leveraging is accelerating, I would say it's certainly 1928."[8]

Tisch had called it, but only in terms of what happened in stocks, and this time only for a short period. Stock prices bounced back quickly, recovering to precrash levels within 17 months. No depression followed; in fact, it took three years for a recession to happen. By that time, the stock market had run up to 3000.

Immediately after the crash, however, the future still looked frighteningly uncertain, and Tisch turned this fear to his advantage in arguing for approval to sell CBS Records. On the eve of what could be a punishing economy, $2 billion in cash was downright alluring. Whether Tisch believed the crash was prelude to a full-blown depression probably wasn't a major factor in his desire to raise cash at CBS. In fact, immediately after the crash, he loaded up on stocks that had been pounded down to bargain prices, betting correctly against the depression scenario.

Tisch's fundamental goal in wanting to sell CBS Records had less to do with macroeconomic theories than with practical investment common sense. His strategy was the same as it had been in all his other successful businesses: Maintain high liquidity, as long as doing so promised to generate a return that was as good as or better than having the money tied up in some other, probably riskier asset (like a record company). He had the same attitude about debt. It wasn't worth carrying debt, unless the money owed was invested in a way that stood an excellent chance of generating a better-than-average return, net of the debt's carrying cost.

While Tisch was busy betting on a rebound after the crash, the market's apparent fragility was a factor in the CBS board's decision, on November 18, to take Sony's $2 billion offer. With that sale, Tisch had succeeded in doing largely what everyone feared Ted Turner would have done, had he gained control. He had stripped CBS of everything that wasn't broadcasting. Had CBS gained anything, after all, by turning to Tisch to escape the Atlanta entrepreneur?

"When you're running a business, you've got to run a business," Tisch said. "You have to make sure that you can survive, whether business gets a little better or a little worse. Maybe Turner would have done the same things. I don't know. But all three networks have done the same things. We were first was our only problem."

Having Tisch manage the asset sales surely was preferable. Turner—who spent $18 million on advisers in a noisy, futile effort to gain control—would have needed all those sale proceeds to retire debt. Tisch had amassed more than $3 billion of cash at CBS. Within a year of taking over, Tisch had made CBS nearly failure-proof, at least in the short term. It could afford to trail in the ratings for a long time while it worked out a long-term strategy to regain and hold the lead.

That, however, wasn't the prevailing view. In its November 23, 1987, issue, *New York* magazine painted an unflattering portrait of Tisch in his dealings with Bill Paley. It portrayed Paley, the godfather of quality television, as frustrated with Tisch's lack of programming skill, and Tisch as having no use for the 86-year-old Paley. In Tisch's view, the magazine asserted, Paley was "useless baggage," an annoying obstacle with nothing to contribute. Such characterizations weren't likely to win Tisch any friends among CBS's employees, many of whom held Paley in awe for his industry-defining instincts and had viewed his return as chairman with relief.

Tisch denied ever referring to Paley in such unflattering terms: "I never said Paley was 'useless baggage.' What I said was, wasn't it sad how no one seemed to care about him anymore?"

The sale of CBS Records was portrayed as just another insult hurled in Paley's face, the way some reports had it. Soon after the sale was approved, Yetnikoff described a tearful Paley, in his wheelchair, reminiscing about the struggling record company he bought in 1938 for $700,000 and built into an innovator, a cultural institution, and the industry leader. Now Tisch had traded it away to the Japanese for cold, impersonal cash—and perhaps not enough of it. Within months of the deal, it would become apparent that CBS Records was on its way to another year of stellar earnings, leading some industry analysts to suggest CBS could have gotten $3 billion, possibly even $4 billion. Perhaps, but as Tisch said, "That was Walter's deal."[9]

Said Tisch of Yetnikoff: "When he was here, he was a sick man. He was on drugs, he was on alcohol. I made one big mistake. I must admit one mistake. I should have fired Yetnikoff the first day. I take blame for that. . . . Yetnikoff and his ilk was what I sold when we sold CBS Records. As for the price, we did a lot of due diligence. Morgan Stanley a year earlier priced it at $750 million. We sold it for $2.5 billion to $3 billion."

WEATHERING THE STORM

All the unfriendly attention Tisch was attracting failed, however, to distract him from the process of rebuilding CBS. LeMasters may have prevailed in his bid to succeed his boss as Entertainment president, but only because other, more sought-after candidates eluded Tisch. Bochco wasn't the only outsider considered for the job. One of the alternatives was Jeffrey Sagansky, the president of Tri-Star Pictures, who had been Brandon Tartikoff's deputy at NBC in 1983–1985, when Tartikoff was doing for NBC what CBS needed in 1987: building the foundation of a first-place network. Tisch recognized the importance of being number one.

It was becoming increasingly clear, as cable and VCRs continued to erode the network audience, that the television business now had room for only one of the three traditional broadcast networks to be profitable. Being second or third was rapidly becoming financially untenable. It was also clear that, for Tisch, CBS was no temporary assignment. Citing his declining involvement at the company he had helped found, the Loews board, at Tisch's request, had cut his annual salary to $200,000 from $750,000—coincidentally, the salary he was now earning at CBS.

As part of his effort to consolidate power at CBS, Tisch sought to have his brother, Bob—essentially co-owner of his CBS stake—named a director, as well as lawyer Arthur Liman, the linchpin in forging the Tisch–Paley alliance. The board rejected both candidates. They could not, however, prevent Larry Tisch from granting Jay Kriegel a permanent role. Kriegel had been operating under a consulting contract. On December 13, he was named senior vice president in charge of external relations, government affairs, and special projects, formalizing what he already had been doing. "He's very effective," a CBS source said at the time. "Larry trusts him completely."[10]

The bond between Kriegel and Tisch was powerful, and with Tisch's media notices almost uniformly negative, it made sense to institutionalize Kriegel's role as a handler. Kriegel knew Tisch well. He knew that, in print, his strengths frequently came off sounding like weaknesses. Tisch was quick to say what was on his mind. He took some care in his choice of words, but he was uninhibited and, at times, impatient in his attempts to help the press get it right.

Tisch's strength was in managing financial situations; Kriegel's was in managing the media. It was a natural combination. Tisch, who once was confident of his ability to handle the press, needed an agent in the high-profile world of network television.

The sale of CBS Records, for example, hurt Tisch on Main Street but extended his heroic reputation on Wall Street. Standard & Poor's Corp. upgraded its rating on CBS debt because of the sale. Meanwhile,

Loews Corp. and CBS would notch huge profits from 1987—$696.2 million and $452.5 million, respectively—although, in the case of CBS, much of that reflected asset sales and interest income from its cash holdings. It wasn't hard to find analysts willing to say it troubled them to see CBS, stripped of prior money-makers, depending on an investment portfolio to prop up profit, having narrowed the focus to a broadcast business that was struggling to keep itself out of the ratings basement. As long as Tisch's people were running it, CBS was in good hands financially. Despite its current weakness, it was on solid footing to stage a long-term turnaround strategy.

Kriegel's work, however, was cut out for him. On the face of it, Tisch was easy to second-guess. Everything he had done was open to public criticism. A multitude of questions begged for answers that only time would provide: Had he sold CBS assets too cheaply? Had he crippled the broadcast business's ability to compete? Was he turning CBS into a money manager? Did he have any idea where he was taking CBS? For the time being, all of Tisch's successes with CBS were related to the cost-cutting, debt-trimming, cash-raising process. It was hard to convince the world that these moves would make for a better future and not just a cheaper, perhaps higher-yielding one.

The "vision thing" was where Tisch took his biggest thrashing. Companies like Warner Communications Inc. were moving toward logical integrations of entertainment media—capturing the profits from a book that gets made into a movie and yields a soundtrack album, a line of licensed products from a movie like *Batman*, or a TV series. Such vertical integration captures a larger share of the profit by using each derivative opportunity from a single creative effort. CBS was doing the opposite. Instead of looking for ways to do integration better, it was abandoning the concept all together.

As if to cast further doubt on Tisch's vision, Sony, after taking possession of CBS Records in January 1988, announced plans to enter the motion-picture business. Perhaps, over time, Sony would end up being the fully integrated communications giant CBS could have been. It was a test of Tisch's willingness to stick with a plan that made sense to him—again, regardless of what was in fashion. The business press seemed inclined to portray Tisch's moves as lunacy—a love of cash taken to dangerous extremes—but it wasn't hard to see the virtue of fortifying and rebuilding the core business, then focusing the cash hoard on ideas for expansion.

Tisch was learning rapidly that building the core business depended heavily on gaining access to creative talent. ABC was about to overtake CBS in second place with such creative hits as "Moonlighting," "The Wonder Years," "China Beach," and "thirtysomething"—all programs that appealed to the most coveted prize in the ratings war, the baby-boomer/yuppie generation. CBS's audience was dominated by the boomers' tightwad parents, a prudent and therefore less desirable generation for many advertisers. The younger generation was more actively consuming, more willing to spend money—and use credit—for self-gratification.

Tisch's reputation was not that of a builder. Many of his own directors shared the popular view held by affiliates: he had no plan to take CBS back to first place. At the January 1988 board meeting, Tisch resisted any suggestions that CBS's $3 billion in cash be applied to such acquisitions as TV stations or cable properties. Instead, he suggested ways CBS could boost its return on the money through aggressive Wall Street investment strategies, something the board decided he shouldn't do without its full approval.

THE SONY LAWSUIT—AND CBS'S COUNTERSUIT

Meanwhile, it was becoming apparent to both sides that the $2 billion Sony paid for CBS Records was a bargain indeed. CBS sought to collect an additional $100 million under an arbitration agreement that allowed for such an adjustment as part of the sale agreement. A little over a week later, in early March 1988, top CBS Records executives sued CBS and Tisch for "maliciously and fraudulently" shortchanging them to the tune of $1.5 million. It was the opening round in yet another assault on Tisch in what Howard Stringer would later refer to as "the primal scream theory of public relations."

The spat came to a head at the May 1988 annual meeting, held in an auditorium at the Museum of Modern Art. The usual chorus of gadflies turned out to grill Larry Tisch on why CBS television, for the first time ever, managed to finish an entire season—the 1987–1988 prime-time season—in third place and lose 15 percent of its audience. In the course of the meeting, CBS disclosed its countersuit against Seymour Gartenberg and other CBS Records executives. The way CBS's general counsel, George Vradenburg III, characterized the suit rankled Gartenburg enough to say so. Yetnikoff, also named in the suit and present at the meeting, responded by leaving the meeting, motioning for reporters to follow. He was primed to feed them a giant-size helping of juicy anti-Tisch quotes.

"Larry Tisch thinks that everyone is a bellhop at the Regency Hotel," he told them. "He thinks he can push you around and say, 'My lawyers'll sue, my lawyers'll sue ya, my lawyers'll sue ya'." Yetnikoff went on to describe a clash between the two men that was meant to show Tisch attempting to intimidate him and failing.

As Yetnikoff told it to the reporters outside the meeting, the lawsuits resulted from Yetnikoff's stipulation that top CBS Records executives receive $1.5 million in bonuses in the sale to Sony. Yetnikoff claimed to have threatened to derail the deal unless the bonuses were paid. Tisch asked to meet with Yetnikoff in Tisch's office to discuss this sticking point. As Yetnikoff told it to reporters, "He says, 'You're a fucking prick, and I'm gonna tell the whole world you're a fucking prick.' And I started to laugh at him. And I said, 'Why bother, Larry? The whole world knows this. And I'm going to tell the whole world that you are a cheap fucking prick. But why should I bother, Larry? The whole world knows this! Right?'"

Soon, according to Yetnikoff's account, Tisch was shouting at him. Yetnikoff said he shouted back: "'Listen, you! Your yelling at me doesn't mean shit!' I'm generally a classy, cultured guy, but calling me a prick? The head of CBS? So I said, 'Your yelling at me doesn't mean shit, but I have to warn you: If I lose my temper, I could get physical!' I slam my fist, boom, on the table. And he says, 'Let's go to the next point.'"

Tisch accused Yetnikoff of greatly exaggerating the level of volume and profanity in this confrontation—a colorful but inaccurate account.

Still, Tisch's dealings with Yetnikoff illustrated a recurring theme in Tisch's business life: when the person on the other side of the bargaining table isn't playing by the rules, Tisch is vulnerable. He tends not to anticipate the possibility of deception—as in the case of Equity Funding and Franklin National—or of irrationality. Yetnikoff may have hurt Tisch's image temporarily with reporters, but the episode did nothing to enhance Yetnikoff's image either, except to show him as standing up to Tisch.

Nevertheless, Tisch had pushed Yetnikoff to come up with the $2 billion Sony offer, topping Morgan Stanley's initial $750 million estimate of what CBS Records was worth. Tisch had insisted shareholders not be deprived of even a seemingly insignificant $1.5 million, when he thought giving it to the executives was a waste of money. Yetnikoff scored this a victory: he had siphoned off the media from the annual meeting to focus on his Tisch-bashing sideshow.

THE CRITICISM MOUNTS

More bad press for Tisch quickly followed. He was raked over the coals for agreeing, in May 1987, to pay $243 million for the right to broadcast the 1992 Winter Olympics from Albertville, France, outbidding NBC by a whopping $68 million. The media skeptics assumed it would prove to be a money-loser. Tisch, however, was betting—correctly, as it turned out—that, at worst, the weeklong event would capture larger-than-normal audiences willing to sit still for endless CBS self-advertising.

About the same time, with Tisch's blessing, CBS agreed to renew "48 Hours" and "West 57th Street," two CBS News prime-time productions that had won critical praise but were poorly rated. The decision suggested that Tisch understood the value of giving quality programming a chance to build an audience. Like the Olympics deal, it showed he was thinking farther ahead than the next fiscal quarter.

For now, however, he had to endure considerable skepticism. Nowhere was this more evident than at the network's closed-door affiliates' meeting in Los Angeles in June 1987. Tisch had decided to reorganize the CBS Television Network division to help rebuild confidence in CBS. The reorganization carved the division into a marketing unit and an affiliate relations unit. Anthony Malara, who a year earlier had been reassigned to senior vice president, distribution, from president of the old network division, was named president of affiliate relations. Malara had been well-respected by the affiliates, but his rehabilitation to a higher-profile position was too little too late to calm the network's station managers.

Duane Harm, then president of KWTV, Oklahoma City, minced no words. Harm stood up at the affiliates' meeting and suggested that Tisch quit as president and CEO, that Paley be replaced as chairman, and that a real broadcast pro manage the company day-to-day. In the past three years, Harm noted, CBS had dropped to third place and Tisch appeared to be calling all the shots. If that was the case, Harm said, then it obviously was time for new leadership. The audience, about 1,000 strong, representing the network's 206 affiliates, applauded.

Problems with ratings, problems with Dan Rather, problems with having no apparent blueprint for the future—all were on the affiliates' lists of complaints.

"I heard your concerns and disappointments loud and clear," Tisch responded later. "I share your dissatisfactions." Once again, Tisch wasn't allowing ego to cloud his judgment. He was straightforward with the affiliates. He was willing to fine-tune the network division in a tacit admission that he had mishandled Malara and was willing to rectify the situation. Tisch reassured the station managers that, although CBS's profitability was strong, he recognized it was on the strength of its investment portfolio. The paramount goal remained, as ever, to regain the lead at all costs, he told them.

Was Tisch dissatisfied with his own performance? Not likely. The problem wasn't with Tisch; the problem was with the so-called broadcasting experts. What, for example, was Gene Jankowski doing? What was his turnaround strategy? He seemed to be doing his best to satisfy

Tisch's appetite for cutting costs, but without complementing it with is own vision of the future.

Before the end of June, a search was launched to find a successor for Jankowski, the last division manager left from the Wyman years. The choices were Leahy, Neal Pilson, and Howard Stringer. (Peter Lund, by then, was gone.) No outsiders apparently were given serious consideration. Leahy was as much a part of the previous administration as Jankowski; Pilson was seen as lacking the political skills deemed necessary for such a job. Stringer, a superb politician without seeming to be political, emerged as the front runner. He had a relaxed, low-key demeanor combined with a proven ability to face up to harsh realities and execute a business plan.

When Tisch told Jankowski he wanted to name him broadcast group chairman so Stringer could succeed him as president, Jankowski said he was ready to retire. He wanted to start his own business. Instead, he took the title change, a position from which he shopped for TV stations. A year later, he left to launch Jankowski Communications Inc., which invested in local TV stations. In the end, despite his efforts to adapt to the Tisch regime, Jankowski was hopelessly steeped in the traditions of Frank Stanton and Bill Paley.

For Stanton, Jankowski said, "employees would walk through a wall." Their loyalty was won in part by the prestigious image and style Stanton and Paley had worked so hard to construct. "It had a look that was applied to everything from the stationery to the look of the building," he said. "It costs money to do these things, but it enriches the environment." For Jankowski, it was punishing to watch the transition to a management that failed to see the payback for such enrichment.

With Stringer's elevation to broadcast president from news division president, David W. Burke was recruited from ABC to succeed him. At ABC, Burke had been Roone Arledge's number-two news executive. Arledge ultimately used this latest CBS talent raid to justify his renewed pursuit of Diane Sawyer. This time, Arledge succeeded.

As Tisch seemed to be consolidating control and installing his own management picks, the criticism continued. Business publications had little trouble, in this environment, getting insiders to do their own "primal scream." A few months after *New York* magazine ran its "The Tisching of CBS" piece, *Business Week* scared up a few anonymous votes of no confidence from CBS directors. Said one outside director: "We've got an accountant running a creative company."

The accountant, however, was smart enough to keep hunting for the talent he needed to complete what was emerging as Larry Tisch's plan to put CBS back on top. Eventually, he would succeed.

13

Setting the Stage for a Comeback

"Everybody in this building would like to have 20 diversions, all meaningless, so we could say we have a strategy."

—Larry Tisch, June 1990

Larry Tisch was not a complicated man. Neither were his strategies. Even as the business press, CBS employees and affiliates, and even some Wall Street analysts and CBS directors pointed to the network's status in 1988 as proof that Tisch had failed, a fundamental, long-range strategy to rejuvenate CBS already was in place.

The critics suggested that sitting on so much cash ($3.25 billion by July 1988) was a travesty. Was CBS a company or an investment portfolio? they asked. Tisch's answer: "I'm very happy to let it sit. It earns money every day." And while it earned, it stood ready at a moment's notice to be put to work in any other way that made more sense. It also gave Tisch plenty of time to construct the management team that would rebuild CBS. It had always been Tisch's style to support strong, innovative leaders and give them the time and freedom to make their solutions work. Tisch was never the type of executive who had to have his hands in everything. As long as that cash grew, CBS was under no pressure to take rash steps.

219

It annoyed Tisch that no one seemed to grasp the simple logic of what he was doing. His failure wasn't in his plan; it was in his effort to convince anyone that he had a plan.

The press seemed incapable of seeing any depth in Tisch's thinking. He was portrayed as being obsessed with cutting costs and amassing cash, blind to any of the long-term business implications. Rumors persisted that he was shopping around his stake, no matter how many times he denied them. As with practically everything he ever said about his future intentions, he hadn't sworn a solemn vow never to do so. In fact, he steadfastly declined to utter such vows, if only because he believed it foolish to commit himself to anything, as long as conditions were subject to change.

Nevertheless, in a March 31, 1988, memo to employees, he chose uncharacteristically precise language to deny reports he might sell his CBS shares or the network. At the time, Rupert Murdoch was the supposed suitor. "I have met with no one, had no conversation, and have received no offer for the sale of Loews' CBS stock or the CBS network," the memo read. "If you hear or read anything to the contrary, it is absolutely, totally, and categorically untrue."

The memo provided some insight into Tisch's attitude about CBS's poor competitive position. Acknowledging its slide into third place, he wrote: "First place is what counts. And we know it will take several years—not a few months—to get there."

Even with this explicit memo, released to the media, Tisch was hard-pressed to get straightforward coverage. In reporting on the memo, *The Wall Street Journal* was careful to call Tisch's credibility into question. Invoking one anonymous CBS executive, the *Journal* reminded readers of such previous reversals as the decision to sell CBS Records.

CLASHES WITH CBS NEWS

Persistent doubts about Tisch's intentions weren't confined to financial matters. A theory that he intended to bend CBS News to a more sympathetic posture toward Israel—first promulgated by predecessor Tom Wyman—was regaining currency.

At a birthday party, in March 1988, for Fed chairman Alan Greenspan, the conversation turned to the question of whether the presence of television cameras was inflaming West Bank confrontations between Palestinians and Israelis. According to some accounts, Henry Kissinger, the former U.S. Secretary of State, offered the opinion that camera crews ought to be kept out of the area because the resulting video tended to make the Israelis look like the bad guys. Tisch supposedly agreed, later conceding it would be a tough decision if he were the one who had to make it.

For Tisch, this episode represented yet another example of media distortion. "When something gets misreported, it becomes permanent record," he said. "What very simply happened was that we were talking about the television cameras showing riots and stuff like that. We were saying, Were they [those that banned cameras] smart in some countries? It was a question. A rhetorical question. . . . Nobody—neither Kissinger nor myself—recommended that we not have cameras there. That was nonsense."

The tone of the conversation was that Israel should be complimented for not stooping to the level of dictatorships, in which bans on television coverage are common. "If I didn't want cameras in Israel, we wouldn't have to have a bureau there," Tisch said.

The exchange at the party, however, was portrayed as evidence that Tisch's support for Israeli causes was bound to influence how CBS News covered the Mideast. It didn't help that Tisch had been critical of what he perceived as an Arab bias in the ABC News coverage of the troubled region. The underlying assumption was that CBS News, just by being acutely aware of Tisch's strong position, would adjust its focus to suit him.

Yet, when "60 Minutes" ran a critique of the "enormous" lobbying clout of the American Israel Public Affairs Committee (AIPAC) in Washington, none of the media reporters seized on it as proof that the news division remained independent of Tisch's politics. Instead, an exchange between Tisch and "60 Minutes" producer Don Hewitt, a few days after the report aired, was used to show Tisch seeking to intimidate news executives on Israel. Tisch had words with Hewitt and Mike Wallace, themselves Jewish, at a party. He suggested the report reflected Jewish self-hatred, but the exchange wasn't meant as a toe-the-line-or-else warning. Tisch frequently exercised his right to agree to disagree, on nonfinancial as well as financial issues, with people who worked for him.

That, however, wasn't the message the media derived from the confrontation. One news division employee said, "Nobody could believe it—Tisch just went ballistic."[1]

Hewitt knew perhaps better than anyone that Tisch's disapproval wasn't to be taken as a threat. "There was discussion but never any meddling," Hewitt said of Tisch. "He let us know what he thought, but he never suggested we change anything. Any negative feelings I had were confined to the [conservative Israeli] Likud party, and that doesn't make me any more self-hating than being opposed in this country to a particular party makes one a self-hating American."

In *Three Blind Mice*, author Ken Auletta argued that Tisch may have failed to influence such oldtimers as Hewitt and Wallace, but younger, less secure CBS News staffers might not be so strong-willed. Perhaps; but it would be hard to find any media organization where overly ambitious staffers aren't prone to voluntarily or unconsciously compromise their news judgment to curry favor with the boss on pet causes. In the case of CBS News, even Auletta conceded it was hard to find evidence of reports being skewed to please Tisch.

Indeed, "60 Minutes" later aired a report that Israelis—not Palestinians, as Israel had been insisting—had sparked the 1990 riot in Jerusalem that left 17 Palestinians dead. Once again, Tisch expressed his displeasure at the news division for taking a swipe at Israel. He questioned Wallace and Hewitt on the fairness of the report, but they insisted the story was accurate. An Israeli magistrate later reached the same conclusion. No one at CBS appeared to be pulling punches on Israel or losing work for failing to.

CBS's "Major Events" Strategy

Convincing the world that there was more to Tisch than a love of cash would prove to be just as daunting as dispelling the notion that he wanted to turn the news division into a public relations operation for Israel.

Tisch had a soft spot in his heart for large sums of cash, but cash wasn't an end in itself. CBS's huge cash position was there to protect the company from the downside, but Tisch wasn't waiting for the upside to take care of itself. He couldn't afford to. CBS's slide into third place posed a danger to the company's long-term health. It meant, for example, having to provide $65 million in free airtime to advertisers for failing to deliver a certain number of viewers promised during the 1987–1988 season.

More important, persistently lousy ratings, especially with a poorly rated evening news show, increased the danger of affiliate defections. With a winning prime-time schedule several seasons away, Tisch had to concentrate on putting affiliates at ease. To do this, he focused on locking up winning sports programming. At least if he could deliver exclusive access to such premier sports events as the baseball World Series, affiliates would be compelled to hang on. Purchasing the 1992 Winter Olympics, it turned out, was only the beginning. This was not a strategy hatched suddenly in 1988.

Neal Pilson, head of CBS Sports, had proposed this "major events" strategy to Tisch as early as April 1986, during a train ride from Philadelphia to New York after CBS's annual meeting—five months before Tisch ousted Wyman as CEO. With big sports opportunities coming up, Pilson was ready to deal and Tisch was ready to spend. No matter how many cable channels are available to viewers, larger audiences than are attracted by regular programming will always tune in to the live, exclusive broadcast of a major sports event like the Olympics or the World Series.

In December 1988, CBS agreed to pay $1.06 billion for the exclusive right to four years' broadcasts of major league baseball. It was a high-stakes bet, part of an eventual $3.6 billion investment in sports programming. Not only was the network agreeing to an amount that virtually guaranteed it couldn't be profitable, it was doing so at a time when the popularity of baseball seemed to be waning. Tisch, however, wasn't the two-dimensional waste-watcher his critics supposed. He could tell the difference between pointless purchases and those that promised a substantial, durable payback. The baseball contract by itself might not be a stand-alone money-maker. It did, however, stand a chance of generating benefits that would far outweigh any losses from the contract itself.

And losses were likely. Wrote NBC programming chief Brandon Tartikoff: "With a $1 billion-plus price tag, even if we sold every second of commercial time at a premium rate, we estimated we would lose about $100 million a year or more." After decades of owning at least a share of the major league package, NBC decided it didn't need to take such losses. It already was the number-one network, and Tartikoff and NBC president Robert C. Wright agreed it would be better to let CBS spend the $1 billion while NBC spent $20 million to develop competing programming.

For CBS, though, having the All-Star Game, the National League and American League playoffs, and the World Series, starting in 1990, was a crucial opportunity to promote the rest of its schedule. If it could simultaneously get a large share of such sports exclusives and develop competitive programming, the network had a chance to regain audience share. "This is a risk we love to take," Tisch said at the time. "We think the tangibles and the intangibles overcome any risk we take."

CBS suddenly was emerging as the strongest of the networks in sports. It already had the strongest National Football League package, the National Basketball Association, and the final rounds of the college championship basketball tournament. Now it had elements of the baseball season that currently were split between NBC and ABC, with one network airing the playoffs and the other the World Series in alternating years. Although that was proving to be a money-losing arrangement, it wasn't necessarily a foregone conclusion that one network couldn't do a better job broadcasting the whole package. For one thing, might not the network airing the playoffs promote them differently, knowing it was generating interest in the series about to be carried by its rival? The dilemma was that it was important that the World Series be successful on the rival network each year in order to sell ads on the competing network the following year.

For CBS, it was also a defensive move: the network wouldn't be launching a new fall season of regular programming only to be set back by audience losses to baseball being aired on the rival networks. The move pleased the network's affiliates, for whom the cost of the baseball contract wasn't an issue. Top sports events generally attracted a third again as many viewers as the network would get for its regular programs.

This strategy was a major reason Tisch felt comfortable predicting that CBS would bottom out in 1989 and then steadily improve thereafter. The following year, viewers would tune in CBS for an unprecedented array of top events: the NFL's Super Bowl, the college and pro basketball finals, and the baseball playoffs. The trick was to make sure CBS had top-quality regular programming to tout while all these sports events were on the air; only bona fide hit material would make the sports programming effort pay off. In television, no amount of promotion would overcome a clear lack of creativity.

The strategy wasn't risk-free. What if baseball's popularity continued to sag? What if the sports strategy failed to reach women, the demographic group that appeals to advertisers most? One affiliate that had switched to NBC from CBS wasn't even convinced of the value of a baseball championship that went the full seven games. "The World Series, seven nights, wasn't enough of an incentive," said Arnold Klinsky of WHEC-TV in Rochester, New York. "You've got to judge where the network will be in three years."[2]

Klinsky may have been right to act on where he thought CBS would be three years hence, but he would find that he had bet wrong. Three years later, NBC and CBS were well on the way to trading places in the ratings race. Tisch had said that the turnaround would take years and would need a coherent strategy. That he had a strategy—and the ability to get the best people to execute it—was becoming apparent, though not too clearly to the media.

Pilson was so convinced of the value of the 1992 Winter Olympics, he bid for the 1994 version in Lillehammer, Norway, before he knew how well the 1992 event in Albertville, France, would work out. It's not unusual for networks to bid years in advance for Olympics broadcast rights. In this case, however, CBS took a thinly veiled hint on what amount would guarantee a successful bid, and agreed, in August 1989, to buy the 1994 rights for $300 million. NBC and ABC declined to bid at all. In 1994, the Olympics' four-year cycle began the new alternating schedule for the Winter and Summer Games, which would bring some portion of the Games to a world audience every two years.

Pilson's competitors didn't miss the opportunity to call his wisdom into question. In May 1988, when CBS won the rights to the 1992 Winter Olympics, NBC Sports president Arthur Watson said, "You always want to be a winner, but you don't want to commit suicide at the same time." With hindsight, "suicide" would not spring to mind to describe the impact of the Olympics decision on CBS.

But in 1988, Tisch was still the subject of intense second-guessing. "CBS will have none of this year's blockbuster sports events," *Business Week* observed in July, "which pull in viewers and provide networks with powerful leverage that helps them to promote their new shows."

Two weeks later, *Forbes* noted that CBS's market capitalization—including debt and equity, minus all that cash and any tax liability—amounted to just $1.7 billion compared with Capital Cities/ABC's $6.7 billion. In other words, investors apparently believed that, despite having twice as much revenue, CBS wasn't worth even a third as much as Capital Cities. "Thus the market gives much higher marks to the Thomas Murphy–Warren Buffett team at Capital Cities than to the Tisch regime at CBS," *Forbes* wrote, unable to resist the temptation to compare Tisch with two of his closest and most admired friends in the business world.

Media scrutiny did not give equal attention to Tisch's financial successes. In early 1987, he was much maligned for not outbidding

NBC for a CBS affiliate in Florida, priced at $270 million. A year and a half later, he agreed to pay just $59 million for WCIX-TV, an independent station in Miami.

Bill Paley continued to complain about Tisch's lack of programming talent and made noises about finding someone to push out or buy out Tisch. Like all his predecessors, Tisch was no longer useful to Paley, but Paley no longer had the standing, in terms of ownership or board influence, to oust Tisch, and he knew it. As if to drive that reality home, Bob Tisch finally got his seat, in September 1988, as CBS's 14th board member. When the board voted him on, Paley lodged no complaint. It was hard to deny Bob a seat; he was an equal partner in the Tisches' CBS stake.

BOB'S FOOTBALL BUSINESS

Bob Tisch wasn't expected to become a factor in the company's day-to-day operations. CBS was Larry's deal. Besides, Bob seemed to be looking to fulfill some of his own dreams, including owning a professional football team. Earlier in the year, he had considered making a bid for the financially struggling New England Patriots from Victor ("I bought the company") Kiam.

It wasn't the first time Bob Tisch had thought about buying a football team. In 1970, along with former New York Giants coach Allie Sherman, and Steve Ross, then president of Kinney National Service Inc.—later named Warner Communications Inc.—he had tried to buy the New York Jets. Ross, a Brooklyn native who went on to build the powerful Time Warner Inc. publishing and entertainment empire, first met the Tisches in 1960 in his capacity as director for Al Tisch's funeral. In early 1989, Bob Tisch explored the possibility of setting up a franchise in Baltimore; in 1991, he finally got a piece of the NFL, after spending $80 million for a half-interest in the Giants.

Bob's timing seemed inconsistent with the Tisches' reputation as bargain hunters. The purchase occurred just two weeks after the Giants had won the Super Bowl for the second time in three years, which was a bit like buying into the stock market the day it hits a record. A few months after Tisch's purchase, Bill Parcells, who coached the team to two championship victories, quit. As a business, the Giants' potential for growth was limited. It had sold out its 76,000-seat stadium for 15 seasons, so any growth would have to come from raising ticket prices and from such peripheral activities as corporate sponsorship and exclusive broadcast programming featuring players and coaches.

Changing Times

Bob Tisch's ability to finally get a CBS board seat was a reflection of Paley's rapidly waning influence. "Everybody's forgotten Bill Paley," Larry Tisch said regretfully at a cocktail party soon after Bob's election that September. "They don't realize he is still around. I went to an industry luncheon this afternoon and nobody came up to me and asked, 'How's Bill?'"

Tisch wasn't alone in feeling sorry for Paley; Akio Morita, chairman of Sony, also expressed sorrow for Paley, but laid the blame on Tisch. "Larry Tisch is breaking up the company and eating it himself."[3]

Tisch was enduring the treatment usually accorded politicians who are swept in on a wave of popularity and great expectations and turned into targets for ridicule once they get down to business.

By the end of 1988, CBS had more than doubled its profit to $1.15 billion. The lion's share of it—$866.6 million—came from the sale of the records division, and much of the balance—$184.8 million—represented interest earned on its cash. Profit from broadcast operations was weak, as the network struggled through a lengthy writers' strike and costly election-year coverage. It didn't help to be stuck in third place at a time when the big three networks had seen their combined share of the audience shrink to 68 percent. Still, the CBS shares Tisch had acquired three and a half years earlier for $125 each were now worth $171 each, a 37 percent paper profit. Tisch and his fellow shareholders were still being rewarded for holding on.

Tisch knew, however, that achieving nice paper profits for shareholders wasn't proof of any long-term success. A healthy stock price was only a reflection of investor confidence in Tisch's ability to effect a turnaround at CBS. At the end of 1988, the network was in a precarious state.

Its last-place status, no doubt, played a role in Diane Sawyer's willingness to be wooed away from CBS by ABC's Roone Arledge. Tisch wasn't going to let her go without a fight. He asked Paley to intercede, but to no avail. The series of lunches Sawyer had been having with Arledge was apparently more convincing than the several hours she spent with Paley in his CBS office dining room. Arledge's point: CBS wasn't fully utilizing her talents. Paley's counterargument: CBS was where she grew up. Tisch's reaction: he felt burned.

At ABC, Sawyer earned about $1.7 million in the first year of a contract agreed to in January 1989, up from $1.2 million at CBS. She was signed to cohost the weekly news feature program "Prime Time Live" with Sam Donaldson.

Soon after Sawyer's departure, writer Edward Klein reported that Tisch said he felt "personally betrayed"—something Tisch flatly denied. Losing Sawyer to ABC was another public relations black eye for the network; such defections were infrequent in the business. "Confused and defensive" was the way Klein described Tisch, "and there were signs that he might have bitten off more than he could chew." Klein's assessment was that Tisch misread Sawyer in suggesting her main concern was money. Tisch, Klein asserted, "understood little about the tender egos of his on-camera talent."

True, being in front of the camera at peak times, being the center of attention, was a broadcaster's primary measure of success, but Tisch's problem wasn't that he didn't understand this. In Tisch's view, it was common sense that ego was an obstacle to success in business. Why should such egocentricity be tolerated in the broadcast business any more than it was in any other business? It was also his view that Sawyer wouldn't be able to achieve the same luminosity as ABC stars Barbara Walters and Ted Koppel; in retrospect, that assessment appeared to be right.

The Sawyer deal was a blow to morale at CBS in general and to Tisch in particular. Such public embarrassments continued to plague him. Even in a philanthropic act of immense proportions, he seemed incapable of avoiding criticism.

When the Tisches announced, in January 1989, a $30 million gift (a record donation at the time) to New York University Medical Center for biomolecular research, the university faced a storm of outrage. The gift—which stipulated the renaming of University Hospital as the Tisch Hospital—was made possible in part by the highly profitable cigarette business owned by Loews. Critics asked: How could an institution whose mission is to save lives take money from the sale of products that sickened people?

William Cahan, a senior attending surgeon specializing in lung cancer at Memorial Sloan-Kettering Cancer Center in New York, was among those sufficiently incensed to lodge a protest with president of NYU, John Brademas. "Surely, such an action raises questions as to the propriety of accepting funds from individuals," he said, "whose wealth was, and is being, amassed at the expense of our country's health." Dr. Cahan figured that more than 15 percent of the hospital's patients were there for illnesses related to smoking.

The counterargument suggested by one of Tisch's friends was that Tisch had invested in Lorillard in 1968 from the perspective of a stock-market value investor, not a tobacco businessman. How many universities held large stakes in tobacco companies, simply because they fit a certain risk–return formula?

"To single out Larry for doing something that is legal is unfair," said Leonard Stern, a fellow NYU board member.

Tisch himself conceded a certain discomfort related to Lorillard and the health impact. "At the best," he said, "it's painful." But he saw no benefit, either to the general public or to Loews shareholders, to pulling Loews out of the business. "If Lorillard closed tomorrow," he said, "there wouldn't be one less cigarette smoker in America."

Referring to Lorillard, Jimmy Tisch said: "We're on a bucking bronco. All you can do is ride the bronco. There's no safe way to get off."

This predicament was true for all the tobacco companies. As Congress and state legislators in 1994 adopted novel approaches to attacking the industry—most notably, trying to make cigarette makers responsible for the related health-care costs—plaintiffs' lawyers were taking a new approach. Having never won a tobacco product liability case against any tobacco company, smokers' lawyers were now pursuing lawsuits alleging tobacco executives deliberately hid the addictive nature of tobacco and exploited it to boost sales.

With so much controversy swirling around the industry, bailing out wasn't an option. Loews or Philip Morris or RJR/Nabisco or B.A.T Industries might be able to sell its tobacco assets, but the seller would retain liability in any consumer or shareholder lawsuits that might go against it in the future.

Jimmy Tisch summed up this nonsmoking family's attitude about selling a product the federal government estimated cost at least $50 billion in 1993 in medical expenses: "Let informed people make their choices."

PROGRAMMING TURNAROUND

By February, Tisch's projection that 1989 would be the year in which CBS began its rebound was starting to be believable. The network's highly praised "Lonesome Dove" miniseries, based on the Larry McMurtry novel, attracted a surprisingly high 38 percent of prime-time viewers. It was the 15th-highest rated miniseries out of 120 aired since 1975, but CBS probably gave up an additional $5 million in ad revenue by underestimating how well it would do in the ratings.

The series helped CBS tie NBC for first place in the week's total prime-time audience ratings. "CBS's dramatic turnaround in the first quarter of 1989 continues," the network bragged. The victory, however, wasn't complete. The series failed to draw the most desirable viewers: the 18- to 49-year-old set, especially women. Instead, CBS's strength remained in attracting older viewers. "Lonesome Dove," for example, was strongest in attracting men over 54 years old—not the cream of the crop for advertisers.

"We want to tell people which is the most popular network. The public is fascinated by television, and they don't dismiss everyone over

50 years of age as irrelevant," David F. Poltrack, a CBS senior vice president, said at the time. "That's the consumer side. On the business side, we can still be more popular and get less money if we don't have the right kind of people."

Tisch had to be pleased with this faint glimmer of hope. He had been accused of destroying the company's morale and the company along with it. His decision to sell major assets had been branded as shortsighted. Now he could point to proof that his long-term strategy for CBS just might work. Ultimately, his successes were his only way to silence his critics.

Success, however, was still sporadic. Once again, NBC ended the prime-time season firmly in first place. CBS, for the second year in a row—and the second time in 37 years—came in third. There were signs, however, that the situation might be starting to change. In the second half of the season, Candice Bergen, in the critically acclaimed comedy "Murphy Brown," was added to the lineup. Still, the three major networks' combined audience share for the season fell to 67 percent, and the biggest losses were among the most sought-after viewers. More than ever, the pressure to occupy first place mounted.

By the end of May, the networks' combined share had slumped to 65 percent, but CBS managed to barely sneak past ABC and take second place for the second time in a row. It was still well behind NBC. Nevertheless, more bad ratings news lay ahead for CBS.

At the annual affiliates' meeting in June, it was clear that Tisch's message was starting to get through. A year earlier, they had practically booed him off the stage. Now they were patient. "We've had another year to get to know Larry Tisch," said Gary Schmedding, an executive at a company that owned affiliates of all three networks, "and we can see that maybe this guy isn't just in this to buy and sell things."

This newfound respect for Tisch was earned by bold moves that had drawn criticism from other quarters—including paying $1.06 billion for baseball, and an innovative, $20 million promotional program involving Kmart. It also reflected recognition that, for all the cost cutting in the news division, CBS wasn't any less committed to covering news. It had pulled out all the stops in its coverage of the Tiananmen Square uprising and massacre in Beijing, and Tisch reasserted the network's willingness to spare no expense to get such coverage on the air.

Such a commitment was noncontroversial; the Kmart deal was another matter. The discount retailer distributed contest game cards, and viewers had to watch CBS for Kmart commercials to find out whether they had won certain prizes. For Paley, this was the ultimate proof that Tisch had no interest in preserving CBS's reputation for class. (NBC soon after agreed to a similar marketing partnership with Sears, Roebuck & Co.) Still, this was the sort of deal affiliates looked to for proof that the network was doing something to bolster viewership.

When the new fall season rolled around, it became clear that CBS was adopting an approach that would appeal to Larry Tisch's lack of respect for the conventional wisdom. Instead of trying to build a prime-time schedule of shows meant to appeal to the vaunted 18- to 34-year-olds, CBS took the opposite tack, consciously building on the network's first-place rating among older viewers. David Poltrack was certain that these viewers mattered to advertisers. Older viewers, he argued, may not be spendthrifts, but they have more money to spend, and their numbers will swell as aging baby boomers join them.

Tisch let Poltrack pursue this unconventional strategy—an indication of his willingness to give trusted professionals a free hand. Besides, the concept made sense. CBS had always been the network of choice for older viewers. When a network tries to draw viewers to new programs, it promotes them during its top-rated programs. But CBS's top-rated shows—"60 Minutes" and "Murder, She Wrote"—weren't standard fare for young viewers.

Poltrack believed that if CBS could regain the lead among networks by appealing to even more older viewers, a few younger viewers would be snared in the process. It was becoming apparent that the big three networks generally were drawing older people, while cable offerings such as MTV were siphoning off the young and hip.

Not all advertisers thought Poltrack was crazy for pursuing the older set. "For years, David Poltrack was a lone voice in the wilderness, and a lot of it came across as self-serving," Betsy Frank, an executive at

Saatchi & Saatchi, the big ad agency, said at the time. "But I'll tell you, the man was right."

Maybe; but positive results were still nowhere in sight. In October 1989, NBC, for the first time after a record-breaking 68-week run, was not in first place; ABC had benefited from the highly rated "Roseanne." CBS remained buried in third place.

One change that particularly pleased Tisch was David Burke's apparent success in stanching the torrent of anti-Tisch sentiments emanating from the news division's ranks. Tisch's support for Burke, however, wasn't unqualified.

One reason was the way Burke handled yet another incident involving Andy Rooney, the network's star curmudgeon. Rooney had allegedly made a racist remark about blacks to a magazine, the *Advocate*, and sent a letter about homosexuality to the magazine against Burke's wishes. Burke responded by suspending Rooney for three months without pay, starting February 8. Perhaps compounding the situation was the gay community's outrage at this Rooney comment on a prime-time special: "Too much alcohol, too much food, drugs, homosexual unions, cigarettes. They're all known to lead quite often to premature death."

Burke's decision to punish Rooney, however, was proving to be a costly demonstration of political correctness for the network. Three weeks into the suspension, "60 Minutes" dropped from fifth in the prime-time rankings to 11th. ABC rescheduled "America's Funniest Home Videos" to compete head-to-head, and ABC's strategy worked. For only the second time in 12 years, "60 Minutes" was beaten in its time slot. A week later, Rooney's suspension was cut short.

Although Tisch was pleased that the news division was making money, the Rooney affair and another involving Kathleen Sullivan, anchor of "CBS This Morning," were bitter reminders of the near-warfare that had broken out soon after Tisch took over. Sullivan, earning about $1 million a year, got caught referring to CBS as "Cheap Broadcasting Network" on an open microphone (though it didn't make it into a broadcast). Soon word was out that CBS was negotiating to lure Paula Zahn from ABC to replace Sullivan.

As for Burke, too many brush fires were breaking out under his command. Tisch was losing patience, especially since he was hearing that Burke was bad-mouthing him behind his back. At the same time, Burke wasn't working well with Howard Stringer. Without support from his boss and his boss's boss, Burke was essentially developing into a seat-warmer until someone better came along.

About this time, *Fortune* magazine irritated Tisch with its "Has Larry Tisch Lost His Touch?" story, which described CBS as still mired in a torpor of discontent. Raising all the familiar criticisms, the story faulted Tisch for selling off assets too cheaply, being too cautious an investor, and failing to recognize the risk of mismanaging on-air egos. It quoted a "former high CBS executive" anonymously as saying, "The relationship between supervisors and the supervised has deteriorated on all levels." Tisch's response: "Morale is 1,000 percent better than it ever was in the past. Everybody is free and easy. There's no politics, no backbiting." In the news division, he said, "There is peace. There is harmony."

An internal gag memo about the scheduling of bathroom visits was held up as evidence of continuing morale problems, but, although the story's headline asked a provocative question, the writer, Kenneth Labich, knew it was too soon to answer it. Indeed, the article recognized that Tisch's simple plan had a chance to work. It was a good bet that Sagansky would be able to cook up a crowd-pleasing lineup worth touting during the network's major sports exclusives.

At the CBS annual meeting two months later, in May, Tisch once again faced a barrage of stinging criticism. The network had just ended its third consecutive year in the prime-time cellar. "We're a total disaster only in prime time," he countered. "We will correct that." CBS *was* a leader in daytime TV, but its only prime-time program among the top 10 was the decades-old workhorse, "60 Minutes." One shareholder's comment seemed to typify investors' impatience for results: "When you have to go to Kmart to get viewers, that's the bottom of the barrel."

But the news wasn't all bad. For the sweeps week that May, CBS came within a hair's breadth of besting NBC for first place. What helped carry it was a rebroadcast of the original "I Love Lucy" pilot, some movie specials, Connie Chung's celebrity interviews, "Murphy Brown," and "Designing Women." None of this, however, reflected great, new programs—just good competitive counterprogramming versus a leader whose winners were starting to sag.

Tisch was clearly frustrated about the business. "I didn't know what I was getting myself into,"[4] he said in June. He feared the possibility that network television was going to continue to rapidly lose its market share. "The golden days of network television are over." Rumors reported that Tisch literally was losing sleep over his apparent inability to cut the cost of running the network to a level approaching that of such rivals as CNN in news and Fox in entertainment.

"I never lose sleep over business," Tisch protested. "I'm a businessman. I have good days, bad days. But I tell you one thing, when I leave the office, my business day is over. I don't lose sleep over it. I will lose sleep over important things, family things, health, but I don't lose sleep over whether business is better or worse."

For all of Tisch's apparent frustration with the television business and its Hollywood egos, he remained committed to his plan for regaining ratings leadership. Not that ABC and NBC didn't have their own strategies. One major difference, however, was that, unlike CBS, its rivals were hedging their bets by investing in cable-TV ventures. Tisch was convinced viewers tended to stick with a small number of favorite channels, no matter how many choices are available.

Wall Street analysts thought the time was right for a big entertainment production company like Walt Disney Co. to buy a big entertainment delivery vehicle like CBS: a theory that regained currency in 1994 after the QVC merger failed. Tisch resisted the pressures to do something bold or innovative for the sake of itself.

"Everybody in this building would like to have 20 diversions, all meaningless, so we could say we have a strategy," said Tisch in an interview in his CBS office suite. "It reminds me of the hotel we owned, where the service and food were poor, and the manager's solution was always the same—redecorate! I don't believe in that. We have to concentrate on our core business."

Tisch, and CBS, was about to be rewarded for doing just that—and ignoring the critics.

14

Results

"I actually like him more now than I did then."

—Andy Rooney in 1993

Tisch wasn't done shaking things up at CBS. David Burke, for a variety of reasons, was fired as CBS News president in August 1990, two years after having been hired amid much fanfare. With Dan Rather's newscast stuck in second place behind ABC for 33 weeks, news remained a weak spot in the network's schedule, and Burke's efforts to assert his independence irritated both Tisch and Stringer.

He was faulted, for instance, for signing ABC's Paula Zahn to a $1 million-a-year contract as "CBS This Morning" coanchor without consulting higher-ups, a practice that had astonished Tisch when he first took the helm at CBS. The Andy Rooney suspension and reinstatement also was seen as badly managed. The capper was that the news division's budget once again was getting too out-of-hand for Tisch's tastes. By the end of the summer, it had already exceeded its $300 million limit for all of 1990 and the likelihood for heavier spending soared with Iraq's invasion of Kuwait.

Major news events like the Tiananmen massacre and the fall of the Berlin wall tend to run up production costs and do little for ad revenue—especially when a news event warrants preempting regular

237

programs. About the only potential benefit from covering breaking news better than the competition was the ratings boost, which could be significant. The network with the most-watched evening news had a head start in the nightly prime-time race.

Burke's successor was Eric Ober, 48, president of the CBS-owned television stations division and a former news division vice president. The problem with the budget would spark the same reaction it did two years earlier, when Tisch first took the helm: cut costs. It remained to be seen whether Ober would emulate NBC's Michael Gartner, whom Tisch had held up as the model news executive because he delivered cost cuts the day they were ordered.

Cost cutting, however, wasn't Ober's most immediate concern. "My top priority is letting the news organization go about covering the news," he said at the time. "No one has discussed anything about budgets with me." With 1,370 employees, CBS News was still the fattest among the Big Three networks.

How Ober handled budgets wasn't Tisch's main concern either. Leadership was needed. Compared with Ober, Burke was remote with employees and with bosses. Ober was more outgoing and more popular (for example, with the station managers who worked with him), and he worked closely with top executives. The media, of course, couldn't resist noting that Ober was CBS's fourth news president since Tisch's arrival.

GLIMMER OF SUCCESS

Other numbers were beginning to suggest that CBS's three-year sentence at the bottom of the ratings might not last forever. The first night of the 1990–1991 prime-time season, CBS notched a strong first-place showing, well ahead of its nearest competitor, ABC, whose perennially powerful "Monday Night Football" wasn't enough to slow CBS's advance. CBS managed to stay in first through the rest of the week, the first time that had happened since January 1987.

David Poltrack was ebullient. "This is the first of many surprises from CBS," he said. It had been a long time since CBS had managed to win anything but Sunday night in prime-time ratings. Poltrack was distressed, though, that "CBS Evening News" continued to trail ABC.

The Iraqi invasion of Kuwait was a double-whammy for CBS. Not only did it prove to be a ratings test that CBS News would fail, it plunged the country into a recession that, until then, had been merely rumored. The recession put a crimp in advertising budgets, and it came at a time of big advertisers' growing interest in alternatives to network advertising, including precisely focused direct-mail campaigns.

With the proliferation of bar-coded sales data collected at supermarket checkouts, for example, a consumer-products maker could pinpoint stores where a particular product was lagging behind the competition and saturate the appropriate neighborhood with coupons. This eliminated the waste of offering discounts to already-loyal customers. By comparison, network advertising was the scattershot approach to hitting a consumer target.

Driving the point home was CBS's inability that autumn to command high ad rates for its high-priced baseball playoff schedule. Not only were advertisers balking at paying even as much as they paid a year earlier for air time during games, the series themselves faltered in the ratings against the other Big Three rivals. Tartikoff's strategy of airing three miniseries aimed at women was paying off for NBC.

Still, baseball was giving CBS better ratings than the programming it was replacing. It was part of a long-range strategy that would take more than a single year to yield results. Said Peter Lund, who had just returned to CBS's Broadcast Group: "At the end of four years is when the real story will be written."

Whatever the success of the major-events strategy, Tisch's sports-rights spending spree earned him a spot at the top of *Sporting News'* list of the 100 most powerful people in the sports business. "No one has made the impact across the face of sports that the network giant did the last two years," the *News* wrote. "Tisch set the pace for rights fees negotiations that other broadcast networks were forced to follow." Tisch's impact wasn't limited to CBS's rivals. The big spending he unleashed rippled through the finances of advertisers, team owners, athletes, and marketers alike.

CBS STOCK BUYBACK

In late November, it became clear what Larry Tisch wanted to buy with all that money accumulated in 1990, from selling CBS assets. It wasn't cable properties and television stations, as had been speculated. It was CBS's own stock, which was still trading well below what Wall Street analysts believed it was worth. A stock buyback, however, seemed about the least exciting idea for putting the company's cash to work. "Anybody who buys back his own stock has no imagination," J. Peter Grace, head of W.R. Grace & Co., said later. "If management can't develop investment opportunities, they don't deserve to run the company."

Tisch found those words ironic coming from Grace, whom Tisch termed "one of the great failures of American business." Though Grace wasn't referring specifically to CBS, Tisch noted, "The people who bought Loews made 600 times on their money. People who bought Grace are barely breaking even after 30 years. Maybe I have no imagination, but it's worked for our shareholders. We bought back CBS stock at $190 a share. The stock is $300 today. We didn't hurt anybody. We treated every shareholder equally. The best thing for Loews at the time would have been to declare a dividend. But we said forget what our interest is. What's the fairest way to do it and that's what we did."

CBS's stock at the time was under heavy pressure from the network's expectation of an operating loss for 1991. Tisch's response was to cut the dividend, take a $170 million loss on its $1.06 billion baseball contract, and spend $2 billion—coincidentally, what it got for selling CBS Records—to buy back 44 percent of its own shares to bolster the share price. "I'm not sorry we did baseball. Would I do it again at the same price? I doubt it."[1] The buyback, though, was a great deal for shareholders, including Larry Tisch, who with the death of Bill Paley at the age of 89 in late October had added the title of chairman.

Paley's death indirectly brought Tisch around to the buyback idea. CBS had been casting about for ways to invest its cash when Paley's heirs, needing to raise money for the taxes on his $550 million estate, inquired about the possibility of the company's buying their inherited shares. Those discussions led to the buyback, which left Tisch and Paley's heirs with the same size stakes they had held before the purchase. For Tisch, it meant bringing down the effective cost of the Loews 24.9 percent stake in CBS to just $217 million.

The buyback, however, wasn't greeted with unqualified approval by all constituents. CBS Network affiliates were outraged, having just had their compensation payments cut by $30 million, or 20 percent. In their view, their sacrifice indirectly was subsidizing Tisch's decision to enrich himself and other holders. The move renewed speculation that Tisch was preparing to bail out of CBS, perhaps by selling out to that perennially rumored suitor, Walt Disney. Once again, Tisch denied the rumor.

Aside from the theory that CBS was something Tisch bought for posterity, it didn't make financial sense that he would want to sell out. The buyback would reduce the cost of Loews' CBS shares to about $65 each at a time when they were trading at $175. The buyback itself would lift the stock price further. If, as Tisch believed, the broadcaster was poised for a rebound, then a higher share price was even more likely. Even in a worse-case scenario, the stock would have to fall all the way back to a 1990 equivalent of about $130 a share to cause concern for Tisch about the ultimate return on his investment.

Put another way, why cash in an investment that had a large margin for error and plenty of upside potential? Where else would Tisch find a better investment? Indeed, that was why the CBS board decided the buyback was the best possible way to invest its cash. Most important, it was a way to return value to all shareholders without triggering a dividend tax, and still leave $800 million in the company's coffers. Wall Street loved it.

IMMINENT TURNAROUND

Wall Street's approval still failed to gain Tisch much respect among the ranks of those who wrote about the television business. Sally Bedell Smith's biography of Paley was in bookstores within days of

Paley's death. "Perhaps Tisch finally made CBS what it had been all along," she concluded, "a machine of lowbrow mass market entertainment, now shorn of its pretensions." It didn't help that once again, CBS News, for the first time since 1987, was preparing to fire people—up to 50 by the end of the year—and to shut down its Chicago and Denver bureaus.

By early 1991, Tisch was talking about a changed CBS, a company ready for the future—in other words, a company whose employees had finally accepted, if grudgingly, that the good old days of Paley-style extravagance were over and that disciplined cost accounting was here to stay.

As if to underscore the point, Stringer hired McKinsey & Co., the management consultants, "to tackle with some insight the spiraling costs and dwindling revenues that are leading some of us to say, 'Stop the world, I want to get off.'"

The world all the networks wanted to abandon was the one in which cable TV had siphoned off one of every three of the networks' viewers since 1976.

GULF WAR WOES

The high-profile conflict between bean counters and news executives came back to haunt CBS News in full force when the United States and its allies launched the massive bombardment of Baghdad on January 16, 1991, in the first phase of the effort to liberate Kuwait. Not only was CBS trounced in the effort to be the first with live reports from the Iraqi capital, it became the laughingstock of broadcast journalism.

Nearly a half hour after CNN and ABC had started broadcasting vivid live reports of the massive air assault and anti-aircraft fire, Dan Rather was telling his viewers, "There are some indications that American cruise missiles—these are missiles, they are not aircraft with people in them—may have started to attack Iraq." As if to debunk its rivals' eyewitness accounts, CBS suggested the shooting was just Iraqi gunners nervously blasting away at the darkness.

Getting beaten on the biggest story of the year was more than just embarrassing; it pushed CBS News, which had been coasting along in second place, into third place in the evening-broadcast ratings for the first week of the war. By the middle of May, CBS News would rack up a record nine straight weeks in third. "I accept my own share of the responsibility for whatever shortcomings we've had," Rather said at the time. "I tell the people here not to look back, to take each day as it comes and look forward."

The media derided Rather for attempting to spice up his broadcast journalism with jarringly shallow commentary. For example, when President Bush made it official that Operation Desert Storm was under way, Rather offered the observation that war "always brings a . . . a lump to your throat." Perhaps it was true, but saying so wasn't the way to bring that lump to viewers' throats. If, as was rumored, Howard Stringer was casting about for ways to rejuvenate the news, this kind of commentary probably wasn't what he had in mind. Within a month of the outbreak of Desert Storm, Tom Bettag, Rather's executive producer, was out of that job, replaced by Erik Sorenson, executive producer of "CBS This Morning" and a former news director at CBS's Los Angeles station. Bettag would land a few months later at ABC's "Nightline" as executive producer.

Bettag's departure sparked widespread speculation that Rather was vulnerable. Rather was a strong supporter of Bettag's, and both men had a reputation as staunch opponents of further budget cuts, putting them both at loggerheads with Tisch.

RED INK IN NEWS

Coinciding with the decision to oust Bettag was the revelation that CBS News was hemorrhaging red ink while its competitors were managing to eke out profits. It was one reason the entire company posted a 63 percent drop in profit for 1990, despite a 10 percent rise in revenue to $3.26 billion. Soon after, USA Today's stock market columnist, Dan Dorfman, wrote, yet again, that Tisch "has made a definite decision to sell the network." This time, Dorfman noted that CBS could fetch $240 to $275 a share, compared with the $168 it was then trading at.

It wasn't that far-fetched an idea. After all, even at that trading price, Tisch was looking at paper profits of more than $100 a share. At the time, he was practically lamenting having ever bought the stock. For example, he admitted he was "much too glib" in suggesting when he first started buying CBS stock that television was like any other business.[2]

Central to Tisch's thinking was what he viewed as the gradual transformation of the industry to one in which viewers no longer would have any free access to programming. Tisch's argument was that, because of federal limits on network participation in the syndication sales for reruns, the networks essentially were subsidizing the development of material that ultimately aired on cable. At the same time, cable was steadily eroding the large audiences the networks needed to justify bankrolling such program development.

"We're subsidizing our competition," Tisch complained, expressing a thought he apparently wasn't plugged into before acquiring CBS. If he no longer viewed the networks as powerful franchises, the logic went, then perhaps he was beginning to see the wisdom of taking his profit and moving on to some other investment with a less murky future.

At the time, the Tisches were placing heavy bets throughout the then-downtrodden banking sector; ultimately, their bets were unprofitable in the New England regional banks. Wall Street pundits wondered whether they were thinking about a wholesale shift of resources away from the fickle entertainment business and into the relatively sober logic of banking. Investors had been bailing out of bank stocks in droves, fearing a string of failures for a number of reasons—including a growing cancer of bad loans to high-risk businesses like commercial real estate, among the first casualties of the Gulf War-induced recession, and to the tidal wave of companies that were taken private in the 1980s and were now collapsing under the weight of their buyout debts. Exacerbating the banks' woes were increasingly zealous federal bank examiners intent on forcing bankers to come clean about the poor quality of their loan portfolios.

If the Tisches saw these beaten-down giants as great investment opportunities, why not cash out at what might be the top of the broadcast business and get in at the bottom of the banking sector?

That April, a *New York* magazine article suggested Dan Dorfman's
report wasn't too far off base and took it one step further by asserting
inaccurately that Tisch had invited Disney and Paramount Communications Inc., Tartikoff's new home, to make him an offer. But the idea
of a large studio like Disney or Paramount bidding for CBS was out of
the question at the time, because of the syndication limits. Syndication, a $5.7 billion market, was how the big studios profited on the
programs they produced; joined with a network, they would lose that
right. The *New York* article, which carried Tisch's oft-repeated denial
of any interest in selling out, quoted one anonymous CBS official as
saying, "The place is going broke. . . . Given our increasing costs, you
can see our extinction."

Tisch's response: "Utter nonsense."

Still, Tisch once again was demanding more cost cuts. Stringer's
hope of revamping the news operation without losing any more of
CBS Inc.'s 6,650 employees was proving futile. After meetings to find
more ways to trim expenses, it was clear an additional 100 people
would have to disappear from the CBS News payroll of 1,070, and 300
more from other parts of the company.

Tisch's frustrations about the network business weren't limited to
the financial aspects. His role in the celebrity business put him and
his family in the public eye. It was painful, for instance, to have the
unraveling of his children's marriages detailed in *New York* magazine,
alongside implications that members of his brother's family were disgruntled over Larry's supposed failure to give them more of a role in
the power structure overseeing the family fortune.

SIGNS OF A TURNAROUND

By the end of the 1990–1991 prime-time season, CBS again ended in
third place, but Poltrack saw an encouraging sign: much improved

viewership in seven returning programs, including "Murphy Brown" and "Major Dad." At the same time, "60 Minutes" kept chugging along, despite its aging stars. This was the strategy NBC had used years earlier to launch a string of first-place seasons. Rather than depending on instant hits, it made commitments to let quality programs build their audiences over time. If the trend continued for CBS's lineup, 1991–1992 was on track to be a strong season. In addition to increasingly popular regular programs, the CBS Sports schedule included the World Series, the Super Bowl, and the Winter Olympic Games. The major-events strategy Tisch bought into in 1986, coupled with a Tartikoff-style programming approach, was poised to pay off.

Nevertheless, Edward Klein drew some harsh conclusions about Larry Tisch that April in his *New York* magazine cover story. "Eye of the Storm: Life at CBS With Larry Tisch" painted a picture of an insensitive, cursing hothead on the verge of failure because of his decision not to include his brother, Bob, in the CBS makeover. The presumption was that Larry Tisch had botched the CBS turnaround, fulfilling the hopes of numerous businesspeople who supposedly thought this abrasive character had it coming to him. Larry's protestations to the contrary failed to alter Klein's emphasis.

Klein generally seemed to miss the mark with Tisch. A cursing hothead? No. "I've been in about half a dozen meetings in which he gets angry, but it's not very common," said Howard Stringer. "For his annual budget meetings, he never gets angry and for board meetings, you never see him get angry. Usually when he gets angry the common denominator is when someone is resisting an oft-stated idea and he sees you're not understanding what he's saying. And that's not very common."

Insensitive? Larry Tisch was blunt; his words were easily taken out of context and given a harsh spin. But insensitivity suggests a carelessness that was rare in Tisch. Were it so, he would not be so quick to respond to reporters, nor so accessible.

"You can get through to Larry terribly easily," Stringer noted. "If you're an employee in this company, you pick up the phone and call Larry. He's listed in the damned phone directory out in Rye, and so anyone can call him. We found odd sorts of people have called him and complained, and we always hear about it."

The idea of Bob Tisch's being edged out of a CBS role also makes little sense. CBS was always Larry's investment idea. Bob never sought permanent active management, although he did get a board seat. Ultimately, Bob was much more interested in a high-ranking government job.

"I always wanted to be in government," Bob said. When the postmaster general's position opened up in 1986, Bob, an ardent fan of the national political conventions, used his White House connections to be considered for the post. "To be postmaster general for a Brooklyn kid was a big job," he said. That Bob always dreamed of such a job failed to prevent it from being portrayed as a consolation prize arranged by Larry for the CBS job he supposedly wanted and didn't get.

TISCH, THE SURVIVOR

One businessman not anxious to see Tisch stumble was his old friend Warren Buffett. In August, Tisch bought about 1.5 million Salomon Inc. shares. Buffett, a large Salomon holder who had helped protect the firm four years earlier from a feared hostile bid by Revlon Group Inc.'s Ronald Perelman, had just taken over as interim chairman after John Gutfreund's ouster. Gutfreund, star of Michael Lewis's irreverent portrayal of the firm in "Liar's Poker," got the boot in the wake of revelations that top management knew as early as April that the firm had submitted an unauthorized bid two months earlier for Treasury debt but didn't disclose it.

The news had sent Salomon's shares into a tailspin. Buffett's belief that the selling was overdone and that the firm's ability to generate cash essentially was unchanged gave Tisch two powerfully compelling reasons to buy: (1) it was a deeply discounted, valuable asset, and (2) it might help a friend whose judgment had yielded Tisch millions of dollars.

Such investments were proof that Tisch hadn't lost his touch. After six years of association with CBS, "conglomerate builder" no longer was Tisch's main public identity. His strategy, however, was still to be diversified, to buy low, and to hold on as long as the return was respectable.

The stock of Loews continued to benefit from the company's hard-to-categorize nature. While Loews derived hefty profits from Lorillard, it escaped any mention, for example, in a bearish investment report on tobacco stocks in September 1991. The report, by newsletter writer Richard Schmidt, was headlined: "Tobacco Companies: Can You Kill 400,000 People a Year & Remain a Cash Cow Forever?" His point was that the tobacco companies were setting up for a fall, with product-liability litigation continuing, federal tobacco-crop subsidies coming under wider attack, and mounting regulations against smoking in public places and at work places.

Similarly, the *Wall Street Journal* managed to avoid mentioning Loews in a "Heard on the Street" column that took a swipe at hotel stocks because of how slowly they were emerging from a deep slump made even deeper by the Gulf War. If Loews had been mentioned, it might have noted the Loew's Hotels' relative strength, largely because of its conservative investment approach. While many hotel companies went on a building binge in the 1980s, Loew's stayed on the sidelines.

"We have very conservative people running Loews Corp.," Jonathan Tisch had said earlier that year. "I was somewhat frustrated in the late 1980s when we weren't doing deals like everyone else. They kept saying, 'Let's wait.'" Loews waited and, as a result, it sat in the middle of an overbuilt hotel market with plenty of cash and with plenty of desperate developers willing to sell properties at less than what it had cost to build them. In 1991, the average hotel property sale, on a per-room basis, had plunged 40 percent.

The failure of these writers to mention Loews in reports on key elements of its business was one of the intended benefits of diversification. The company was insulated from the stock-price volatility visited on single-industry companies that get lumped into market-moving news and analysis. From the perspective of Loews Corp., CBS was part of that strategy. Because it owned more than 20 percent of CBS, Loews put its prorated share of the network's results on its books, giving the company increased protection from severe profit slumps in any one of its businesses.

During the fall 1991 premiere week, network television once again saw a slide in its combined audience share. CBS had a strong showing, and, as expected, it posted especially strong gains in the 55-plus age group. The network was building audiences for its returning programs, but it had less luck with its seven new entries. Only "Brooklyn Bridge" survived the season, another one of those programs that won rave reviews but needed time to build an audience. By the end of 1991, CBS was clearly holding on to first place in the ratings, powered largely by better-than-expected ratings for a seven-game World Series in which the Atlanta Braves lost to the Minnesota Twins.

The Winter Olympic Games in February 1992 added the necessary momentum to ensure CBS a first-place finish for the entire 1991–1992 prime-time season, its first such showing since 1985 (the year Tisch bought into CBS), despite the misfortune of having to cancel two potential hits because of the deaths of their stars, Michael Landon and Redd Foxx. Part of the network's newfound strength was its lock on Monday night, with "Murphy Brown" and "Northern Exposure."

Even before the crucial Winter Olympics, evidence was mounting that Larry Tisch had no hidden agenda at CBS after all. Despite rampant rumors to the contrary, he had never misrepresented himself about his motives. He reduced the company to its main franchise and supported it with a mountain of cash investments to allow time for a long-term growth strategy to take root. Now that it was working, the critics fell silent, except for the fading echoes of criticism in *New York* magazine and in Ken Auletta's 1991 book, *Three Blind Mice,* which essentially concluded that the Big Three networks were endangered by professional managers too obsessed with cost accounting to understand that the key to success in any entertainment business was producing hits. No amount of financial acumen could make up for a lack of creative talent.

It wouldn't be long before Tisch could look back and say that both Klein and Auletta had written his epitaph too soon. In the total picture, CBS would emerge as one of Tisch's greatest turnarounds.

THE MACY'S LOSS

Even as it became increasingly clear that CBS was on the rebound, Tisch was grasping at straws for ways to deal with a real failure: Loews' 15.6 percent stake in R.H. Macy & Co.

Loews had acquired the stake when the retailer went private in 1986, in a $3.7 billion leveraged buyout, but the burdensome cost of servicing the buyout debt and digesting a bunch of ill-advised acquisitions converged with poor sales in a slumping economy. Tisch had been the only Macy's board member to vote against those acquisitions. When it became clear, in January 1992, that Macy's couldn't pay its bills, Tisch tried to negotiate a deal to get management control of the 133-year-old retailer for a $1 billion cash infusion.

Tisch, however, wasn't in the habit of throwing good money after bad. He wanted interest-rate concessions from other lenders, including Prudential Insurance Co. of America, but Prudential refused. Within days, Tisch yanked his offer. Immediately after, Macy's filed for bankruptcy court protection, and Loews lost an opportunity to manage one of its sicker investments back to health. Failures like this, however, didn't generate much heat for Tisch. Without the mystique of celebrities, television, and Hollywood, a large but crummy investment like Macy's was, for Tisch, just another garden-variety bad bet that warranted scant analysis and criticism by the media, which tended to place more emphasis on institutions that collapse with celebrities inside.

Still, the Macy's investment would prove to be Tisch's biggest single loss, though proportionally it would be much less painful financially than the Equity Funding loss nearly 20 years earlier, when Loews was a much smaller entity.

One success was about to unfold: the Winter Olympics in Albertville, France—something the *Los Angeles Times* had called "a financial albatross for the networks." Television writers carped that the 15-day, 116-hour extravaganza was doomed to financial failure, but with Paula Zahn and Tim McCarver anchoring the entire event, the ratings were strong. CBS consolidated its first-place spot in the prime-time season rankings, which ultimately was more important than whether the event by itself was profitable.

The total cost per program hour to air the Olympics was triple the cost for an average regular series, which has rerun potential, but the event fulfilled its mission not only in cementing affiliate support but also in boosting morale within CBS. At the same time, Jeff Sagansky was winning the praise of critics for giving quality shows like "Brooklyn Bridge" time to attract more viewers.

On April 14, 1992, CBS executives celebrated ending the 30-week season in first place for the first time since 1985. They wore T-shirts mocking the media with the legend, "Mired in First Place." It was a respectable showing: CBS finished the season with 13.6 percent of U.S. homes with TV sets, according to A.C. Nielsen. NBC was slightly ahead of ABC, 12.3 percent to 12.2 percent. NBC was somewhat less than gracious in defeat, arguing that the 30-week season format for ratings measurement wasn't precise, and that what really counted was the full-year program schedule.

CBS officials noted that NBC expected to post strong ratings with a special episode of "Cheers," featuring Johnny Carson, and final episodes of three other successful series, including "The Cosby Show." "It's like a going-out-of-business sale," a jubilant Larry Tisch carelessly told reporters.

The comment may have betrayed some overconfidence, but CBS's first-place showing would prove to be no fluke. It was the fruit of Tisch's commitment to a long-term business plan of keeping the company financially sound while it built a durable foundation of talent to fill its program pipeline for seasons to come.

The David Letterman deal drove home the extent to which Tisch was willing to go to recapture CBS's status as a powerhouse willing to pay up for talent to fortify every segment of its schedule. When NBC failed to turn the "Tonight Show" over to Letterman, whose popular

"Late Night" show followed on NBC, CBS seized the opportunity to mount a serious challenge to NBC's decades-long dominance of the 11:30 P.M. to 12:30 A.M. time slot. It took nine months, but Stringer, with Tisch's blessing, lured away Letterman, whose comedy of sarcasm and the offbeat appealed to the 18- to 34-year-olds advertisers favor. He was given a staggering $42 million contract, or $14 million a year for three years, to go head-to-head against "Tonight," which comedian Jay Leno had inherited from Johnny Carson. At the time, Leno was earning just $3 million a year.

Tisch's critics were quick to point out the economic folly of the contract, even though it wasn't unlike the deals Bill Paley had cut in the old days to steal such top talent as Jack Benny from NBC. Immediately, it became apparent the Letterman deal was another masterstroke. Nearly two months before the first Letterman show aired on CBS, ad space on it for an entire month was sold out. Air-time prices equaled those of the Leno show, and some advertisers supposedly offered twice the going rate for time in the show's CBS debut. With so much overheated media hype, Letterman's "Late Show" swamped "Tonight" the first night, as expected, and after a month and a half it still held the ratings edge. Indeed, in terms of the ratings, the "Late Show" remained dominant.

The $50 million of annual profit Letterman had generated for NBC was now coming in, at a minimum, to CBS—at considerable expense to NBC. By the middle of 1994, nearly a year after the switch, CBS's newfound dominance in the late-night time slot was cited as the biggest single reason for its surging ad revenue and profit.

One of the questions asked at the January 1993 news conference announcing the deal was whether Tisch would be the target of the kind of biting humor Letterman had aimed at NBC and GE management. Tisch was nonchalant at the prospect.

The Letterman coup was emblematic of Tisch's triumph over artificial adversity. Being made fun of wasn't threatening, unless you had a large, fragile ego. Far more threatening to Larry Tisch were the years of relentless criticism of his business judgment, which had the potential to damage his credibility sufficiently to alienate the people whose cooperation he needed most to make a success of his tenure as CBS chairman.

"Two years ago, if you asked about Larry's relationships with Hollywood producers, you'd have to say it was very, very bad," said nephew Steve Tisch, himself a Hollywood producer connected to such hits as "Forrest Gump." "Today it's very, very good. Of course, it helps to be number one, but more importantly Larry was advised and learned to leave Jeff [Sagansky] alone."

Not that no one in Hollywood was willing to slam Tisch. Veteran TV-movie producer Lee Rich remained highly critical of the businessmen who had taken over the networks. "I'd get rid of everybody who runs" the networks, he said.[3] "You can't have General Electric running a network. They make refrigerators. . . . Larry Tisch running a network? Come on. You got to be kidding."

In fact, Tisch *was* running a network, but he was doing it by finding the right people and letting them do their jobs without second-guessing. That he was able to do so should come as no surprise. Throughout their careers, the Tisches let capable managers manage without hovering over them. They hovered only when things appeared to be going wrong, and they richly rewarded successful managers—not themselves. Sagansky, for example, was paid a total of $6.1 million in 1992, nearly four times Tisch's compensation from CBS.

Sagansky's programming skills amounted to the network's financial lifeblood. They meant higher ad rates, helped give CBS first crack at many of the best producers in Hollywood, and were the ultimate response to the company's own malcontents. Even Andy Rooney, perhaps the loudest voice of internal dissension, got the message.

When Tisch first took over, "I did feel the way things were handled left something to be desired," Rooney said. "He fired so many people who were my friends. But he's just a very practical businessman. The rumor was he lost his temper over my comments, but I never heard directly from him about it. I doubt if he would hold a grudge. After all, as long as I'm doing my work, I doubt he would care what I said. I actually like him more now than I did then."

The very fact that Rooney remained at "60 Minutes" was a reflection of Tisch's ability to put matters of business ahead of ego. Tisch was unwilling to let Rooney's near-mutinous comments in 1987 cloud his business judgment, thereby earning Rooney's respect, even though Tisch felt no need to do so.

In retrospect, Rooney, who once accused Tisch of letting the network's moral mission be practically erased by business considerations, was at a loss to explain his success.

"The same things seem to happen over and over again to the same people," Rooney observed. "Whatever business he gets, he seems to be a success at. I have to think it's not luck. The differences now between NBC and CBS are startling, though the news divisions have suffered the pressure of having to get ratings."

Rooney conceded that it certainly was a pleasure to work for an organization that managed to maintain its quality and still make money. Rooney was speaking from the "60 Minutes" perspective, where the Don Hewitt news feature formula had survived practically unchanged over 25 years, largely because of its relentless profitability.

Dan Rather may not have gone after Tisch quite as directly as Rooney did in the early going, but he seemed not to grow as comfortable with him as Rooney had. In September 1993, he spoke out strongly, if not specifically, against network management for its role in supposedly degrading the mission and product of broadcast news.

He criticized executives who "freely take an hour that might have been used for a documentary and hand it over to a quote-unquote entertainment special about the discovery of Noah's Ark that turns out to be a 100 percent hoax." The day Rather made these comments in a speech before a broadcast news group in Miami, CBS announced it would air a one-hour special based on one of the more outrageous of the supermarket tabloids, supposedly including a segment on Noah's Ark.

Rather, who earlier in the summer went from being sole anchor to being co-anchor with the popular Connie Chung, decried the pressure from corporate executives for news directors to air "more fuzz and wuzz"—material selected not to inform but to entertain. It was a thinly veiled criticism of his own network's management. Rather's colleagues in the TV news business hailed this gutsy self-analysis, but at least one critic felt it showed a lack of familiarity with financial reality.

If the ratings and other audience feedback indicated "that news from other countries, economic news and serious, substantive news of any kind would bring in more money than game shows or crime shows, America would have an hour's worth of such nourishment every night," wrote TV critic Walter Goodman in the *New York Times.* "The problem faced by Mr. Rather and his allies is that mass merchandising does not permit much in the way of boutique programming. That's the reason for public television."

THE CABLE CHALLENGE

The fact that Goodman felt comfortable making such an observation was perhaps proof of just how successful Larry Tisch and his counterparts at the other networks had been at getting the world used to the idea that television was a business, not a charity. The public trust of the television airwaves was a notion born of an oligopoly. The public had to trust private enterprise to use its airwaves not just to turn a profit but to provide a public service. Television, however, was no longer oligopolistic, a fact Tisch hadn't fully grasped when he acquired CBS. Now broadcast television was steadily losing market share to programming that traveled by wires and satellite. In the future loomed an even wider array of options, with giant telephone, cable, and production companies forging powerful alliances in a world where programming could be delivered over phone lines as well.

Changes in the marketplace were happening so fast that federal limits on broadcasters were rapidly approaching obsolescence. As if to underscore just how outdated those limits were, the cable companies' growing dominance over the Big Three networks became crystal-clear in August 1993, when the networks backed down from their demand that cable channels pay fees for carrying their broadcasts. CBS was the last holdout in this battle, after first demanding fees and then failing to get any other form of compensation. "We are at a loss as to what the cable industry does want," Tisch said, "short of our abject surrender." In the end, from a ratings perspective, the networks perhaps needed the cable channels at least as much as cable needed to be able to run network-affiliated stations.

"That was a disaster," Tisch said of the cable-fee battle, but he wasn't so sure what CBS had to gain from having its own cable channel, especially if the television viewer of the future will have 500 choices. Even in a universe with one-tenth that number of channels, gaining a market share a fraction of the size of a broadcast network takes six or seven years. "At the end of six years, you end up with 40 percent of the country," Tisch said. From a ratings standpoint, which is how advertising is sold, "You're no place," Tisch said.

Even if your cable channel is in 100 percent of homes with cable, "It's nothing. You're not competitive. You can have losses in the first five years of $150 million to $200 million. And then you're still no place. And the other thing that's happening out there, if you believe in the future and you believe in the superhighway and the 500-channel universe, is that every new cable network today doesn't take away from the three or four networks, it takes away from each other."

Ultimately, Tisch was betting that the broadcast networks would remain the dominant producers of new programs for television. The cable channels depend heavily on reruns, but the audience for reruns isn't growing. At the same time, CBS's own market research found that, no matter how many channels a viewer has access to, the average person's capacity for what he or she can pay attention to is 7 to 10 channels, including ABC, NBC, CBS, Fox, CNN, and maybe ESPN.

Once again, Tisch was betting against the conventional wisdom that the networks would wither away. "Someone has to buy the new programming," he said. "That's the job of the networks. We'll go out of business if we don't have new programming. The cables can't afford it, so they live off our leavings in a sense. But how many people can live off the same leavings?"

President Clinton's administration, recognizing that the world of television was changed, made it clear, in September 1993, that it favored lifting the prohibition against networks owning and syndicat-ing reruns, further strengthening the networks' hand.

"It saves free television for the American people," Tisch asserted, "because it enables us to continue to produce new programming. If we couldn't own the show and get the back end of the show, we couldn't produce new programming. The logical conclusion to lack of new pro-gramming is everything becomes pay-per-view."

When Bell Atlantic Co. announced its $33 billion acquisition of Tele-Communications Inc. (TCI), the cable-TV giant, the broadcast networks saw the deal—which eventually would fall apart—as the final piece of evidence it needed to prove it was time for the govern-ment to free them from all regulations. Wall Street agreed. Shares of the network owners climbed; investors assumed deregulation would naturally follow.

Just as Warren Buffett—who in 1993 rose to the top of *Forbes*'s rich list, with a total net worth of about $8.3 billion (Tisch ranked about 38th, with a mere $1.3 billion that year)—remained committed to keeping a large stake in Capital Cities/ABC, Tisch professed an undy-ing commitment to CBS. "Television networks are a business that's tougher but still very good with very good management," Buffett told *Forbes.* "It generates a lot of cash." Echoing words spoken by Tisch 15 years earlier, *Forbes* wrote, "Buffett doesn't buy stocks; stocks are an abstraction. He buys businesses . . . ."

As businesses go, CBS was back on the fast track as 1993 drew to a close. Advertising sales were on the rise and its number-one prime-time position was firm for the year. When it posted record profit for the 1993 third quarter, the stock was trading at $285 a share. Larry Tisch had done right by the company's owners. The stock was trading well above the level analysts once said it was worth, back when the company was perceived to be in play—and that was before Tisch had trimmed away everything that wasn't broadcasting.

Approaching his 72nd year in 1995, Larry Tisch had disappointed those in the media who, for whatever reason, hoped to see a fabled business genius stumble. What few observers seemed to understand was the possibility that Tisch's aggressive, sometimes abrasive demeanor wasn't motivated by a desire to intimidate for the sake of intimidation. He simply lacked patience for anything that didn't make sense. Time and again, he demonstrated an unflinching willingness to quickly admit an error and make the appropriate adjustment. He trusted his instincts, no matter what the business. As CBS began to regain its prowess under his leadership, it tickled him to think that, by and large, if a new TV program didn't appeal to him, it probably wouldn't appeal to enough other people to make it a success. For Larry Tisch, instinct wasn't seat-of-the-pants; it was the bonding of logic and common sense guided by unshakable values acquired in a lifelong crucible.

What makes it hard to describe Larry Tisch as a tycoon, despite his billions, is that, unlike so many other wildly successful builders of corporate empires, the extent of his wealth wasn't generated by the need to compensate for some hidden personality flaw, real or imagined. In him were found no double life, no skeletons in the closet, no shattered lives, no deep-seated insecurity, no need for the approval of some hard-to-please, long-since deceased parent, no greed, no fraud, no craving for social acceptance, no insatiable ego taking credit for every success, no trampled victims on the path to the top, no shattered marriage, no compromised personal values.

Perhaps the greatest proof of all this was that, as Larry Tisch entered his 70s, many people at CBS now seemed just as apprehensive about his inevitable departure as they once were about his arrival, even though the success they had experienced under his guidance was far from guaranteed. From them and from the rest of his empire, Larry Tisch had gained respect.

15

Endgame

"I came into the world poor. If I go out poor, what's the difference."

—Larry Tisch

By early 1994, Larry Tisch was looking for a way out of CBS. Even as the network was basking in its return to first place and the restoration of its status as the Tiffany network, he was growing increasingly frustrated with the industry's persistently quirky challenges. In the television industry, success requires seemingly opposing executive qualities: the ability to impose order on creative forces that tend to be eccentric, and the ability to impose strict cost-accounting discipline, without stifling creativity.

Tisch wasn't a programming genius and never intended to be one. As head of CBS, however, he needed to know enough to recognize a programming genius when he saw one. He was a finance man now overseeing assets that totaled $45.85 billion at year-end 1993. He knew that his ideal successor at CBS—a relatively small, although high-profile part of his empire—would be a true entertainment executive with a solid track record as a businessman.

But Tisch was in no rush to step out of the limelight at CBS. It wouldn't happen until all the conditions were right, and it would depend largely on finding the right successor. None of his sons was

259

interested or qualified. Jimmy was no more cut out for the entertainment business than his father was—Andrew, even less so. Danny's and Tommy's strengths were as money managers more than as operating managers.

Howard Stringer might have seemed a logical choice, but as Stringer himself acknowledged, CBS needed a CEO who, like Tisch, was a substantial owner and knew his way around the financial markets. Indeed, in February 1995, Stringer took himself out of the running by resigning to head a telephone-company venture to offer entertainment, information and interactive services supplied to televisions over phone lines. He was succeeded by his second-in-command, Peter Lund. Jeff Sagansky, like Stringer, had made himself somewhat of a hero at CBS as head of entertainment, but he wasn't a major holder and had already left the company, eventually to become president of Sony Software at Sony Corp.

What got Tisch thinking it was time to move on was a sobering dose of network business reality in December 1993: the Fox network outbid CBS for the exclusive right to broadcast National Football Conference games. What upset him wasn't so much that, after 38 years, CBS was about to lose the franchise. It was the outrageous amount of money Fox agreed to pay for it: $1.56 billion for a four-year package, an amount that meant Fox would lose perhaps as much as $155 million a year, according to some estimates. CBS had learned its lesson with baseball.

In Tisch's view, Fox had done another maddeningly illogical network deal, coming in the wake of CBS's bungled attempt to force cable channels to pay for carrying its broadcasts. In what other industry would a single company invest so much capital in a property guaranteed to lose money? Not that Tisch wasn't willing to do the same. The amount that he was willing to lose, however, was limited to about $50 million a year. Airing the football games had helped solidify CBS's Sunday night dominance with its highly profitable "60 Minutes," but Tisch was willing to commit what he had saved by not matching Fox's huge bid to an all-out effort to program against Fox— and against NBC, which won the contract for the slightly less desirable American Football Conference games.

The concept of paying for the privilege of losing hundreds of millions of dollars was beyond Tisch's powers of reasoning. The whole network business seemed intent on defying logic. To Tisch, it wasn't logical that cable companies should be able to carry the network's wealth of original programming for free. Similarly, it wasn't logical that the networks should have to pay local stations cash compensation to carry the network programs these same affiliates needed to attract large audiences.

Never one to lick his wounds over any business setback like the loss of football, Tisch would take a cue from Brandon Tartikoff, who, when CBS grossly outbid NBC for major league baseball, committed the resources necessary to develop programming in competing time slots, and for a lot less money, to reach a different, equally desirable audience—young women. In the meantime, however, it rattled CBS, still trying to bask in the warm glow of its recently retrieved number-one rating, that a piece of its fragile formula had been shattered.

Now Tisch, who already knew he didn't want to stay at CBS forever, was more open than ever to doing the right deal to extricate himself from this less-than-logical environment. He still spent 50 percent of his time in the comfort of Loews, a company far less frustrating to run than CBS, built as it was according to Tisch's view of what made sense, and operated according to logical principles. Eight years at CBS as CEO was enough.

"He was a bit tired of it," son Jimmy said. "He understood that the economics of the business were deteriorating, and he understood that he wasn't with the program in terms of cable." Fox's football deal brought it all back into sharp focus.

Enter Diller

About that time, Tisch began to wonder why Barry Diller, head of QVC Network Inc., the home-shopping cable giant, and former head of the feisty, profitable, low-cost Fox network Tisch admired so much, was wasting any time pursuing Paramount Communications.

Diller, like Michael Gartner at NBC, was one of those bottom-line-oriented media executives Tisch frequently cited as proof that what he was trying to accomplish at CBS could be done without significantly hurting product quality. Diller's success in turning Fox into a lean, profitable operation was legendary, as were his programming instincts.

Diller, a college dropout, was a product of the mail room at the William Morris agency. He worked his way into a job as a programming executive at ABC-TV and rocketed into the top programming job in 1969. In 1974, still in his early 30s, he became chairman of Paramount Pictures, where his understudies included Michael Eisner, the future chairman of Walt Disney. Diller moved to Twentieth Century–Fox in 1984, and, under new owner Rupert Murdoch, built the Fox network into a successful operation with entertainment geared to the young adults advertisers generally value the most.

Diller, however, wanted more than the thrill of victory. He wanted ownership, and that wasn't possible at Fox, a unit of Murdoch's News Corp. empire. Indeed, when Diller left Fox in February 1992, his stated goal was to achieve greater autonomy, as well as greater profit participation than was possible at Fox. The assumption at the time he left was that he might not be satisfied until he was in control of an even bigger media property. NBC, however, was viewed at the time as the only potentially available property.

"Barry is hands-down one of the two or three most brilliant creative and business executives in Hollywood, and to have him move out of a position like this clearly creates a void," Jeffrey Katzenberg, chairman of Walt Disney's studio, said at the time. "That void could set a whole lot of dominoes in motion, and who knows where it all will lead?"[1] In his opinion, Diller still had "plenty of mountains left to climb."

The next "mountain" Diller took on, however, left a number of media watchers scratching their heads. Diller bought into QVC Network Inc., based in West Chester, Pennsylvania, a far cry from Hollywood. He might have gained greater autonomy, but over what? Granted, QVC's well-heeled cable co-owners—Comcast Corp. and Liberty Media—made it a potential cable-TV powerhouse, but by itself, it wasn't enough of a challenge for Diller. The appeal was QVC's mandate for Diller to use his new position to expand into programming.

It took Diller less than a year to identify a target to accomplish that. In the fall of 1993, QVC went against Viacom Inc. in a bidding war for Paramount Communications, one of Diller's former stomping grounds and one of the nation's biggest and most diversified publishing and entertainment concerns, encompassing a prolific movie and TV studio and Simon & Schuster, the book publishing giant.

When Viacom, which owned MTV and Nickelodeon, won that five-month war in February 1994, Diller's comment was short and intriguing: "They won. We lost. Next." Again, the speculation began over what Diller would go after. He impressed Wall Street by resisting the temptation, in bidding for Paramount, to offer more than he thought it was worth, and QVC shares rose on the news that Viacom had won. Amid all the speculation about what was next for Diller, the one deal possibility everyone seemed to miss was already in the works: CBS.

Why not CBS? Even before Diller lost his bid for Paramount in February, he and Tisch had discussed the concept. The assumption was, however, that Diller would never be able to raise the $6 billion or more necessary to buy out CBS in an all-cash transaction. The idea of finding a way for Diller to take over CBS, however, stayed alive. It was an enticing "next" deal for Diller to pursue after his failed run at Paramount. Indeed, it would be a crowning achievement in Diller's career.

For Tisch, meanwhile, the network business wasn't getting any easier, although he would claim it was better to face new challenges for the excitement of it than to get bored. In May, he got a little more excitement than he may have wanted. Once again, the challenge came from Fox, which announced it would invest $500 million in New World Communications Group Inc., in return for which 12 stations owned by New World—eight of which were CBS affiliates—would switch their affiliation to Fox. CBS would be left with just over 200 stations carrying its programming.

Again, what upset Tisch about this deal wasn't so much the loss of the affiliates; they would be replaced quickly enough. It was the prospect that it would drive up the network's costs. Fox's willingness to pay such a premium for affiliates would make it that much harder for CBS to continue its efforts to cut the amount of money it had to pay affiliates for airing the network's programs.

"It all sort of welled up within him," Jimmy said. It was mind-boggling to Larry that any of the networks would take what ultimately seemed to be such a self-destructive course. How could the networks hope to improve profitability if any one of them chose to keep inflating its fixed costs? It might not be a problem in a strong economy when ad spending was on the rise, as it was then, but what would happen at the next inevitable sign of economic weakness? The cost structure would remain high and the losses in a downturn would be that much deeper.

To Tisch, the industry once again was showing its proclivity for a lack of spending discipline. It was out of control. What the industry needed were managers like Barry Diller—people known for being fiscally conservative without hurting the ability to identify and acquire hit shows.

Tisch had known Diller for 20 years, beginning when Tisch was still in the movie theater business and Diller was in the movie production business at Paramount. With Fox once again sending shock waves through the network industry, and with Diller essentially available and casting about for a bigger challenge, Tisch's and Diller's destinies seemed bound to intersect. The question was: How could Tisch hand the reins over to Barry Diller without Diller's having to scrape together billions of dollars?

Enter Tisch's old friend, takeover lawyer Marty Lipton, who had represented Diller in his Paramount bid.

Lipton and Larry Tisch had known each other even longer than Tisch and Diller had. Lipton was probably more comfortable with Tisch than with Diller, who seemed to intimidate Lipton. Ten years earlier, Tisch and Lipton had worked as a veritable tag team to get Gordon Getty the best possible price for Getty Oil in Texaco's ill-fated winning bid over Pennzoil.

"The genesis of the deal was during the course of the Paramount–QVC–Viacom fiasco," Danny Tisch said. "During that period, I spoke to Marty Lipton who was representing QVC and said, 'If you think that's attractive, you should take a look at CBS. I can't believe Paramount is worth anywhere near these numbers.'" The ultimate price Viacom paid was $10 billion. "You ought to be able to do a transaction at CBS," Danny told Lipton.

It didn't take long to shelve the idea of an all-cash bid. Such an offer would amount to a takeover, a change of control that would trigger intense—and typically glacial—scrutiny by the Federal Communications Commission. Even with FCC approval, Diller wouldn't have been able to succeed without saddling CBS with a potentially deadly load of debt.

Besides, Larry Tisch did not want to subject CBS to an open auction—a near certainty in the event of a takeover bid, no matter how generous the offer was. As Danny noted, "CBS wasn't really for sale, quote unquote."

Tisch's relationship with Lipton put Tisch in a unique position to negotiate with Diller with minimal obstacles. Both Danny and Larry consulted with Lipton on how a deal might be structured to give Diller management control and a solid chunk of equity without necessitating the FCC's blessing.

By June 10, 1994, Lipton had the basic elements in place. QVC and CBS would merge in a deal valued at the time at $7.1 billion. It would be structured as a true merger, with CBS shareholders getting a $175-a-share dividend and a share of stock in the new company, which would retain the CBS name. QVC holders would get a combination of common stock and nonvoting preferred in the new company. In the end, CBS holders would own 53.6 percent of the merged entity. Loews Corp. would retain a 10 percent stake, half its premerger stake.

It was the quintessential Tisch deal—the ultimate example of his situational, commonsense investment style. For Tisch, CBS never posed any real downside risk. With this deal, however, Loews stood to collect pure profit of $550 million in cash from the dividend and end up still owning 10 percent of a new, presumably more powerful CBS— a stake valued at roughly $700 million. Not bad for an initial investment of which, by the time Diller came along, Loews had already recovered all but slightly more than $200 million. The terms included nonvoting preferred shares for QVC holders, to keep the FCC at bay.

Danny, who had initiated the first purchases of CBS shares by Loews with a call to his father nine years earlier, loved this deal. "Marty came up with this new structure and sat down with my father and myself and Jimmy at Loews and went over the new proposal," Danny said, "and we could find nothing wrong with it." From the very beginning, the primary goal was to find a way for Diller to take the helm and give CBS a new, strong leader just when it needed it. Under Lipton's proposal, Diller would take over as CEO and president, and Larry Tisch would stay on as chairman no longer than two years.

"I had no intention of being here forever," Tisch said. Still, as was often the case in how events unfolded in his empire, "I never had an endgame strategy before this."

The one wild card in the success of the deal was Comcast, which owned about 15 percent of QVC. The plan was to take the proposal to Comcast's president, Brian Roberts, to seek his support and then go forward with an announcement. It was assumed no opposition would be voiced by John C. Malone, the chairman of Tele-Communications Inc., which controlled Liberty Media, a 17 percent owner of QVC.

A leak, however, pre-empted that plan—a leak most likely from the Diller camp, according to the thinking of non-Diller sources involved in the deal. Wednesday evening, June 29, the Associated Press ran an item saying the *Los Angeles Times'* Thursday editions would report that CBS was in merger talks with QVC. Jimmy Tisch got word of the story from the CBS newsroom. Within minutes, a *New York Times* reporter got him on the phone seeking comment. It forced the two companies to make a joint announcement the following day, robbing them of the opportunity to control the presentation of the plan to Comcast.

Still, Tisch and Diller were ebullient. The photo of the two together on the front page of the *New York Times* prompted more than one observer to suggest the headline should have read, "Separated at Birth," a reference to a *Spy* magazine feature pairing celebrities who bore strikingly similar features.

No one could possibly object to this best of all possible arrangements. "I've never seen a deal that was so well accepted," Tisch said. It wouldn't take long, it was assumed, for Comcast to get over being left out of the loop and warm to the idea of joining forces with a legendary giant like CBS.

The day after the deal was announced, Tisch said he took calls throughout the day from Wall Street analysts, none of whom had a negative thing to say about the merger. Small wonder. Practically overnight, CBS seemed to have gone from being a network facing new competitive pressures with a 71-year-old CEO who was getting tired of it all, to a bigger, broader, financially healthy operation on the cutting edge of cable with one of the industry's most respected leaders, a 51-year-old dynamo.

"We knew it was a deal that made a lot of sense and that people's imagination could have fun with the possibilities," Danny said.

Jimmy wasn't so sure. He had worried about the advisability of his father buying into CBS back in 1985. Now he worried about the advisability of his father selling out to Diller. He feared Larry's image would come through badly tarnished.

"I knew of Larry's desire to be out of the CEO role at CBS, but I wanted to make sure his image wasn't completely and irrevocably tarnished in the getting out," Jimmy said.

Heightening his concerns was Larry's suggestion when they discussed how to word the news release jointly announcing the proposal: "Let's talk about how much Diller can save by cutting costs."

"But no one cares about expenses," Jimmy protested. "We need to talk about how great this will be in terms of programming." Jimmy later added, "Till the end, Larry was never a broadcaster, though in a larger sense, Larry was right" to focus on costs, just as Diller had at Fox, though not at the expense of programming.

In the end, the mutually congratulatory news release quoted Larry as saying the new company would remain "devoted to the creation of first-rate original programming." No mention of cutting costs.

Indeed, the euphoria was so infectious, Jimmy's concerns about the effect on Larry's reputation quickly vanished. In a single stroke,

CBS was about to silence the doomsayers regarding the network's failure to establish a cable-TV beachhead, as well as settle the question of management succession in a way that tended to put employees at ease.

The mainstream media had to stretch to find something negative to say. Some reports suggested that, although the deal seemed at first blush to make sense, the announcement made no reference to exactly how the two companies would be better off together than apart. Besides, everyone was quick to point out: Didn't this proposal amount to hanging a for-sale sign on CBS? And weren't there plenty of Wall Street investment bankers already feverishly shopping around their services to anyone who might be even remotely interested?

Both Tisch and Diller played down the possibility. Anyone else who would come in with a credible bid would have to deal with the FCC, which probably couldn't rule on a change-of-control question before the QVC merger would be completed. Few mainstream beat reporters failed to note that the for-sale sign effectively had also been hung on QVC.

COMCAST AS SPOILER

It quickly became apparent that Comcast wasn't thrilled about being forced into bed with a traditional rival, a broadcaster. And Diller's deal with Comcast and Liberty was that all three had to agree before a deal like this could be cleared. At the same time, Diller was starting to annoy Tisch with endless demands.

"The chemistry got bad," said one person close to the negotiations. "Barry negotiates like a bully. 'If I don't get this and that, the deal's off.' That doesn't sit well with Larry."

Diller was insisting on getting stock options for certain nonexecutive employees, not the kind of issue one allows to get in the way of the opportunity of a lifetime. But Diller was abrasively demanding. The sense was that he wanted to assume the throne like an anointed king. He failed to see the value of keeping his ego in check during talks with Larry, who had always viewed an overinflated ego as an obstacle in business.

By July 12, the night before the CBS and QVC boards were scheduled to vote on the merger proposal—with both boards poised to recommend that shareholders accept it, and with no one expecting any major opposition—Tisch already was exasperated with Diller. Then Comcast blew it all away.

Less than two weeks after Diller and Tisch got engaged, Comcast offered $44 a share, or about $2.1 billion, for the QVC shares it didn't own. The offer was about $6 a share sweeter than the value the CBS proposal put on QVC. In a stroke, the CBS–QVC deal was "separated at birth."

Tisch's immediate response, after learning of the Comcast deal that evening during a CBS board dinner, could be summed up in five familiar words: They won. We lost. Next. In this case, "next" meant immediately resolving to launch another big buyback of CBS shares—3.5 million at $325 each—and walk away from QVC. Tisch wasn't interested in a bidding contest with Comcast, and the love fest with Diller already had soured. Larry Tisch didn't need to do the deal that badly.

By the time Jimmy reached his father at the board meeting, it was all settled. "No Sturm und Drang," Jimmy said. "Zip zap. It was done."

The ease with which Larry Tisch walked away from this deal of deals reflected the level of exasperation he had reached with Diller, which in turn reflected how badly Barry had played his cards in failing to understand Larry's lack of patience for being browbeaten about details, no matter how big or appealing a deal was.

For Larry Tisch, life would go on, with or without Barry Diller. Attempts surely would be made to find Diller another way back into CBS. Tisch wasn't the type to hold grudges, nor was he likely to let Diller's abrasiveness in negotiations cloud his appreciation of Diller's unique prowess in network management.

Regardless of the outcome, what Tisch needed to make his exit from CBS work was now clearer than ever.

In the meantime, the CBS saga brought to light Tisch's best qualities, both in the successes and the failures. "It's the ability to make a deal when a deal isn't there," Jimmy said, a statement that applied both to his father's earliest foray into CBS and to his dance with Diller. The first purchases of CBS stock back in 1985 were part of an elaborate tax strategy in the tradition of risk arbitrage. "No one except Larry saw this as a long-term deal," Jimmy said. But to Larry, CBS was a tarnished trophy property capable of regaining its luster.

In the QVC deal, there was no deal—that is, no all-cash buyout—and it was typical of Tisch that, when Comcast weighed in, he simply folded his hand. No crying over spoiled deals. Another one was sure to come along. CBS had plenty of deals to work on to meet its new challenges.

Just one day after abandoning the CBS–QVC plan, the network unveiled an agreement with Westinghouse Broadcasting Co. that would convert three stations to CBS affiliation and set the stage for future joint purchases of other stations and for program production and local ad sales.

No matter how fast the picture changed, Tisch adjusted with speed and grace. This was the way he did business. It was the way he played bridge, as Warren Buffett had noted years earlier. For Larry Tisch, the connection between business and cards was seamless.

Said youngest son Tommy of his father: "He is fundamentally and psychologically a bridge player. Many people in business like to play the cards they don't have in their hands. My father plays the hand he is dealt—not what he wants."

The bridge analogy extends throughout Tisch's business style. He didn't worry about the cards he didn't get. He accepted that he didn't control the deck, and he didn't want to deal from the bottom of the deck. Bridge had always been a constant in his life, and his business day frequently would melt into an evening of bridge without any change in his mental processes. In both worlds, Tisch "has no illusions about the hand he is dealt," Tommy said.

His involvement with CNA Insurance, for example, had resulted initially from a bad investment by Loews, but he figured which elements of CNA he could control and focused on them—resisting the fad, popular at the time, of using such an operation as a foundation for creating a supermarket of all manner of financial services. The majority view on a given business strategy was of little interest to Tisch, except to the extent that he could profit on it either by betting with or against it. Taking an unpopular approach, however, was never a worry. He never craved the support of the crowd, although he enjoyed it on the rare occasions when he had it. He certainly had it for the QVC deal, yet he showed no bitter disappointment or ego deflation when it failed to materialize. It was, after all, a business decision, not a bid for popularity.

"With my father, there is a sense of constantly accepting the world as it is, realizing there are certain things you can or can't have an impact on," Tommy said. "In adversity, he is among the most supportive people. He'll never sell you out when you're down, and whether it is in market terms or personal terms, when somebody has adversity, he is there."

As manager of the Tisches' family and foundation money, Tommy frequently experienced his father's strong tendency to be supportive, especially when the chips were down. "If a position is down, he encourages you to trust your instincts and double the position," he said, "and when things start running away on the upside, he's less inclined to value that." When Tommy's bet on Boston bank stocks proved to be too early, "This is a major disaster," he said.

Larry's response: "I came into the world poor. If I go out poor, what's the difference?" Tommy was quick to remind his father that the same couldn't be said for his sons.

The flip side to Tisch's ability to adapt quickly to an ever-changing reality was his inclination to adopt whatever insight he gained from the last person he spoke to. "He learns from everybody," Tommy said. And learning from everybody was what Tisch seemed to enjoy most about his life. He went to work every day not to do work but to interact and learn and get ideas. "He doesn't particularly like work, but he finds business fascinating," Tommy said.

While Tisch thrived on picking other people's brains day-to-day and enthusiastically repeating their nuggets of wisdom, he was not tentative about his own views. "It's hard to knock him off course, but he is constantly listening and modifying his views on the margins," Tommy said.

Part of what Tisch loved most about the hotel business in the early days of his business career was the people he met coming through the lobby. That was how he met Nate Cummings at the Americana in Florida—a chance meeting that ultimately led to the creation of Loews Corp. as a latter-day conglomerate that depended only marginally on the hotel business for its cash flow.

What was enjoyable to Tisch about his coffee-shop meeting with Cummings back in the late 1950s wasn't the prospect of making more money, but the excitement of exchanging ideas about business. What separated Tisch from many other successful businesspeople was the lack of greed in his motivations.

If greed had played a greater role, Tisch would have been a different kind of investor. Ultimately, even Tisch would admit he was not necessarily the world's greatest investor. Loews portfolio manager Joe Rosenberg would say that the best trades Tisch ever made, much like Warren Buffett, were things he never sold.

Pursuing the next big Wall Street killing was never an obsession for Larry Tisch. "He never went off and chased other gods than the comfort of being around his family," Tommy said. "Wealth has been a by-product of what he enjoys."

INVESTOR'S ADVOCATE

Perhaps more than any other deal, the Macy's bankruptcy saga underscored the qualities that set Larry Tisch apart in the community of the super-rich. Like many of the most successful people in business, Tisch possessed exceptional intelligence, a superb sense of timing, and a bridge player's approach to problem solving. Where Tisch departed from the majority, however, was in his motivations. As *Fortune* magazine had once observed, Tisch was a radical driven by an almost religious commitment to the rights of shareholders.

This commitment—as opposed to any lust for personal financial gain—drove Tisch's activism as a Macy's director in the negotiations that ultimately led to its acquisition by Federated Department Stores. Soon after Federated had made its initial move on Macy's, Tisch became outraged at what he saw as Macy's management's efforts to maintain its hold, even at the expense of stockholders. His ire emerged at a board meeting in early 1994, after learning that Macy's chairman, Myron E. Ullman III, was working in secret to cut a friendly deal with two big bondholders on a plan to emerge from bankruptcy without necessarily valuing Macy's at what Tisch considered a fair price for the company's long-suffering shareholders.[2]

Ullman denied any effort to keep directors in the dark about his plan, but it was too late. Tisch had decided Ullman was looking out for Ullman and mounted a full-scale—and ultimately successful—rebellion against the chairman. In Tisch's view, Ullman was trampling the rights of shareholders to entertain the best possible offer for their company. In large part because of Tisch's activism, Macy's value was set at $4 billion, nearly 30 percent higher than the $3.1 billion initially envisioned when Macy's plan for recovery first began to take shape after its January 1992 bankruptcy filing.

Throughout this widely reported clash, the press failed to note that Tisch personally had little to gain. Indeed, he stood to lose nearly all the $80 million Loews had invested in Macy's debt, regardless of his efforts on behalf of shareholders. It was the largest single investment loss Tisch would incur in his entire business career.

"I helped other investors more than myself," Tisch said. "My investment was gone, but I was a director and, as a director, I wasn't going to stand by and allow this company to be stolen from creditors."

It was a role Tisch had played repeatedly. On the board of Grand Union, the grocery store chain, more than 25 years earlier, Tisch's campaign for a higher bid in the midst of a takeover fight led to a 10 percent boost in the offer. "If you're a director, you have to take that role seriously," Tisch said. "A lot of directors don't have a clue as to valuation, and it's hard to argue if you don't understand. In American business, there are a lot of professionals but very few people who really understand the markets, risk-reward, and real-world valuations."

For Tisch, the stewardship of wealth—maintaining the delicate balance between protecting it and making it grow—was the point, not personal wealth. Stunning successes delighted him, and they happened often enough that stunning failures failed to elicit much more than a shrug. His sense of self-worth wasn't tied up in the bottom line of each and every deal, nor did he share his fellow billionaires' appetites for lavish life-styles. Spending a fortune was anathema to his mission as the enemy of corporate waste. He and Billie lived well below their means. They seldom indulged in lavish vacations. They avoided the trappings of obvious wealth. No Rolls Royce. No personal aircraft. No trophy real estate or vacation villa. No South Sea islands. No high-priced decorating binges.

To Larry Tisch, it was common sense to *add* value to every enterprise he undertook—not to spend it. He defied conventional wisdom and resisted any temptation to follow the herd on Wall Street. At the same time, he was unfettered by any fear of failure or by any reluctance to acknowledge his own fallibility; such concerns are the mark of an overdeveloped sense of self-importance. Larry Tisch's brilliant career could be summed up in one of his own favorite expressions: "Now let's be practical."

Notes

Chapter 3

1. As quoted in *The Money Masters*, by John Train (New York: Harper & Row, 1979).
2. Broadcasting wasn't the only medium that interested the Tisches. By 1982, they would make a bid for *The New York Daily News* at the invitation of the paper's owner Tribune Co., but would back out after being outbid by Joseph Allbritton; who also backed out, ultimately leaving the paper's fate to Robert Maxwell, an eccentric British financier who later disappeared from his yacht off the Canary Islands, leaving his overleveraged empire to collapse.
3. William R. Shelton, "The Tisches Eye Their Next $65 Million," *Fortune* (January 1960), p. 132.

Chapter 4

1. Charles G. Burck, "How the Tisches Run Their Little Store," *Fortune* (May 1971), p. 208.
2. *Business Week* (August 26, 1972).
3. *Fortune* (May 1971).
4. Ibid.

Chapter 5

1. "Italy's Howard Hughes," *The Wall Street Journal* (February 17, 1972), p. 1.

Chapter 6

1. *New York Times* (February 18, 1973), Sec. III, p. 1., Col. 1.
2. *Business Week* (November 1, 1976), p. 64.

Chapter 8

1. Leonard H. Goldenson, *Beating the Odds,* (New York: Scribners, 1991), p. 455.
2. Thomas Petzinger, Jr., *Oil and Honor: The Texaco-Pennzoil Wars,* (New York: G.P. Putnam's Sons, 1987).
3. Stratford P. Sherman, "CBS Braces for the Tisch Touch." *Fortune* (October 13, 1986), p. 63.

Chapter 9

1. Edward Klein, "Eye of the Storm," *New York* magazine (November 15, 1991), p. 26.
2. Ken Auletta, *Three Blind Mice,* (New York: Random House, 1991), p. 56.

Chapter 10

1. Ken Auletta, *Three Blind Mice,* (New York: Random House, 1991), p. 169.
2. Ed Jones, *Prime Time, Bad Times.* (New York: Doubleday, 1988), p. 481.
3. Ken Auletta, "Gambling on CBS," *New York Times* (June 8, 1986), p. 35.
4. Linda Sandler, "Heard on the Street," *The Wall Street Journal* (October 24, 1985).
5. CBS wasn't the only one of the networks facing hard business realities. ABC already was getting measured for a leaner future. And on December 11 RCA agreed to be acquired for $6.28 billion by General Electric, whose hard-driving chairman, John F. Welch, Jr., didn't like being in a business unless it had a solid shot at being the best in its category. Anything else was a candidate for the auction block, and, under Welch, General Electric had dumped lots of also-rans along with thousands of employees.

   Any fat at NBC would be detected and removed in the interest of maximizing profit. Never mind that NBC already was RCA's best profit center and was in the process of taking over as the number-one network in ratings, under the guidance of Grant Tinker, NBC's entertainment division president, and legendary programming chief Brandon Tartikoff. It wasn't Welch's habit to be satisfied with the status quo, no matter how well it worked.
6. Ken Auletta, "Gambling on CBS," *New York Times* (June 8, 1986), p. 35.
7. George Russell, "The Man Who Captured CBS," *Time* (September 22, 1986), p. 68.

8. Peter J. Boyer, "At CBS, a Feeling of Relief," *New York Times* (September 11, 1994), Section IV, p. 6.
9. George Russell, "The Man Who Captured CBS," *Time* (September 22, 1986), p. 68.

Chapter 11

1. Ken Auletta, *Three Blind Mice*, (New York: Random House, 1991), p. 249.
2. George Russell, "The Man Who Captured CBS," *Time* (September 22, 1986), p. 63.
3. *Time* see note 2.

Chapter 12

1. *New York Times* (February 7, 1987), Section I. p. 50.
2. Peter J. Boyer, *Who Killed CBS*, (New York: Random House, 1988), p. 328.
3. Peter J. Boyer, "Sadness Turns to Anger Over CBS Dismissals," *New York Times* (March 9, 1987), Sec. III, p. 14.
4. Ibid.
5. "From Murrow to Mediocrity," *New York Times* (March 10, 1987), Sec. I, p. 27.
6. Peter J. Boyer, "Sadness Turns to Anger Over CBS Dismissals," (March 9, 1987), Sec. III, p. 14.
7. Subrata N. Chakravarty, "Revenge of the Antisuits," *Forbes* (December 11, 1986), p. 49.
8. Ken Auletta, "Gambling on CBS," *New York Times* (June 8, 1986), The Business World Special Section. p. 35.

Chapter 13

1. Kenneth Labich, "Has Larry Tisch Lost His Touch?" *Fortune* (February 26, 1990), p. 99.
2. Dennis Kneale, "Seeking Ratings Gains. CBS Pays Huge Sums for Sports Contracts," (October 10, 1989), p. 1.
3. Sally Bedell Smith, *In All His Glory*, (New York: Simon & Schuster, 1990), p. 607.
4. Edward Klein, "Eye of the Storm," *New York* magazine (April 15, 1991), p. 26.

Chapter 14

1. Edward Klein, "Eye of the Storm," *New York* magazine (April 15, 1991), p. 26.
2. Ken Auletta, *Three Blind Mice*, (New York: Random House, 1991), p. 565.
3. Robert W. Welkas, "The Secret of His Success: Lee Rich Gives the Public What It Wants," (November 10, 1992), Part F, p. 1.

Chapter 15

1. Laura Landro, Thomas R. King, "Diller Steps Down at Fox and Murdoch Takes the Reins," *The Wall Street Journal* (February 25, 1992), p. B1.
2. Stephanie Strom, "Derailing a Big Bankruptcy Plan," *New York Times* (July 29, 1994), p. D1.

A Note about Sources

More than 100 people were interviewed in the course of researching this book. Many of them requested anonymity. Many others, not mentioned here by name, served mainly to confirm or to correct previously reported events and quotes. Still others were reluctant to cooperate, because this was an unauthorized biography.

After the first draft was completed, however, Larry Tisch and his family agreed to be interviewed and responded openly and freely during the numerous times they were contacted with follow-up questions. These conversations proved to be the most important and enlightening. Besides Larry, family sources included his wife, Billie; his four sons, Andrew, Daniel, James and Thomas; his brother, Bob; his cousin, Elizabeth Drew; and to a lesser extent, his nephew, Steve, and Billie's brother-in-law, Martin Cohen.

Among others who were helpful in varying degrees were: Lisbeth Barron, George H. Buckwald, Warren Buffett, Sam Christopher, Neil E. Derrough, Raymond L. Dirks, Vernon Gay, Stanley Goldblum, Kevin Goldman, Duane Harm, H. Erich Heinemann, Don Hewitt, Eugene F. Jankowski, Henry Kaufman, Jack Lamping, Paul Luftig, Norman Pearlstine, Thomas Petzinger, Andy Rooney, Rabbi Nesson Scherman, Andi Sporkin, Leonard N. Stern, Howard Stringer, Neal Zoren, and Sidney Zweben.

Index